I0643057

The Politics of Information

The Politics of Information

Problem Definition and the Course of Public Policy in America

FRANK R. BAUMGARTNER
AND BRYAN D. JONES

The University of Chicago Press
Chicago and London

FRANK R. BAUMGARTNER is the Richard J. Richardson Distinguished Professor of Political Science at the University of North Carolina at Chapel Hill. BRYAN D. JONES is the J. J. "Jake" Pickle Regent's Chair in Congressional Studies in the Department of Government at the University of Texas at Austin. Together, they are the authors of several books, including *Agendas and Instability in American Politics*, also published by the University of Chicago Press.

The University of Chicago Press, Chicago 60637
The University of Chicago Press, Ltd., London
© 2015 by The University of Chicago
All rights reserved. Published 2015.
Printed in the United States of America

24 23 22 21 20 19 18 17 16 15   1 2 3 4 5

ISBN-13: 978-0-226-19809-5   (cloth)
ISBN-13: 978-0-226-19812-5   (paper)
ISBN-13: 978-0-226-19826-2   (e-book)
DOI: 10.7208/chicago/9780226198262.001.0001

Library of Congress Cataloging-in-Publication Data

Baumgartner, Frank R., 1958– author.
 The politics of information : problem definition and the course of public policy in America / Frank R. Baumgartner and Bryan D. Jones.
    pages cm
 Includes bibliographical references and index.
 ISBN 978-0-226-19809-5 (cloth : alkaline paper) — ISBN 978-0-226-19812-5 (paperback : alkaline paper) — ISBN 978-0-226-19826-2 (e-book)   1. Federal government—Information resources management—United States.   2. United States—Politics and government—1945–1989.   3. United States—Politics and government—1989–   4. Policy sciences—United States.   I. Jones, Bryan D., author.   II. Title.
 JK271.B36 2015
 352.3'80973—dc23

                                                    2014014262

♾ This paper meets the requirements of ANSI/NISO Z39.48-1992 (Permanence of Paper).

We dedicate this book to our students—from today, from yesterday, and from quite some time ago!

Contents

Preface

This book follows a research path that we began in 1987 and which has led us into a number of studies of many types. We began with a suspicion that political science had overestimated the weight of inertia and stability in the policy process and, by studying a number of individual policy issues over time, were able to develop a theory of punctuated equilibrium in order to explain not only the obvious stability that characterizes most issues most of the time but also the periods of abrupt change. Tracing the route of individual policy histories over time remains the single most approachable and common path to theory building in this area.

Our discovery that we could develop quantitative indicators of the agenda status of an issue, as well as how it was framed in the media and government discussion, led to a proposal to the National Science Foundation to create comprehensive indicators of U.S. federal government activities from approximately 1947 to the present. The result of that and subsequent grants has been the creation of the Policy Agendas Project (http://www.policyagendas .org). This resource now includes over 1 million observations, allowing anyone with an Internet connection to analyze trends in U.S. federal policy activities, including congressional hearings, laws, presidential speeches, and a growing collection of other indicators from 1947 to current times. The large datasets available allow us to investigate the patterns of stability and change that characterize government in all domains. It would not have been possible to create this resource without the continued efforts of dozens of collaborators and students. It has also led to some unorthodox methodological approaches. Indeed, since our first focus on tracing the path of individual policies over time, with the data resources that the agendas project makes available, we have gone well beyond this approach. While stochastic modeling does not allow us to understand much about any particular policy domains, it allows new insights into the general patterns of change that characterize them all. We are convinced that a combination of close study of individual policy issues and broad overviews of the general patterns of attention in government will lead to the greatest number of insights; we know that no single approach alone can be as useful as a combination of approaches.

Some of the most exciting projects we have been involved in over the past years have been associated with a network of colleagues, collaborators, and, now, friends who have replicated the U.S.-based Policy Agendas Project across many different political systems (see http://www.comparativeagendas .info). Studies we have done with them, and others they have done without us, relating to budgets, legislative activities, executive actions, and the impact of elections on policy priorities have reassured us that our U.S.-based findings are far from unique. Indeed, to the extent that much of what we describe here is due to general characteristics of human cognitive processes, our approach has the potential to be universalistic, applicable, we suspect, in any large and complex organization (whether in government or in the private sector, though to our knowledge these ideas have not been tested in nongovernmental settings). It has been a true intellectual pleasure to work with others gathering evidence and collectively puzzling over the best ways to answer questions about democratic governance, human attention, and policy change in a manner consistent with what the data show. This has led us to refine some of the ideas with which we started over twenty-five years ago and to develop new ones.

The organization and prioritization of information has become increasingly central to our studies. Governments are complex adaptive organizations, but to what are they adapting? We made the case in *The Politics of Attention* that processing information within policy-making structures invariably leads to a disjoint pattern of policy outputs, because attention implies inattention, and inattention to important developments in the environment can build up and cause a scramble to address them. We used the phrase "error accumulation" to describe this process: information that is temporarily ignored because of information overload or institutional resistance eventually accumulates and surpasses a threshold where it can no longer be ignored, leading to a rapid "catch-up" that often leads to a policy punctuation.

Any study of the role of information in policy making should, it seemed to us, rely on information. Or maybe our interest in information came from our insistence that we give pride of place to observation and measurement in analyzing government. Cause and effect are easily switched in the human mind. We have spent over twenty-five years focused on developing new indicators of what the government does. In this book we continue our focus on observation. Certain patterns jump out from any analysis of the huge range of behaviors and trends we review here. But just as we note that political leaders often trade off the scope of their jurisdictions for an illusion of control, we can make the same argument regarding our own profession. We certainly do not believe we have given the final word on the developments we explore here. We have taken the observations as they fall out, and we have not limited our purview only to a narrow slice of the political world. By taking on such a broad set of observations, the patterns we observe as well as the explanations we develop for them will be very general. It will fall to us in other projects and to others in the future to delve into some of these arguments in greater detail, exploring how they manifest themselves in detail during the day-to-day or year-to-year functioning of individual policy domains, agencies, and policy communities, and to understand the role of individual leaders in pushing the system in this or that direction.

In creating the infrastructure that is now the Policy Agendas Project, we have been constantly mindful of the advantage of a comprehensive approach: We do not cherry-pick our examples but seek to look at policy developments and patterns across the board. At the same time, we are aware of the importance of mixing large-scale quantitative approaches with more intensive, qualitative assessments of individual policy domains, none of which can generalize. Further, because of our desire to be comprehensive in gathering information about government activities, we have made decisions not to study certain things that we know are important but that logistically simply cannot be measured comprehensively: framing effects and policy positions (ideology) are the two most important elements we have not measured systematically. These important variables require so much contextual knowledge about each individual policy domain that we rely on a back-and-forth between the broad patterns and the individual policies in order to study the effects of these important variables. While the Policy Agendas Project creates an infrastructure that allows unprecedented studies of the patterns and dynamics of government attention, it is not the last word on politics. We recognize its strengths as well as its limits and we seek to go beyond it when the situation requires. For the most part, however, our investment in infrastructure and measurement has made possible entirely new types of analyses, and we develop these further in the chapters to come.

We cannot defeat complexity. We must address it head-on. We hope that this will be a first step in a new literature in public administration, and political science more generally, that takes complexity more seriously.

Acknowledgments

We have many debts, as those familiar with the scope of the agendas project and its comparative extensions will clearly understand. Readers of this book will see without a doubt that we have relied on a great number of students and collaborators over the years. In *The Politics of Attention* (2005b) we tried to list a great number of our students as evidence of our thanks. If we missed any, we hope we have recognized you here. In any case, we could not do the work we have done without the help of the following students. We have tried over the years to repay our debts to our students by providing mentoring, advice, skills, experiences, and publication opportunities, and many of the students in our list below are now tenured professors in the United States and abroad, a point that gives us great satisfaction. Let us begin by thanking these students who have worked on the agendas project over the years and in many cases become close collaborators on various projects with us: Jeffery C. Talbert, James L. True, Glen S. Krutz, Michael C. MacLeod, Kelly Tzoumis, Chris Koski, Christian Breunig, Sam Workman, Tracy Sulkin, Michelle Wolfe, Edward T. Walker, Erik W. Johnson, Sebastien G. Lazardeux, Jon Moody, Derek A. Epp, John Lovett, Shaun Bevan, Tim La-Pira, Trey Thomas, K. Elizabeth Coggins, Mary Layton Atkinson, Amber E. Boydstun, Max Rose, Heather A. Larsen, Paul Rutledge, Andrew W. Martin, Michelle Whyman, Rebecca Eisler, and Annelise Russell.

One of the great joys of the agendas project has been its progressive extension to other countries. This book does not make use of the powerful analytic capabilities that come from the growing comparative agendas project; we have explored those issues in other publications and look forward to doing so in greater detail in the future. But let us mention a number of collaborators here and abroad who have helped us over the years to understand the politics of information in important ways: John Wilkerson, Christoffer Green-Pedersen, Peter May, Christopher Wlezien, John D. McCarthy, Stuart Soroka, James A. Stimson, Laura Chaqués Bonafont, Anna M. Palau, Luz Munoz, Jeffrey M. Berry, Beth L. Leech, Sylvain Brouard, Stefaan Walgrave, Emiliano Grossman, Martial Foucault, Abel François, David Lowery, Virginia Gray, Peter John, Peter B. Mortensen, Frédéric Varone, Roy Gava, Pascal Sciarini, Amy Mazur, Isabelle Engeli, Peter B. Mortensen, Michiel Neytemans, Arco Timmermans, Gerard Breeman, Will Jennings, Grant Jordan, Robert Repetto, László Zalányi, Péter Érdi, and Joe McLaughlin.

Chapter 4 on the analytic institutions of the executive and legislative branches follows from a remark by David Brady at a presentation that Jones made to the Stanford Political Science Department. Brady suggested that there was a political and historical story underlying the information processing analysis that Jones presented. Also related to this chapter, but more broadly, the authors owe a large debt to the late Walter Williams, who taught Jones much about the history of policy analysis and whose book, *Honest Numbers and Democracy* (Williams 1998), is a forceful defense of policy analysis in government. We also consulted several congressional scholars who aided us in understanding the longer-run dynamics of the institution. We are particularly indebted to Sean Theriault, Joe Cooper, and Larry Dodd for their comments on this material.

We also gratefully recognize the following National Science Foundation awards that have supported the development of the Policy Agendas Project: SBR 9320922, 1994 to 1998; SBR 0111611, 2002 to 2007; and SES 1024291, 2010 to 2013. Many students have benefited from these funds, and we are pleased that our Web site has become a source for thousands of users each month from around the world and provides the resources for them to learn about and analyze the actions of the U.S. government.

Will Winecoff, now assistant professor at Indiana University but a graduate student at UNC–Chapel Hill when he got involved, produced the graphics for the book. John Tryneski and Rodney Powell have earned our heartfelt thanks for working with us on another Chicago book; we are pleased to have been working with both of them for twenty years now, on several projects. It is a pleasure to work with such professionals.

Finally, we appreciate John Wilkerson, Scott Adler, and Chris Wlezien, who read earlier versions of the manuscript and improved it immeasurably with their comments.

PART I

"Seek and Ye Shall Find"

Picture yourself an analyst with decades of experience in a federal agency charged with fighting poverty. You probably know a lot about the issue. You have seen programs come and go; you have tracked the ups and downs of the poverty rate; you have seen the political parties wax and wane on the issue; you know what innovations and experiments have been tried out in the various states; you understand the various contributing elements to poverty; you know which programs have been more and less successful in fighting aspects of it; you understand that some of them have unintended consequences; you can see gaps in the safety net; you know that political realities preclude certain policies that work in other countries; and you can see gaps in the commitment of elected officials to push for a renewal of a national war on poverty. In sum, you have a strong understanding of the complexity of the problem—as you should, since you have spent your entire career working in the trenches of a bureaucracy focused on nothing but this problem.

Now imagine yourself an opponent of increased government spending. You have nothing personally to object with the values of our federal poverty official described above, but you think taxes are too high, that there are too many programs, and that if we have not solved poverty with all the effort that has been put into it by government over the past fifty years, perhaps it is simply something that government cannot solve, period.

How do these two individuals approach the question of information? For the first, the causes of poverty are endlessly complex, and the myriad solutions to the issue vary in their effectiveness, cost, and approaches. The more we learn about the connections between poverty, education, transportation, job training, and other contributors, the better we may be able to address the problem. The more we gather information on the effectiveness of various public and private solutions to the problem, the more accurately we can calibrate our public policy response. The more information we have, the better we can justify and choose among competing solutions and programs.

The second individual may view any additional study of the causes of poverty with suspicion. Most likely, he or she may argue, it will come from a source with a vested interest in spending more money to combat the problem. If a study documents that the problem is more severe the previously recognized, will this not simply be used to demand greater spending? If it shows that a given program is more effective than the other, will not the old program remain while the new program grows dramatically? Is it not likely that wishful thinking, or social norms, will press to enact well-meaning programs to solve a national problem even if evidence suggests we do not really know what works, or if the solutions do more harm than good? No one wants to rain on the parade, but who is going to suggest we should not throw money at a problem that simply cannot be solved, or that we should not duplicate efforts already going on in the states, for example?

These dilemmas are at the heart of our book. We argue here that information is at the core of politics. We focus on complex problems with no simple solutions: war, peace, economic growth, educational attainment, and, yes, poverty assistance. We argue that the search for information is tightly connected with the implementation of solutions; therefore, our attitudes and curiosity about the nature of a social problem are closely tied with our beliefs about the value of government responses to the public policy challenges we face. With the collection of a diverse array of information about a complex problem, we discover its manifold dimensions. Understanding the multiple aspects of a given public policy problem, we justify solutions and government programs designed to attack this, then that, aspect of the problem. As we do so, government grows. But it does not grow in a neat, orderly manner. It grows organically, as different elements of a problem emerge and as our understanding of the causes and possible solutions to it arise out of professional communities of experts, social movements, the business community, other governmental agencies, and academic disciplines. Agencies and programs proliferate with slightly different missions designed to address different parts of the larger whole. Problems then emerge with regard to the coordination of these disparate institutions. Calls for "leadership" and "clarity" proliferate. And leaders attempt to impose control. A key element of what we point out is that central to any effort to impose control is one to limit, or censor, information. Declaring some aspects of a problem out of bounds for discussion, or beyond the purview of what we can do today, is central to most efforts to impose clarity, hierarchy, and efficiency in government.

The three chapters that make up Part One develop these arguments in greater detail. But the idea is very simple: The more you look for problems, the more you find. The more you seek to understand the complexity of a given problem, the more complex you find that it is. With each discovery of the nature of a social problem comes at least the possibility (not the certainty) of creating a government program to help alleviate it. With greater understanding of the multiple dimensions of complex problems, we see the proliferation of targeted programs. These trends cannot continue forever because important political actors object to the accumulation of too many overlapping agencies and they seek to impose order. Our approach to the growth of government, and the limits to this process, are new enough that we spend three chapters explaining our ideas first in the abstract and then with reference to more examples and historical cases. In Part Two, we shift to a more quantitative and empirical approach driven by the resources of the Policy Agendas Project to document the pattern of growth in the U.S. federal government with a focus on the post-1947 period. Part Three concludes with the theoretical implications of what we think is a new way of approaching the question of government growth and its causes.

P1

P2

P3

"The more you look for problems, the more you find." → relate to Casey and letter writing → "five alarm" of high volume of letters = what happens when gov closes eyes to problems but media is looking

→ what is funct of media? they need problems to look for?

1

Search, Information, and Policy Agendas

Good government requires sound mechanisms for detecting problems and prioritizing them for action. But the <u>better the performance of the search mechanisms</u>, the <u>more likely is public policy action on the problems de-tected</u>. And the more government action, the larger and more intrusive the government. We call this tension the *paradox of search*.

This is not just a theoretical proposition. We show in this book that in the United States, this tension has contributed to an arc of policy develop-ment in which the policy agenda, the arena of serious dialogue for possible government intervention, expanded to a peak, which we can locate defini-tively as occurring in 1978. Then the policy agenda contracted throughout our period of study, which ended in 2008. We do not claim that search alone caused the arc, but we show correspondences in data we have assembled and coded through the Policy Agendas Project that strongly indicate how cen-tral search was in this historical development and how these mechanisms became part of the ideological dialogue in the period.

In this introductory chapter, we explore the paradox, showing that it in-volves at its heart a <u>tension between allowing full and free participation in the detection and discovery of public problems and orderly government</u> in which policies are carefully implemented through hierarchies. One can have <u>order and control, or</u> one can have <u>diversity and open search processes</u> and "participatory democracy." In theory these could occur in continual bal-ance. This does not, however, work out so well in practice.

can you be gathering into w/o realizing?

Handling Complexity in Problem Definition

In dealing with complex social problems with many underlying dimensions, governments must attempt to understand the issues. To understand a complex issue, governments must gather information about the issue. It is straightforward to seek out expertise on a problem that is well understood and for which known solutions exist. But how does one gather information about a problem one does not completely understand? One way to do this is to break down a large problem into its component parts and attempt to make progress one part at a time. When governments focus their attention on one element of a problem, they often can make progress in alleviating it. Food stamps do indeed allow millions of poor Americans to eat at least somewhat more nutritiously than they would if the program did not exist. But when we create a program to focus on one element (say, nutrition) of a complex and interconnected issue (say, poverty), it is not long before advocates point out that other elements or dimensions of the problem also deserve attention: housing, transportation, job training, tax structures, health care, education, personal responsibility, work ethic, equal opportunity, and family structure are also important parts of the poverty puzzle, to be sure. In an issue as complex as poverty, the more one focuses attention on the myriad dimensions of the issue, the more information one gathers, the more one understands the multidimensional character of the issue, and the more one might be tempted to create a range of public policy programs designed to address different elements of it. Poverty is not unusual with regard to its complexity. Health care or fostering economic growth or protecting national security are equally complex, for example. The more one thinks about how to address a complex social problem, the longer the list of potential ideas that might justify a new government program.

Governments face not only complex individual problems but also multiple problems, and these problems are not prioritized. That means that when they make progress, say, on poverty, some actors might say they are paying insufficient attention to, for example, the environment, health care, national defense, or the space race. There is no simple way to prioritize the diverse problems governments face. So the issue of complexity does not stop with matching solutions with multiple consequences to multifaceted and ill-understood problems. Politics is often about getting government to focus on one topic rather than another. Even if the topics are not directly in conflict with one another, all topics compete for space on the agenda.

Gathering information about complex problems, prioritizing those problems, and understanding the myriad repercussions that current policies may have on different elements of society, the economy, or other sectors require that we organize diversity into the process of gathering information. A greater diversity of information is better in helping to understand extremely complex issues and for balancing diverse priorities: information should come from as many different angles as possible. But implementing solutions and doing so efficiently requires clarity of organizational design and a clear mission. Thus, the goals of understanding the complex world around us are in fundamental conflict with the need to act. The conflict between complexity and control is at the heart of this book, and it explains fundamental tensions at the core of government since its inception.

Judging Government's Performance

Should government be so consumed with defining problems? Not according to many analysts. We can judge government performance through two fundamental lenses. The first concentrates on democratic accountability, and in particular on the correspondence between what government does and what its citizens want. Here the question is the connection between citizen preferences and public policies. A second perspective focuses on the extent to which government solves the problems it faces. These are obviously not the only standards, but they are the most prevalent, both in the political science literature and in general discourse about government.

Both of these standards are quite obviously incomplete. What if citizen preferences are based on faulty or even misguided information? What if such policies have terrible economic, environmental, or social consequences? These and other aspects of the *preference satisfaction* approach have been thoroughly aired in the political science literature.

Less explored is the standard of *problem solving*. The key focus is on how governments detect, prioritize, and address a dynamic flow of changing challenges for the system (Jones and Baumgartner 2005b; Adler and Wilkerson 2012). Here the incomplete nature of the standard is also clear. Problems are in part subjective and in part objective, and any policy solution to a problem will have clear distributional effects. Nevertheless, the problem-solving approach has much to commend it. Ranking of problems by citizens, such as in Gallup's long-running query about "the most important problem facing the nation," indicate a great deal of consensus on problems. The approach focuses on questions of how a political system processes information, because information is a requirement of sound problem solving (Jones and Baumgartner 2005b). Most importantly, much of politics is not about matching policies to preferences but rather centers on the definition of problems and the design of policy solutions. And the approach makes clear that citizens can have preferences for what problems should be addressed as well as what policies should be enacted (Jones, Larsen-Price, and Wilkerson 2009).

This study, and our work more generally, is located solidly within the problem-solving perspective. In following this thread, we have increasingly come to see governments as complex adaptive systems (Jones and Baumgartner 2005b). A complex adaptive system is one that interacts dynamically with its environment by processing and responding to information and adjusting to external changes in its environment in ways that are often not proportional to the changes in the environment (in technical terms, nonlinear) and involve whole series of variables changing together such that it is hard to isolate the effect of a single one of them. The problem-solving perspective, which has a long tradition in political science, meshes well with the burgeoning literature on complex systems in other fields of inquiry.

Underlying the problem-solving perspective is an approach to understanding individual behaviors in complex organizations in which participants are seen as boundedly rational actors who are generally goal oriented but are constrained by their biological and psychological inheritances (Jones 2001). They struggle with allocating attention to the most pressing issues, become attached to solutions independently of how much they contribute to goal attainment, and become confused when faced with longer chains of causation. When the boundedly rational individual meets the complexity of modern government, the result is heightened uncertainty about the course of the future. Within this frame, the organizations that they inhabit can facilitate or inhibit the solving of problems.

A major issue in such a perspective is the complexity of modern problems facing government, and the complexity of problems (by which we mean multi-attribute situations with unappealing trade-offs) has been a (maybe the) major key to our studies. The problems facing modern governments are hard, in two senses. They involve unpalatable trade-offs, or they conflict with the values and preferences of participants such that governments must deny the problems or rethink their preferences. This can be difficult for democratically elected politicians if their constituents do not similarly update their preferences in light of emergent problems.

Information is critical for problem solving, and hence how governments recognize, organize, and respond to information is essential to understand public policy, the outputs of government activities. In particular, we have explored the role of information in causing the policy responses of governments to alternate between calm and incremental adjustments to changes in their environments and disjoint and episodic disruptions to the ongoing adjustment process.

In previous research, we examined the effects of the processing of information on government policy actions (Jones and Baumgartner 2005b). There we explored the impact of the ongoing, dynamic flow of information on a system that was conservative, in the sense that it reacted slowly to changing information signals indicating problems in the environment. That is, mostly political systems underreact to information. They do so because of the bounded rationality of political actors and because of the institutional friction built into the decision-making system. But occasionally the flow of information signals cumulated to reach crisis stage (a process we termed "error accumulation") and major policy punctuations occurred. Sometimes the policy punctuation was preceded by major electoral shifts; sometimes not.

In this book, we turn to the frontend of the information processing in those complex adaptive systems we call governments. We want to understand what organizational mechanisms are involved in the detection of signals and the definition of problems that lead to policy action. We focus on the search mechanisms that governments employ, either consciously or unconsciously, to detect problems, prioritize them among competing issues, and design solutions for those problems.

The term "search" implies active recognition that problems may exist and that governments have established mechanisms for doing this. But in some cases search can be a side consequence of arrangements established to further other goals, in particular the ambitions of office-seeking politicians. We show in detail how the search mechanisms within congressional committees developed both as a conscious information-processing system within congress and as a consequence of changes in the electoral coalitions pushing for reform during the early 1970s.

Three Questions

We organize our exploration of search and information gathering in government by positing three key questions. Taken together, these three questions constitute what we call the paradox of search.

IS SEARCH NECESSARY FOR GOOD GOVERNMENT?

This seems obvious. If government ignores problems that emerge from its environment, it cannot act adaptively to address those problems. But if we return to the two standards for judging government above, it is not. In the preference satisfaction approach, there is no role for search, except for the search that politicians engage in to discover the preferences of their citizens for policies (Gilligan and Krehbiel 1989, 1990). It is not difficult to reconcile search with preference satisfaction by treating it as just another policy and by pointing out that policies may be endorsed or refuted by electorates after they are put in place. But that treats an essential component of policy making as an afterthought. Here, we want to bring search up for explicit scrutiny and give it a prominent place in the analysis of democratic decision making.

ARE ORDER, CONTROL, AND HIERARCHY THE ENEMIES OF SEARCH?

There is a solid literature based on small group observations and experiments that indicate more diversity leads to better decisions (Page 2008). Indeed, Fishkin's (1991, 2011) notion of deliberative democracy builds in diversity of perspectives and a venue for discussion of those perspectives. Elinor Ostrom (2005) has shown in the lab and in the field that diverse perspectives can be reconciled to solve problems. But in large systems these orderly processes tend to fail, and the analysis breaks down here as well. Ostrom and others point out that many decisions can be accomplished within smaller units, which allows both for more deliberation and more homogenous preferences. But if there must be decisions at the larger and more diverse collective, then the analysis is less relevant.

Yet, surely decisions based on diversity and deliberation are generally better than those based on top-down hierarchy, at least over many issues and longer time spans. Hierarchies at some point must stifle search to solve the "analysis paralysis" (too much analysis leads to decision paralysis) problem. Or, in another language, we expect better decisions on average in diverse systems, even large-scale ones, if there are ways to reconcile these diverse preferences and perspectives.

But what if a class of citizens has more information and expertise than others? Should its perspectives be given more weight? If so, then are not order and hierarchy better for assessing and defining problems? This is an age-old question that we cannot answer, but we can make progress by dividing search processes into two types, which are appropriate in different situations. In many, if not most, cases, these situations can be clearly defined. In problem definition and prioritization, diversity is almost always desirable. In solution search, expertise is almost always the preferred way.

IS SEARCH THE ENEMY OF GOOD GOVERNMENT?

This question is the polar opposite of the first. But there are three factors that would suggest that in some circumstances search can undermine elements of sound government.

First, government can overinvest in the search process, just as it can overinvest in any policy activity (Jones, Thomas, and Wolfe 2013). Sometimes the trade-offs between fostering search and good government are crystal clear. As we write, the United States is in a major discussion over the role of the National Security Agency's (NSA) data mining techniques used to detect potential terrorist threats. Debates center on the intrusiveness onto the personal liberties and privacies of U.S. citizens versus the threats to collective safety. The more intensive and comprehensive the search by government, the more intrusive are its effects on citizens. Less debated, but probably just as important, is the enormous expense of NSA's search techniques, a debate that is taking place almost without regard to weighing the monetary cost of the search versus the expected value of threat detection.

Second, search implies that if a problem is found, the probability of government action will increase. It can be hard to stop some sort of policy proposals from gaining traction in many circumstances, especially if the problem can be shown to be severe and directly relevant to citizens' lives. The extensive and intensive activities of NSA are instructive. We explore this issue in detail in this book, and show how the linkage of problem to solution, and therefore of problem-search to subsequent government action, helps us understand the development and structure of the U.S. government throughout the postwar period.

The tight link between finding and acting also has implications for governance. For every problem, there is generally a proposed solution, and more often than not that solution involves more government. More programs imply more expenses, more taxes, and more intrusive government. One approach is simply to refuse to engage the search process. But that leads to festering problems that can grow to large-scale crises. The search process invariably is linked to the disjoint course of policy making. Lack of search will lead to fewer problems being found until a crisis demands action in an "error accumulation" process (Jones and Baumgartner 2005a, 2005b). Search leads to finding problems, and the better the search process, the more problems will be found. The more problems found, the more government policies will be put in place to address them. This can result in more government, which in turn may lead to countermobilization by those who worry about too much government regulation (and often their first target is information-gathering efforts). We take no position here on how much government is the "right" amount. But we do show here that the consequences of increasing search processes is associated with more extensive government activities and that these patterns tend to spill over into other policy areas in a self-reinforcing process. And limiting search leads to a downward spiral of lower government activity.

Finally, search can undermine orderly government. If, as we suggested above, in many circumstances adequate search implies diverse voices, then search can detract in particular from the orderly implementation of policies. It may seem simple to limit diverse voices after the adoption of a policy, but that assumes that policy development ends at one point and then implementation begins. Policy is an ongoing process of adoption and modification, and diversity is as important in implementation as in policy adoption.

Search and Policy Agendas

The major issue in the study of policy agenda setting centers on how a situation comes to be defined as a problem that government could have a role in addressing (Cobb and Elder 1972; Kingdon 1995). As government has expanded and moved into more areas of life, agenda setting has come to be associated with the allocation of attention to the various issues that government could potentially address (Jones and Baumgartner 2005b). In either case, the agenda-setting stage is viewed somewhat similar to a filter that influences the probability of government action. When a situation comes to be viewed collectively as a problem, the probability of government taking action moves from nil to some positive probability.

Crossing this barrier is facilitated when government sets up explicit organizational mechanisms for detecting and defining problems. If these systems are effective, then they detect problems. If they detect problems, then the probability of government action is increased. The more areas in which such mechanisms exist, the broader the policy agenda space within which action may occur.

This would be a simple problem if the decision-making mechanisms of government with high probability addressed only those problems that crossed some threshold of severity, neglecting the rest. Unfortunately, in a boundedly rational world fraught with uncertainty and in which attention is a scarce resource, the more common reaction is "alarmed discovery" (Downs 1972). Risk-averse public officials, fearing retribution, electoral or otherwise, may act when action may not be necessary.

A powerful psychological mechanism joins the risk-averse motivation for officials charged with detecting potential problems worthy of policy action. Modern decision psychologists refer to the connection between interest and observation as _confirmation bias_. Over and over again, in the laboratory and in structured observations, studies have shown a tendency for people to find evidence that supports their preconceived notions. Even in good-faith data gathering, analysis, and interpretation exercises, biased results occur (Ben-Shakar et al. 1998; Nickerson 1998). Daniel Kahneman (2011) notes that most of the time our minds work like lawyers, seeking out evidence to present to the court (our consciousness) that will exonerate our client (the preconceived notion). That is, we are hardwired to find what we are looking for. Political scientists Milton Lodge and Chuck Taber (2012, chapter 7) have amassed considerable experimental evidence that supports motivated reasoning, in which citizens seek out information that confirms prior beliefs about political objects, as well as evidence that people are biased toward disconfirming information that conflicts with prior beliefs. In effect, by putting people in charge of finding problems, we make it more likely that they will do so regardless of the evidence.

Lack of policy action when it is desirable is clearly possible as well, in which officials neglect clear signals of coming problems. Governmental mechanisms that add resistance to change, such as is built into the American system requiring concurrent majorities to pass laws, make the lack of action even more probable. We have studied the consequences of this previously (Jones and Baumgartner 2005a, 2005b). Here we address the other side of the equation: when policy action is initiated and the policy agenda expands as a consequence.

Search, Diversity, and Order

The paradox of search arises because search is tightly linked to finding, and finding is connected to action. The tight link between seeking and finding has two separate implications. First, avoiding confirmation bias is of great utility. While there is no magic solution, search based in diversity makes the process less subject to confirmation bias. Organizations may avoid the confirmation bias by including discordant views in the decision-making process (Page 2008). Proper search is best pursued through diversity and openness. The paradox of search, however, is that with diversity comes loss of control. Control is necessary to forge workable solutions, but control can be detrimental to broad searching. Disorder is valuable when engaging in search, especially in those areas where the problem space is unclear and the means–ends connections are uncertain. Order and control are the enemies of search. Yet we repeatedly hear calls to eliminate this diversity in governmental reorganizations; command, coordination, and control are almost invariably highly regarded, whereas disorder and diversity are seen as the hallmarks of poor governance. These characteristics may be bad for implementation of well-understood policies, but they are beneficial for search in areas where social complexities are great.

SEARCH AND INFORMATION

How do governmental search processes relate to questions of information processing in policy making? Search implies an active role in detecting problems that implies intentionality, whereas information processing is a much broader concept. There are many ways that government officials acquire information that do not involve active search. In effect, information processing requires attention, and explicit search procedures provide for regular attention to potential problems.

Information itself is an elusive concept. It is difficult to define without incorporating attention and problem definition (Jones and Baumgartner 2005b). A major difficulty is that a situation may suddenly become relevant to government even though it has not changed much, if at all. Is there new information? In one sense, there is not; nothing significant in the policy-making environment has changed. But in another, it is new, because as awareness of the situation becomes more widespread among governmental officials, it offers the potential of new perspectives and different interpretations.

Given that government addresses highly complex problems that are constantly shifting, poorly understood, and for which proven and effective solutions are often impossible, there is a logic in fostering a highly diverse search for relevant information—this can help leaders gain greater insight into the multiple aspects of the complex problems they face, and to assess the relative importance of the diverse problems that demand attention. But with conscious awareness of information often comes action, and in the context of government, action often means more and overlapping programs. There is nothing inherently negative about this—often we need to address different parts of a social problem. Different agencies and programs focus on different elements of an underlying problem. But just as search leads to new programs, the accumulation of programs can lead to problems of overlap, coordination, and control. So we expect a trade-off between the values of information and those of control. They are in constant tension.

We do not underestimate the difficulty of enacting policies once a problem enters the realm of explicit policy debate. Participants bring cognitive biases to the debate, often colored by preferences and ideologies. Information relevant to the problem can be addressed in a variety of ways, including outright denial of the validity of the information (not necessarily wrong, given the uncertainty of any information relevant to social and economic problems), interpretation according to one's preferences, and admission that the problem is real and needs to be addressed. How this plays out is often only tangentially related to the initial information.

Nevertheless, it is likely that search procedures make action more likely by steering information into the policy process. This information can take a variety of forms: statistical evidence about the state of the world (such as the unemployment rate), qualitative information about the severity of a problem or the effectiveness of a solution, anecdotes and personal stories that motivate professionals or that mobilize the public, and indictors of how constituents are viewing the emerging situation. Information may relate to the severity of a given problem or to the feasibility or cost of a solution. It may relate to the plan of a government official to engage with a particular issue or to disengage, signaling to other actors that action on that topic is more or less likely. So, information may relate to the problem, the solution, or to the process of policy making itself.

Much of the information governments gather comes from their own systematic and costly efforts: a nation's intelligence services are a vast information-gathering bureaucracy, for example; the Bureau of Labor Statistics is another large information-gathering organization. But governments also have a lot of information thrust upon them. This comes from scientific and corporate discoveries that make new things possible; it comes from advocates seeking to justify a given policy proposal; it comes from journalists; it comes from social movements and interest groups; it can come from anywhere. We will see that governments have very different attitudes toward information: it may be welcomed, subsidized, legitimated and routinized, or restricted, controlled, and censored. It is hard to eliminate, however. And it keeps on coming.

Information has somewhat different roles in simple versus complex problems. Governments deal with many simple problems, such as providing clean water, maintaining roads, and trash collection. We can refer to these as "engineering problems," meaning these are problems for which we understand how to provide a solution. By contrast, "complex problems" are those where we may not even understand the nature of the problem itself, much less be aware of an effective solution. Our focus is on complex problems, but it does not lessen the importance of our arguments to note that we also expect governments to deal with thousands of engineering problems in a routine manner at the same time as they attack the complex ones that are our main focus. Complex problems are poorly understood. They are problems where implementing a solution can make another problem worse. They are problems like global warming, economic growth, national security, poverty, homelessness, health care needs, and other run-of-the-mill issues of government concern.

How governments structure their own information environments is an important key to understanding how they grow, how they contract, and how they are controlled. Institutionalizing the collection of information so that the environment can be systematically monitored is the typical solution of governments everywhere, but these systems are only as good as the institutional design surrounding them. Gathering systematic information on the wrong elements of the problem, or only on a subset of the relevant aspects of the problem, is not effective. As governments institutionalize attention to multiple elements of a complex problem, they create problems of coordination, control, and implementation. Overlapping bureaucracies dealing with different parts of the same problem create their own problems of coordination. And a focus on gathering more and more information about the nature of the underlying problem can take resources away from implementing those solutions to parts of the problem where we know, at least, they are effective in their own domain. Thus, we have a fundamental conflict at the core of all government: the complexity of the task environment requires more information on diverse elements of the various issues facing it, but control of government and the implementation of effective solutions require clarity.

The Great American Agenda Bubble

Underlying the search dynamics that we trace in this book is a historical dimension. Coming out of the Second World War, many Americans felt that anything was possible, and that government could lead the country into a brighter and brighter future. Historian James Patterson (1996, 8), after touching on some disquieting trends, summarized the general public mood as one of grand expectations: "Together the American people had produced magnificently, fought valiantly, and destroyed their evil enemies. They would join harmoniously to make things better and better in the years ahead." The development of the capacity of government to detect and solve problems was part of this general sense of progress in addressing America's problems and developing its potentials through government.

This can-do attitude led to increases in the capacities to detect problems but it also led to government growth as government grappled with increasingly difficult problems and devoted resources to address them. Using the resources of the Policy Agendas Project, we show changes through time in the diversity of information incorporated into politics, and we link these clearly to the growth and consolidation of government. Government grew and then consolidated in a long arc that began with a massive increase in the span of issues addressed by Congress beginning in the 1950s, peaking in the late-1970s, and declining until the end of the period of measurement in the mid-2000s. By the end of the period, the span of issues addressed had contracted to about the same level as at the beginning of the period. However, we also find residues of this bubble in the programs and agencies created in the period, and in the oversight functions of congressional committees. What we call the "Great New-Issue Expansion" cut a great arc of activity through most of the postwar period and in its wake left a strong administrative state.

We do not think the strong and vitriolic conservative countermobilization that began in the late 1970s can be understood without reference to the American agenda bubble. Much of the attack centered on information: social science, planning, social analysis, and even data collection were dismissed, in many cases because they led to more government programs. But, ironically, conservatives strongly supported some of the most intrusive policies of all, in particular those justified by reference to national security and crime control.

Policy-making structures that are well-developed for the consideration of the diverse nature of potential problems are at increased risk for policy overreactions. Similarly, policy-making structures designed to foster agenda denial are at heightened risk of underresponding. These tendencies are at least partially decoupled from the distribution of policy preferences in these institutions. Some policy makers would rather examine problems and run the risk of overreaction, even if they are suspicious of addressing these problems with government programs. More importantly, all policy makers are caught up in the agenda bubble, whatever their policy preferences.

WHAT IS TO COME

Our analysis uncovers an unavoidable paradox: The more sophisticated the governmental search processes, the more problems government finds. The more problems government finds, the more it devises remedies to solve these problems. If we try to limit the scope of information so we can control a program or so we can control government intrusion, it is more likely that problems will fester, grow, and become crises that are even more expensive to address. Not all problems become crises, so it is safe to ignore some. But which ones? It is not all that easy to decide.

The rest of this book is directed at exploring the two parts of the paradox. Chapters 2 and 3 lay the groundwork for making the case that organizations must address both the discovery and prioritization of problems, on the one hand, and direct expertise toward solving them on the other. Diversity is key to discovering problems, but control is the key to directing expertise to solving the problems. Chapter 4 shifts to the historical development of these devices. It examines the development of explicit policy analysis and information gathering in the executive and legislative branches from the Second World War to the election of Barack Obama in 2008. We show that after years of increasing commitment to analysis and an expanding role in providing "honest numbers" for policy choice (Williams 1998), a turning point occurred in 1978, with extended declines afterward.

Chapter 5 turns to Congress, using the approaches developed in Chapters 2 and 3 to analyze the search behavior of the congressional committee system, the legislative branch's premier search mechanism. The chapter shows an increase and then decline in diversity in the search process during the postwar period in the United States. Chapter 6 ties the developments described in Chapters 4 and 5 to agenda dynamics, showing how many indicators of agenda expansion peaked at the same time as did systematic search procedures in the legislative and executive branches.

Chapter 7 shifts toward the second part of the paradox. The chapter traces the increase in the breadth of government activity following increases in the diversity of the search process described in Chapter 6. With more issues on the agenda, we saw a broadening of government into new areas of life and a thickening of its activities in established areas. Chapter 8 rounds up the "usual political suspects" and shows how partisan divisions cannot account for the patterns we observe in the earlier chapters. Chapters 9 and 10 explore the ramifications of the paradox of information and control.

2

Organizing for Expertise or Organizing for Complexity?

Universities are forever arguing about reorganization. How well does the existing structure of academic departments and programs fit the production of new knowledge—that is, how well does what universities teach fit the knowledge that is being produced? Much new knowledge is produced at the edges of disciplines; how can that be incorporated? Are the fields of study within disciplines no longer representative of what the discipline does, and hence obsolete? Should several departments be combined into a school in order to achieve coordination and "synergy"?

All arguments about organizational changes in universities and elsewhere are propositions about attention. Somehow the current structure does not get professors and students focused on the right elements. Arguments about coordination and synergy are essentially claims that the "right" focus cannot be preordained but that it will somehow magically emerge if the proper organizational boxes are put together.

It is tempting to dismiss such debates as arcane academic disputes that have little relevance to the day-to-day operation of the organization. But we argue in this book that these considerations are critical—and not just to universities. Changes in organizational structure, and in particular what tasks are performed by what parts of the organization, are ubiquitous in society. *Jurisdictional assignment*—fitting the parts of the organization to the complex tasks it faces—consumes a very large amount of time and energy in any organization. Moreover, because organization focuses attention and attention is necessarily partial, these actions have important consequences for how well things get done. These academic debates are not just academic.

In this chapter, we explore the organization of government and its relationship to the paradox of search. Structures that are organized to bring expertise to bear on a well-understood problem are often not the best structures for detecting and prioritizing problems in complex and dynamic environments. This tension is responsible for considerable instability in government policy making. Here is how we think it works: There are many forces that move a political system toward equilibrium.[1] Political equilibrium involves the decentralization of policy making to experts and interested parties, along with only sporadic intervention from the higher levels of government. Devolving to experts allows a division of labor and the creation of independent bureaucracies able to function simultaneously without mutual interference. The more the system relies on a set of linked systems comprised of experts, the more able it is to adjust policies routinely to the development of conditions within those subsystems. This works well as long as the problems are well-understood and no dramatic adjustments are needed.

If the problem space is evolving more quickly than the organizational structure can possibly adapt to, then we have an inherent tension. Organizations, whether they are universities seeking to establish "interdisciplinary" centers for learning and research better adapted to the way problems are "really" faced or governments seeking to bring their bureaucratic structures in line with evolving understandings of the underlying problems, are constantly playing a game of catch-up with the shifting nature of society. Some organizations really are well designed to deal with the problems they face. We see few major reorganizations of agencies with relatively simple tasks: the municipal water department, for example, has a clear mission. The problem space is not changing radically, so the organization is typically not under great strain. On the other hand, many organizations, or networks of government agencies, face complex problem spaces that they do not even fully comprehend and for which each solution creates a new problem. In these environments, we see more constant churning of organizational design. We often see a tension between the desire for clarity and clear organizational rules and procedures and that of finding the proper fit with the environment and the problems the organization seeks to resolve. Organizational shifts are resisted, often repeatedly, until finally they are abandoned or adopted in the face of what must be overwhelming evidence that the "old system" is no longer working as it was designed to, or that "new ideas" and "new approaches" are needed in order to address the new en-

---

1. In *Agendas and Instability in American Politics*, we developed the notion of a set of partial equilibria associated with policy subsystems, and showed that these partial equilibria could be disrupted by shifts in the attention of macropolitical actors—in the United States, Congress, the president, and the political parties.

vironment. Organizational change is sticky, but the environment is constantly evolving.

Of course constraints—legal, political, and economic—may cause a mismatch between problems and organizational forms even when a better organizational form, in the sense of matching the nature of the problem, exists. More problematic, however, is that problems are often extraordinarily complex, implying that different organizational forms are optimal for different aspects of the problem space. Not only are problems complex, but the problem space facing government is highly dynamic. Subsystems of experts are good at adjusting to minimal to moderate changes in the local environment, but not so good at mediating among emerging priorities.

An Old Debate in Public Administration

As agencies are created to follow the developing problem space, the issues of supervision and control become increasingly important. In the 1940s, Herbert Simon wrote a paper for the *Public Administration Review* entitled "The Proverbs of Administration." Simon made the devastating point that for every known principle of administration one could generate a second principle, usually contradictory, had as much validity. One of the proverbs dealt with the "span of control." Administrative theorist Luther Gulick contended that no administrator had the capacity to efficiently supervise more than a certain number of subordinates, and he recommended sharp limits on the number of units reporting to any individual supervisor. Simon countered that limits on the span of control for any one administrator necessarily implied more levels to the organization, and more red tape. "If it is granted, then, that both the increase and the decrease in the span of control has some undesirable consequences, what is the optimum point" (Simon 1946, 58)?[2]

Scholars of administration after Simon tended to dismiss management principles, in part based on his stinging critique. The uncritical acceptance of Simon's critique lasted for almost half a century, until modern students of public administration began to reexamine it (Hammond 1990; Meier and Bohte 2000, 2003). Meier and Bohte stress the limits on the supervisory ability of administrators as the span of control increases and show empirically

2. Actually, organizations need not expand levels very much, because the system is subject to combinatorial mathematics. If we limit a supervisor to seven subordinates, the addition of one level to the organization allows an agency head to supervise forty-nine subordinates. Still, in very large organizations, such as government departments, the complexity of organizational design is undoubtedly a concern.

its role on organizational outputs. But the broader point of Simon's article, mostly missing from contemporary and modern interpretations, is the absence of equilibria in designing organizations. There is no optimum point in the trade-offs involving specialization, problem prioritization, supervision, and control. Gulick isolated the right factors, but perhaps erred in assuming they could be easily implemented.

Robert Dahl, in his 1966 American Political Science Association Presidential Address, examined the proper role of the city in the future of democracy (Dahl 1967). His approach was organizational: too large a governmental unit, and individual democracy meant little; too small a unit, and the problems the city faced could not be addressed within the jurisdiction. Dahl blamed the structure of problems rather than the lack of technical skill in solving them:

> Whether the obstacles that prevent us from achieving tight closure on solutions lie in ourselves—our approaches, methods, and theories—or are inherent in the problems is, paradoxically, one of these persistent and elemental questions for which we have a number of conflicting answers. For whatever it may be worth, my private hunch is that the main obstacles to closure are in the problems themselves—in their extraordinary complexity, the number and variety of variables, dimensions, qualities, and relationships, and in the impediments to observation and data-gathering (Dahl 1967, 953).[3]

Reorganizations occupy so much of the public discussion because we have limited organizational forms with which to work, while problems are variegated and changing. March and Olsen, in their study of government reorganizations, write:

> The effectiveness of political systems depends to a substantial extent on the effectiveness of administrative institutions, and the design and control of bureaucratic structures is a central concern of any polity.... Politics operates within highly structured situations (e.g., budgeting) using repetitive, routinized procedures, and it operates within un-structured, relatively rare situations (e.g., revolutions) using ad hoc and unprogrammed procedures. Much of political life, however, is neither so regular as budgeting nor so unusual as revolution (March and Olsen 1983, 281).

They find that most reorganizations fail to achieve the lofty purposes of the reorganizers, and frequently fail more in more fundamental ways.

Often we assume away the complexity of the problem space through over-simplification, force-fitting it into some organization of experts overseen

---

3. The problem of matching organizational form to problem is a major theme in the urban politics literature. See V. Ostrom, Teibout, and Warren (1961); Bish (1970); E. Ostrom (1976).

by hierarchy. That is, we force-fit a problem in detection and prioritization into one of subject-matter expertise. This frequently leads to organizational forms that are maladaptive—that is, they overattend to some aspects of the problem space while underattending to others. By organizing expertise, we invariably organize attention. Organizational forms focus collective attention to part of the complex problem space. This can (and generally does) lead to the overinvestment of resources in some areas and the underinvestment in others. Organizing attention implies setting priorities (Jones and Baumgartner 2005b).

Organizing Information in the Face of Complexity

Governments are inherently complex organizations. They face multidimensional problems with difficult trade-offs that are often ill-understood, they pursue diverse goals using a wide variety of means, and they must incorporate divergent political interests that citizens of a diverse society inevitably have. Seemingly obvious conclusions about how to organize an administrative structure that work very well in an environment where goals are shared and mechanisms of achieving them well understood make less sense in an environment of complexity. In simple settings, hierarchical control and clarity in the distribution of tasks are important. In settings of complexity, too much control can cause relevant dimensions of a choice to be unintentionally eliminated from consideration. In simple environments, too many participants with differing viewpoints can lead to confusion. In complex environments, a greater range of considerations will generally be associated with better decisions. Where we do not understand exactly how to achieve our goals, or where the goals themselves are multiple, some fluidity is important. Deliberation where participants are not allowed to bring up dimensions of the issue not welcome by the leaders is dictatorship, after all. Democratic participation demands openness. More generally, however, the complexity of the social problems facing governments demands that we incorporate more rather than fewer dimensions of consideration into the process. Not only is an open process more compatible with democratic principles but also it is likely to lead to better decisions. Democracies may work better than other forms of government because they guarantee a wider range of social inputs than an autocratic leadership that suppresses dissent.[4] But the need

4. An enlightened dictator would have multiple sources of information about evolving problems and issues in society. The difference might be that the dictator alone would decide on the response. But all governments would work better with a greater range of

for wide-ranging information is in constant struggle with another goal: the need for organizational clarity. Clarity makes sense when tasks are simple, but not when they are complex.

THE TEMPTATION OF CLARITY

Surely, one might think, clear lines of command and straightforward rules of decision making are the *sine qua non* of effective administration and decision making. Certainly, there must be right and wrong, better versus inferior solutions to recognized social problems, and the job of a government administrator or elected official should simply be to pick the best. Decisions should be made by experts, and they should have enough information to choose the best outcome, with the authority to exclude "outsiders" who might want to muddy the waters by introducing "extraneous" or "superfluous" considerations. Certainly, these experts should be able to exclude from participation those pranksters and neophytes whose only goal may be to produce stalemate. Who is not frustrated in seeing those without expertise or knowledge enter into a debate, such as when naysayers arguing that climate change is not occurring gain coverage in the media, or when baseless assertions gain traction in the blogs or the mainstream media? Surely, false and extraneous information need to be excluded from responsible public debate.

Before we jump too quickly into the temptation of clarity, we should consider the types of public policy problems that lead to debate and those that are, in fact, clear. Delivering the mail is relatively clear. Purchasing boots for the army is relatively clear. Providing clean drinking water to a community requires passing some technical hurdles, but the task is clear. Acquiring information about the financial needs of incoming college students is feasible. But these relatively straightforward issues are rarely the stuff of fundamental political debate. We refer to these routine administrative problems as "engineering" problems in the sense that no great theory of government is needed, just the implementation of known technologies. Indeed, in such instances, clarity is appropriate. And, indeed, relatively straightforward policies exist for doing these things and the government implements thousands of such policies on a routine basis every day.

Simple problems are rarely the stuff of public debate. If we all agreed on the severity of a given problem and officials knew precisely how to solve it, there would be little room for public discussion. Debates center on issues

---

information, so it is not clear that this discussion is related to democratic versus other forms of government.

that are either the objects of conflicting interests and opinion, or on what can be called "wicked" or "complex" problems: problems such as eliminating poverty, where the range of relevant dimensions of the underlying issues is so great, and the various potential ways of resolving the problem are multifaceted. Or debates center on the possible trade-offs between attention to issues: Should we send a man to the moon (a complicated engineering problem, but in the end still an engineering one), or should we use those funds to solve some other problem? If a problem is complex, or if the debate is about relative priorities among incommensurate problems, than establishing "clarity" may not be a useful solution. This, of course, does not mean that one allows chaos in the administrative structure. But history shows that even well-intentioned plans to funnel information inevitably lead to ignoring many aspects of complicated issues, as attention focuses on just a few of the most prominent dimensions.

ORGANIZING FOR CENSORING

One common way of simplifying decision making in government is censorship. That is, leaders often use rules of standing, distinctions between experts and outsiders, or other criteria to censor or eliminate unwanted components of the information stream. Often this is a sin of omission—in the face of complexity, decision makers must focus their attentions. And, when they do not have a full understanding of the problems they face, they may well inadvertently ignore some streams of information that prove later to be important. (Donald Rumsfeld referred to these as the "unknown unknowns" of governmental life.) Inevitably, moving forward requires assessing what information is relevant and designing organizational routines to bring that information front and center. Other information is simply irrelevant by definition. So one form of censorship is based on cognitive limitations and the need to prioritize. We even have a term for the operation of this organizational dynamic: "that was not even on the radar screen."

Twenty-six years after the Space Shuttle Challenger exploded during liftoff on January 28, 1986, Roger Boisjoly, an engineer with Morton Thiokol, died (Martin 2012). Boisjoly had repeatedly warned that the seals on the shuttle's booster rockets could fail in cold weather. He testified before a presidential panel on the disaster and released a memorandum he had written warning of the potential disaster. Within the company and at NASA, Boisjoly was ignored and finally explicitly overruled by top management. After the disaster he was prohibited by Thiokol from doing space-related work, shunned by his colleagues, and suffered headaches and depression. The story of Roger

Boisjoly is depressingly familiar. Groups have informal methods for sanctioning norm-violators, as the work of Elinor Ostrom and her colleagues has repeatedly shown in both field observations and laboratory experiments (Ostrom 2005). Ostrom was the leading student of the emergence of cooperative behavior in the absence of formal organizational incentives, situations in which the provision of collective goods can be thwarted by "free riders." It is true that the emergence and enforcement of informal norms can facilitate overcoming collective-action dilemmas. This can operate for group gain, but it can act to the detriment of a broader collectivity, especially when valid points of view are suppressed. Even federal legislation to protect whistle-blowers has had limited success. Bringing unwelcome information into a public policy debate can be very difficult. But it is also hard for leaders to evaluate thousands of bits of information constantly coming to them. So the struggle between complexity and control is not peculiar to the Challenger disaster: it is a constant tension in governments everywhere.

CENSORING IN REORGANIZATION: HOMELAND SECURITY

When the United States was attacked on September 11, 2001, by al Qaeda, a failure of intelligence was apparent. According to the commission that investigated it and suggested reforms, too many divergent agencies, each with a particular mission, but none with an overall vision, shared responsibility for gathering intelligence, analyzing it, and acting on it. Further, as the commissioners write, the relevant structures of government were designed for the Cold War and therefore naturally focused on established states, measured such things as annual industrial output, and observed potential enemies as "threats emerged slowly, often visibly, as weapons were forged, armies conscripted, and units trained and moved into place. Because large states were more powerful, they also had more to lose. They could be deterred" (9/11 Commission 2004, 362).

According to the commissioners, the government mischaracterized the problem of external threats to U.S. security, organizing its agencies to solve a problem that was no longer pressing and failing to create new structures to deal with the emergence of a new but as yet poorly understood threat. In making their recommendations for restructuring government agencies for the new challenge, the 9/11 commissioners focused on the need to understand properly the problem before defining the solution, and they emphasized the need for radical, not incremental, changes. In suggesting changes, they wrote that the "attacks showed, emphatically, that ways of doing business rooted in a different era are just not good enough. Americans should not settle for incremental, ad hoc adjustments to a system designed generations ago for a world that no longer exists" (399). Each of their recommendations starts with the word "unifying" until the sixth and last one, which focuses on "strengthening" the FBI and homeland defenders (399–400).

If one wanted an example of what we described in an earlier book as "institutional friction" and of the disproportionality of government response to sometimes slowly evolving problems (Jones and Baumgartner 2005b), one need look no further than this analysis. Institutional inertia ensured that institutions designed to achieve one set of goals were incapable of shifting their focus to a new set, especially since the signals coming into the system were changing slowly and were poorly understood. Institutional missions do not change easily, especially when those institutions have all the prestige, economic importance, and political influence of the U.S. military and its associated industrial complex; such actors can easily dismiss critics who might suggest that they are designed to fight a threat that no longer exists as being "soft on defense," a charge that is never welcome in U.S. politics. The inertia that characterizes the policy process is institutional, bureaucratic, and associated with lobbying and economic interests that mobilize to protect established programs; it is not only cognitive in origin. But no matter what the sources of friction, one consequence is that when change comes, it is overwhelming. The 9/11 attacks seriously undermined established structures by their manifest incapacity to adapt to the suddenly obvious new reality. So, dramatic rather than piecemeal changes were justified. And the commissioners called above all for clarity: a unified organizational structure with a clear mission.

The commissioners responsible for investigating the 9/11 catastrophe have written one of the best, most lucid, engaging, and perceptive investigative reports in the modern history of the U.S. government. Their analysis of the linkage between the definition of the nature of the problem and the organization of government agencies designed to address it is fundamentally on target. Their suggestions that the complex and confusing mixture of diverse agencies with a piece of the counterterrorism pie should be better coordinated can hardly be contested. And their idea that piecemeal and incremental reforms must give way, given their catastrophic failure, to dramatic shifts, can hardly be countered by any reasonable argument. In the last chapter, entitled "How To Do It: A New Way of Organizing Government," the commission calls for "Unity of Effort" in a variety of circumstances, but the solutions that they propose are unlikely to be successful. Or if they are successful, they will result in neglect and decay in other areas of overlapping responsibility. They illustrate precisely what we mean by the struggle between information and control.

Indeed, the U.S. government was in the midst of a natural experiment with exactly what the commission advocated—the creation of the Homeland Security Department. In the wake of the 9/11 attacks, the Bush administration, with the strong support of Congress, tried mightily to get the diverse agencies of government responsible in any way for "preparedness" to focus their attentions on the terrorist threat. Organizationally this was accomplished first by establishing the Office of Homeland Security in the White House, followed by the creation of the Department of Homeland Security in 2002. Peter May and colleagues examine the changing demands of policy makers in the area of preparedness—preparing the country to detect and mitigate a variety of disasters, from hurricanes and tornadoes to civil defense and terrorist attacks. They write that

> [t]he evidence we provide shows that the Bush administration was very successful in focusing agency attention on the administration's antiterrorism agenda. But the centralized attention to this agenda and the way that it was reinforced within the DHS overloaded circuits at the top. Attention to nonterrorism-related programs was crowded out, as was evident in reduced preparedness efforts for natural and technological disasters and from the problems so evident in the failed response to Hurricane Katrina. . . . In addition, the manner that attention was organized at top levels of the DHS fostered oscillation in grant programs, distrust among intergovernmental partners, and meddling from above (May, Workman, and Jones 2008, 519).

The effect of the creation of the Homeland Security Department and the continual hectoring of agencies involved in disaster preparedness to focus more on terrorism by the staff of the Secretary and by White House operatives was to censor information and limit preparedness for more regular disasters. May and colleagues write that "agencies have two basic ways of organizing attention. One consists of delegated authority and the use of formal routines. The other involves centralized authority and the use of informal procedures. To delegate or centralize is the question" (518). In this case, centralization was the answer. But centralizing a complex mission inevitably creates a cognitive overload, and therefore censoring. Indeed, increased centralization in administrative departments is often associated with a focus of attention on one mission among the several that constitute a modern government department. May, Workman, and Jones found no evidence that agency personnel tried to undermine the centralized demands coming in to their agencies, even though they did send ample warnings of the consequences of the centralization. That is, asymmetric information was a part of the story only in that it was correct. It did not undermine the centralized command to focus attention on terrorism preparedness—the central authorities were able to impose their policy preferences with little or no interference by line bureaucrats. The lesson here is that centralized authority and delegation are inevitably in tension and that the risks of overcentralization can be as great as those of delegation. Centralization risks overload while delegation risks lack of coordination. There is no proper balance between these, which is why we observe agencies lurching from drifts toward delegation with an occasional lurch toward overcentralization. The response to 9/11 within the huge range of agencies that are now said to be related to the new concept of "homeland security" is an excellent example of the danger of overcentralization. But the catastrophic failure of the security apparatus leading to the attacks in September 2001 also illustrate the shocks that explain why attention became so suddenly focused on the need to "fix" a system that obviously was not working.

Is Government an Organized Anarchy?

In 1972 three organizational theorists began an influential article with the words "Consider organized anarchy." They went on to suggest that perhaps government is such an environment (Cohen, March, and Olsen 1972). As they defined it, an organized anarchy has: a) "problematic preferences" (that is, multiple conflicting goals); b) "unclear technology" (it does not know how to achieve its goals); and c) "fluid participation" (the people in charge continually come and go) (1). Their initial description of an organized anarchy can be understood as a simple statement of the obvious: in a boundedly rational environment, we cannot expect models of organizations based on comprehensive rationality to work very well. They write: "Significant parts of contemporary theories of management introduce mechanisms for control and coordination which assume the existence of well-defined goals and a well-defined technology, as well as substantial participant involvement in the affairs of the organization. Where goals and technology are hazy and participation is fluid, many of the axioms and standard procedures of management collapse" (2).

The model was originally developed to describe higher education: What university president could state clearly *the* goal of a modern research university? Once a few important goals were agreed to, how would they be achieved? If every university understood how to maximize student learning, Americans would be a lot smarter. And if each school knew how to recruit and support top-flight researchers, we would have made much more scientific advancement. The simple point is that these are difficult problems for which people can disagree on the best ways to achieve them. And who has a right to be on the ad hoc committee? That is, should professors, administrators, outside experts, or perhaps students and alumni participate in making decisions in a modern research university? It is not so clear. It seems obvious that universities have multiple goals, unclear technologies for achieving the goals, and little continuity of participation in decision-making venues. In the context of government, which of course has an even more diverse array of goals than a university, the applicability of the ideas should be even clearer.

The implications of these elements of decision making within complex policy-making environments are often ignored in many neo-institutionalist approaches to the study of government. Neo-institutionalists often assume fixed preferences and authority structures, eliminating fluid participation (but see Ostrom 1986). The reason this is done is to explore the ramifications of the incentive structure in such systems. In the standard principal-agent approach, an agent, such as a federal bureaucrat, has information that a congressional oversight committee, the principal, does not, and is able to use that information to forward the agent's preferences at the expense of the principal's. But that requires an assumption of fixed authority structures and fixed preferences, something the organized anarchy perspective denies.

Preferences are about the value people place on goals. But often goals are vague or incommensurate with other goals; if goals are vague or incommensurate, so preferences will be. Policy makers, political parties, and even voters are constantly attempting to reach a solution to a problem that cannot mathematically or logically be solved: we want low taxes but good services nonetheless; few regulations but no business excess either; progress on environmental priorities but not stifling of business competitiveness. In sum, we often collectively want A and ~A at the same time. So, far from starting out with a single goal, we start out with many goals and many contradictions among them. Preferences are not only unclear but they are often mutually contradictory. If we focus on achieving one of them to the exclusion of others, we find that we create other problems. It may or may not be possible mathematically to find the right balance among all the competing goals that may exist in a complex environment like the U.S. federal government, but it is unrealistic to expect any human institution to define a clear set of goals and stick to them. In a complex environment, we simply focus on a few goals until we are forced to shift our focus to some others because they become more urgently threatened.

The second part of Cohen et al.'s formulation is important as well. In their terminology, we have "unclear technologies." In government this means that we often do not know which policies work. Will an increase in unemployment compensation reduce poverty, or, on the contrary, will it stifle the incentive to seek new employment? In practice, what our lack of knowledge about the effects of complex public policies means is that advocates are constantly trying to convince us either that a given policy, laudable though its goals may be, is a colossal waste of money, or that another policy, not yet proven, could indeed solve some problem.[5] The technologies of many public policies are indeed unclear. This lack of clarity opens the door for proponents to present information on one side of the issue or another.[6]

Finally, authority structures are not clear—that is, in any decision, participants are fluid. This may be the concept that many readers will have the most difficulty accepting. Similarly, most political leaders think that manipulating the lines of authority and changing the jurisdictional assignments with them can clarify a complex and confusing organizational arrangement. It seems clear: surely there is a division of labor in politics. The secretary of agriculture cannot make foreign policy, and the secretary of defense does not make education policy. To say that there is some structure to government does not, however, indicate that participation is constant or that the rules of authority are clear. Rather than a clearly defined hierarchical pattern in which supervisors have a greater range of power than subordinates and each has clear lines of authority to those below, we have something much more ambiguous. Political leaders may attend to whatever problems they think will improve their position with the voters. Agencies, congressional committees, and individual political leaders shift in their attention, not randomly, to be sure, but with considerable freedom to prioritize this rather than that issue at any given time. Interest groups, social movement leaders, journalists, and others, of course, are much less constrained. As issues rise and fall in salience, a wider then a narrower group of political

5. In *Agendas and Instability in American Politics* we showed this dynamic at work in several case studies. Pesticides, at the beginning, were said to be the cure for human disease, poverty, hunger, and the position of the United States in the world. Similarly, civilian nuclear power in the 1940s and 1950s was supposed to produce the cure to such problems as economic scarcity and clean drinking water for all, as well as eradicate worldwide poverty (Baumgartner and Jones 2009).

6. In those cases where we actually do understand how to accomplish a given goal, such as, for example, delivering the mail, the issue often promptly leaves the political agenda, as there is no longer any reason for controversy. We referred to these as "engineering problems" above.

actors intervenes, and occasionally the public becomes aware of issues that otherwise would be treated within specialized arenas of governance, among experts. So, participation does indeed seem quite fluid in politics. If participation were fixed, the same institutions would always decide issues. In fact, we see some structure, but a lot of fluidity.

Hierarchy and jurisdictional assignment matter, because they channel both participation and attention. We can see this most vividly when jurisdictional assignments are changed. Attention allocation can be shifted via organizational charts, and if the new pattern of attention allocation becomes routinized (something people are very good at doing, and bureaucracies reinforce this tendency), then the new arrangement becomes permanent. The Joint Congressional Committee on Atomic Energy really did gain a monopoly of control of all matters related to nuclear power from the early postwar years until 1976, when it was disbanded. Why was it disbanded? Because congressmen not on the committee considered that it did not reflect the full range of views that needed to be part of the debate (see Baumgartner and Jones 1991, 2009). So preferences are related to structures. As we have previously written, the dominant policy image associated with a policy is typically reinforced by a controlling institutional venue of decision making. Shift the venue, and the image is likely to change. Alter the image, and the venue may be shaken. Image and venue are mutually reinforcing, which makes them powerful when stable but potentially rapidly unstable when one begins to change (see Baumgartner and Jones 2009). Here, we generalize this idea we originally laid out more than twenty years ago as the tension between complexity and control. It is a general, unavoidable characteristic of government.

Conflicting and overlapping jurisdictions are never called for in designing ideal organizational structures. Nevertheless, somehow they keep coming back. The empirical evidence suggests: a) they cannot be fully avoided; b) they have become more and more common as government has grown over the generations; and c) they should not be avoided, as they play a key role in ensuring the consideration of multiple sources of information. The range of perspectives that comes with fluid rules of participation is associated with better decisions and the consideration of a wider range of information.

In the complex and dynamic environment faced by governments, attention is a key variable in the model. Cohen and his colleagues note, "Since variations in behavior in organized anarchies are due largely to questions of who is attending to what, decisions concerning the allocation of attention are prime ones" (1972, 2). Attention shifts tend to be interdependent. Attention may shift to those issues where a credible case has been made that a solution may actually work, or where new information comes in to suggest that a currently active solution is not working at all and is in fact wasting money. Solutions can feed back into problem definition. The availability of solutions affects the likelihood of attention being focused on a given problem.

The involvement of one political leader may suggest to others that this may be a more important issue than they realized, so it can increase the interest of others, triggering a cascade of attention and participation. These interdependencies, the mutual interactions among the parts of the policy process, especially among political leaders who often respond rapidly and en masse to the same information or to the actions of those they see around them, are essential to the punctuated-equilibrium model. Without interdependence, we would not see the cascades, mimicking, and positive feedback processes that occasionally interrupt the routine decision-making process of government. Cohen and colleagues modeled this process as one of completely random couplings, and in his later work John Kingdon (1995 [1984]) followed up on this formulation. A more contemporary description of these interdependences would perhaps have used the language of complexity rather than that of randomness. To suggest that issues are hugely complex does not mean that they come together with no order. In fact, there can be a complex structure to the interactions, but they may be highly interactive and embedded within a network of connections that makes it difficult to predict the precise movements of the system. So Cohen and others may have been on the right track even if today we understand complexity as something more than the randomness they described.

Fits and Starts: The Struggle between Information and Control

The U.S. government, with separation of powers, federalism, and "overlapping institutions sharing power," is a paragon of redundancy. Some would say waste. But the apparent inefficiencies of overlap, shared jurisdictions, and unclear lines of authority are also the means by which large amounts of information enter the political debate. Where one institution develops an incomplete perspective on a complex issue or follows a policy that ignores important elements of social need, another is likely to raise the question. While no institutions deal perfectly with those social issues that are under their jurisdiction, the conflict and competition inherent in the overlapping structures of government ensure that no single view dominates all government agencies. Competition based on shared, even conflicting, mandates is central to the structure of government, and always has been. A monopoly of detailed technical information in the hands of a single agency is the most efficient solution to the division of labor that is necessary in any complex organization. But in situations where the problems are not mere technical ones but require value judgements or experimentation with various approaches, it can create a dictatorship. Redundancy is therefore an important element of organizational theory, but an unpopular necessity.

A constant in the history of U.S. government has been complaints about inefficiency. Not only are efforts to create "clarity" in government likely to fail, but they go against the spirit of separation of powers, federalism, and messiness that have informed the very structure of the U.S. government from its earliest days. The ideas apparent in the structure of government as designed in the eighteenth century have become even more important as the U.S. government has grown from a very modest size, dealing with only a few core items, to its current scope. The framers appreciated redundancy, overlap, and restrictions on the power of any individual actor, creating a system at ease with ambiguity more than two hundred years ago. It is even more important today, in an era of massive overload of information, to embrace these ideas even when they frustrate leaders who would be tempted to call for a chimerical "clarity" in public life. The problems facing government simply do not allow it.

The idea that redundancy and overlap harbor surprising value in public life is not new in the study of public administration. Martin Landau, writing in 1969, began an article on the value of redundancy in public administration with a discussion of an emergency landing in an airplane. Talking to the pilot afterward, he writes, he was reassured that, while the rudder had ceased to function, the pilot was able to fly the plane using other means. Luckily for the passengers, "a commercial airliner is a very redundant system, a fact which accounts for its reliability of performance; a fact which also accounts for its adaptability" (Landau 1969, 346). He contrasts "rationalist" perspectives on the design of public institutions with "redundant" designs. The essential difference is the degree of understanding and mastery of the environment. Where the problem is an engineering one, strict rules of organizational clarity would be appropriate.

> The logic of this position . . . calls for each role to be perfected, each bureau to be exactly delimited, each linkage to articulate unfailingly, and each line of communication to be noiseless—all to produce one interlocking system, one means–end chain which possesses the absolutely minimum number of links, and which culminates at a central control point. For the public administration rationalist, the optimal organization consists of units that are wholly compatible, precisely connected, fully determined, and, therefore, perfectly reliable (354).

For Landau, this might be fine in some settings, but in public administration, "organizational systems of this sort are a form of administrative brinkmanship. They are extraordinary gambles. When one bulb blows, everything goes. Ordering parts in series makes them so dependent upon each other that any single failure can break the system" (354). Such a decision-making process would work in the case where "the environment has been fully and correctly described . . . preferred state conditions are unequivocal . . . [and] the instruments necessary to produce preferred states are at hand. Said alternatively, certainty exists as to fact and value, instrumentation and outcome, means and ends. All that needs to be known is known and no ambiguities prevail" (355). In a later article Landau notes that "duplication of function and . . . overlapping jurisdiction [are seen as] waste" (Landau 1971, 424). In a complex technological environment, such as moon flight, he notes, we design redundancy into the system to ensure it can adapt to partial failures, but in government it is "treated as contrary to common sense, and removed as soon as circumstances permit" (424). Finally, he concludes that the "theory of redundancy is a theory of system reliability" (427).

Landau's critique is virtually identical to that of Cohen and colleagues: by assuming clarity and understanding, we fundamentally misapprehend government. More importantly, the framers of the U.S. Constitution, as Landau notes, expected ambiguity rather than clarity in mission. Rather than design a system for maximum efficiency when dealing with known problems with known solutions, they sought a self-correcting system capable of dealing with messy problems for which the best solutions would continually have to be sought:

> Experience, Madison wrote, has taught mankind the necessity for auxiliary precautions: these were to be had "by so contriving the internal structure of government so that its several constituent parts, may by their mutual relations, be the means of keeping each other in their proper places." The principle of action and reaction, of checks and balances, turns out to have been, in organization terms, the principle of inter-woven and competing redundancies (Landau 1969, 352).

Public administration scholars since Landau have continually appreciated the frustration of political leaders who seek "clarity" and the value in maintaining multiple sources of expertise in government. The U.S. government was designed by a set of thinkers who seem to have had a great understanding of ambiguity and a level of comfort with conflict. They expected factions to be present, for the men and women of government not to be angels but rather individually ambitious humans, and that there would be diverse viewpoints on all matters of public discourse. The system that they designed, compared to others, incorporates the elements of redundancy that Martin Landau so appreciated. But the U.S. government, like any other, features a continuing struggle between those who "clarify," "streamline," and "take control" and those who understand the value in redundancy (or who simply protect their own turf when attacked).

The system occasionally settles into routine patterns where all accept the status quo, perhaps not because they are pleased with it but because they know it is so powerful that fighting against it will be fruitless. Where the dominant party is unassailable, it can pay few dividends to fight against it. During other periods, however, the previously powerful are weakened by widespread recognition that the status quo may not be the best possible situation. Challengers promoting new ways of thinking are no longer silent. Rivals to the powerful seek to supplant them. Occasionally significant changes occur. This process can occur at any level of the political system. The self-organizing nature of the process means that stability and powerful changes can alternate whether we look inside of small niches of the policy apparatus (for example, deep within an administrative structure dealing with such questions as the best way to promote learning among preschool children, the most cost-efficient means of collecting taxes, or the best strategies of community policing), at higher levels of the policy-making apparatus (say, the level of a cabinet secretary), or even at the government as a whole. Very similar dynamics are clearly at work at each level of aggregation. The struggle between information and control affects the ability of policy communities to maintain support and consensus about "best practices" in their respective policy niches, our expectations about the size of the federal government, and everything in between.

Once in power, government officials typically want to exert their authority by consolidating control. In the struggle between clarity and information, any victory for clarity will be short-lived. While we cannot create a governmental structure that can fully solve the problems of overabundance of information or comprehensively assess the myriad challenges that face a modern government, we can certainly put blinders on. These blinders, in the form of restrictive definitions of what is appropriate to consider and what is superfluous, may allow administrators to make clear decisions. But inevitably they will define out of considerations aspects of complex social problems that will eventually rear their heads. Minority viewpoints, unwelcome news, and nagging problems do not go away when ignored; often, they simply accumulate. Governments do a better job when they incorporate even what they prefer to ignore.

The U.S. Constitution as a "Pantheon of Values"

Shortly after his retirement, Supreme Court Justice David Souter gave a commencement address to the class of 2010 at Harvard (Souter 2010). He used the opportunity to reflect on the inherent struggle between ambiguity and control, not just in politics but also in the text of the U.S. Constitution. He writes that "the Constitution contains values that may well exist in tension with each other, not in harmony." After briefly describing the conflict in the case of the *Pentagon Papers*, which put in stark contrast the competing values of freedom of the press and the need to protect national security, both unquestioned constitutional values, he writes:

> The explicit terms of the Constitution, in other words, can create a conflict of approved values, and the explicit terms of the Constitution do not resolve that conflict when it arises. The guarantee of the right to publish is unconditional in its terms, and in its terms the power of the government to govern is plenary. A choice may have to be made, not because language is vague but because the Constitution embodies the desire of the American people, like most people, to have things both ways. We want order and security, and we want liberty. And we want not only liberty but equality as well. These paired desires of ours can clash, and when they do a court is forced to choose between them, between one constitutional good and another one.

He suggests that these difficult trade-offs "are, after all, the creatures of our aspirations: To value liberty, as well as order, and fairness and equality, as well as liberty." Finally, he gets to the crux of the matter, the trade-off between incommensurate values and the clarity that would come if we could only value one of them above all others:

> I have to believe that something deeper is involved, and that behind most dreams of a simpler Constitution there lies a basic human hunger for the certainty and control that the fair reading model seems to promise. And who has not felt that same hunger? Is there any one of us who has not lived through moments, or years, of longing for a world without ambiguity, and for the stability of something unchangeable in human institutions?

Justice Souter is clearly responding to the strong intellectual movement on the Court to embrace an "original intent" model of judicial behavior in which judges would not be so "activist" but rather simply implement what the Constitution says. By pointing out the inherently conflicting goals of liberty and equality, or freedom and security, for example, he stresses that even at the most basic level the goals of government are inherently in conflict, oftentimes mutually contradictory. Since the government is designed to serve so many different purposes, some of which are in conflict with one another, we cannot understand how governments work if we do not appreciate the concept of ambiguity.

Information and Organizational Form

In this chapter, we have focused on some basic ideas about complexity and organizational responses to it. Periodic efforts to establish clarity through government reorganizations have eliminated certain overlaps and redundancies of the kind Landau discussed, but—just as he suggested—these redundancies are not mere inefficiencies. Rather, they are a necessary part of allowing information to flow into government. As government has grown, it has become involved in a greater range of activities, and the boundaries among thousands of independent agencies and actors in the system have become more blurred. As numerous partially independent organizations have developed their own operating procedures, norms, policies, and areas of expertise, a wide range of perspectives has become institutionalized in government. This strengthens the informational capacity of government, but makes it harder to manage.

3

Information, Search, and Government

Governments are awash in more information than they can possibly analyze. It comes from their own agencies (as these monitor developments within their jurisdictions), from outside advocates promoting various policy stances (usually the status quo), and from events of all magnitudes ranging from traffic accidents to wars, epidemics, economic surprises, technological advancements, and environmental catastrophes. Some of the information is designed to have a political impact, as when a lobbyist or a think tank publishes a study suggesting that a certain policy option is particularly effective, costs more than anticipated, or will have unintended consequences. Such studies seek to affect how political leaders assess the likely cost or effectiveness of a given policy and thereby to push policy dynamics in a certain direction. Or they may seek to draw attention to a particular aspect of the problem that has received little attention. Other studies make the case that a problem is more serious than realized, thereby promoting the idea that government should be more active in efforts to solve it. Some information that becomes relevant in a political debate is not generated by such a process, however. For example, new scientific discoveries or inventions can alter the cost or effectiveness of a given policy. Or new data on economic trends, poverty, immigration, or crime may demonstrate that a problem is getting much worse and therefore increase pressure for action. Real-world events such as oil spills, financial crashes, and social movements demand attention, whether government officials would prefer to focus on them or not. And some of the news is good (such as new inventions or studies that show that a particular treatment for cancer may be more cost-effective than previously understood), whereas some of it is bad. In the realm of politics, media, interest groups, and politicians themselves are continually monitoring the mood of the electorate, as well as particular groups that may be crucial for election or campaign funds (Kingdon 1995; Stimson 1999). Oftentimes this political information weights the importance of the issues facing government, helping to allocate attention to some issues at the expense of others (Jones and Baumgartner 2005b).

Governments respond, in fits and starts, to this flood of information that washes over them and which they create every day. There is so much information, and it changes so often, covering so many topics of interest, that no government can incorporate it all into its routine decision-making processes. Further, governments are often expected to address problems for which no proven solutions exist. So they try even though they may not have a clear idea of what really works. And yet at the same time all governments seek to gain control of their environments. They do the best they can to control and funnel information by setting out rules and procedures to prioritize the most important bits of news and channel it to the top, with specialized agencies dealing with relatively routine developments within their respective jurisdictions. But because the world is complex and unpredictable, and because of the inherent struggle among political actors who seek to have their policies adopted, governments never succeed completely in controlling their own agendas. New information sporadically but repeatedly forces their attention from this to that issue or from this to that aspect of an issue to which they are already paying attention. Information determines priorities, and priorities determine actions. The flow of information in politics determines the flow of political life and the dynamics of policy change.

Choosing among Problems, and Picking Solutions

The most complex task that governments face, and one that certainly cannot be devolved to teams of experts, is allocating attention across the various problems that clamor for it. With no systematic indicators that would allow a decision maker to know objectively how serious various issues are, the decision to attend to one problem rather than to another is inherently political. Occasionally, as with Pearl Harbor or 9/11, a foreign military attack unquestionably merits a dramatic response. More typically, however, many problems compete for attention. Some are well understood, but there are no workable solutions. Some are not especially acute, but we may know how to solve them. And some problems are barely even recognized. Choosing among problems is the greatest dilemma facing any government.

Once attention is focused on a problem, of course we need to choose what mix of solutions is best. Different problems, of course, have better and more poorly understood solutions. Some cannot be solved at all; some can be partially ameliorated, but only at some cost in terms of unwanted consequences of the solutions themselves; and some can be fully resolved, if we are willing to implement the right solution. If we consider a continuum from complexity to clarity, then choosing among poorly understood problems is at the far end of the complexity side, and implementing well-understood solutions to a commonly identified problem is at the opposite end. A solution may have logistical issues, but in the terms we used in Chapter 1, these are "engineering issues" and can be solved with the right resources.

The types of information needed, and the organizational structures best designed to work at the left end of this continuum, are those that focus on diversity, openness, and lack of preconceptions. Unfortunately, these are the opposite of what is needed at the other end: clarity, hierarchical control, and discipline. Thus, the search for information and the organization of governmental structures must be attuned to the nature of the problem; there is no one-size-fits-all solution.

Decision makers are best served if formal organizational structures follow the different information types. One is operating in the problem space when trying to define and prioritize diverse signals that may indicate difficulties in the environment. Once the problem is determined, then one is operating in the solution space. Moving into the solution space before having determined exactly what the problem is creates problems of its own. But if the problem is truly complex, one could spend a lifetime assessing it before taking any action, and people demand action on important problems. So, governments routinely act simultaneously in the problem and solution spaces. This should not be seen as a pathology; it is characteristic of how we deal with complex problems.

Unfortunately, the very organizational structures that lead to connecting solutions to problems appropriately can interfere with problem discovery, definition, and prioritization. For problem solving we need the organization of expertise through hierarchy. Hierarchies allow the specialization of function such that experts can interact with experts, and do so in a reasonably autonomous fashion. Higher levels of the hierarchy can mobilize this expertise through task assignment—so long as the problem is well understood. But hierarchy is not the right organizational form for problem discovery or understanding, because diversity of viewpoints is necessary—the very antithesis of hierarchy. The incorporation of diversity in formal organizations requires flat structures and a tolerance for disorder and competition within the structure.

There is a final difficulty. In problem exploration, one can spend so much time and effort in discovery that no problems are ever solved. At some point, there must be a decision-making mechanism that prioritizes problems so that they can be addressed. If information supply and solution expertise are two faces of information, control is the third face. Control involves many things, but at base it is the assignment of problems to experts for solution—that is, it involves hierarchy and bounded jurisdictions. And problem assignment is agenda setting. Control involves choice, and choice means excluding extraneous information. Unfortunately, control for most people implies that they ought to be in charge, and they censor discordant but oftentimes relevant information in order to pursue clear objectives and straightforward implementation.

The disconnect between these two forms of information—solution expertise on the one hand, and problem discovery and prioritization, on the other—leads to great instabilities in policies in even the best governments. How does a decision maker decide when to engage in problem search and when to apply and implement solutions? Given problem complexity in many areas of public affairs, even the best decision maker would have trouble in deciding which approach to apply. But there is a second layer—that of the cognitive capacities of the actors in government—that increases these instabilities. Central control is a major source of this amplification, as higher-level officials are subject to the same laws of human nature as their subordinates. Control is necessary because it provides a mechanism for assigning problems to agencies and for shifting problem priorities. But it leads to the potential of misguided certainty and the illusion of clarity. The tendency for people to overestimate their decision-making capacities is so well-grounded in psychological experiments that it has become a fundamental premise (Kahneman 2011).

Information versus Preferences as the Key Dynamic Force in Politics

If we are sure everybody knows what he or she wants, then lots of difficulties in understanding and analyzing the activities of governments disappear. The only issues concern the reconciliation of these preferences—say, through majority vote or some other decision rule—and then deciding on the appropriate technology for achieving this. This would not be easy in any real political system, as any number of formal analyses have shown. But if we assume that knowing what one wants (and hence what government should do) is not so simple, then we are going to have to figure out exactly what the problem is, and that requires a different set of skills and organizational arrangements.

People often want many contradictory things and they cannot prioritize clearly one set of goals ahead of another—trade-offs among incommensurate goals are very difficult. Much of politics is about how we understand issues. Underlying each preference is a set of attributes or components that structure the preference. If the weights of these components shift, then the preference can shift (Jones 1994). Republicans once advocated a government-enforced mandate to purchase health care, using the argument that people should take care of themselves and not rely directly on government when they failed to do so. As governor of Massachusetts, 2012 presidential candidate Mitt Romney included an individual mandate in his state's signature health care reform. By 2010, when Democrats adopted this proposal for President Obama's health care reform plan, Republicans had abandoned this position, seeing it as a "government takeover" of the health care system. A change in issue understanding caused a radical shift in preferences. In general, preferences are more fluid and dynamic than is often thought, because of this link between preferences and the underlying attributes of complex issues. There is a sizable body of research in psychology that indicates that people do not have fixed preferences, and often do not know what they want until they experience something (Kahneman 2011). Much of this is semantic: if one has a preference for happiness or wealth or good health, that does not tell him or her much about how to get there. To translate preferences into issue positions, we need information.

It is common in politics for people to have general preferences for goals like reducing poverty or promoting a good economic climate. But the technology for achieving these goals is often unclear, so preferences alone do not tell us what policies one might support. Further, at the same time as one has one preference, one has other, possibly contradictory, preferences as well. Those that want to reduce poverty also were forced in late 2008 to admit that they, unbeknownst even to themselves, also had an unrecognized preference to make sure that the largest banks and financial institutions in America continued to function. And when most members of the U.S. Congress voted for what was called the financial bailout, many complained that they were voting "against their preferences" (Jones and Surface-Shafran 2009). If preferences are relatively vague, many times unrecognized, and often contradictory, it is hard to build a theory of decision making on this basis. Further, if the likely success of a given policy proposal in achieving the goal that it sets out is also unclear, then preferences are a further step away from explaining policy choices.

Information and Public Decision Making

Information implies communication, and communication involves *senders* (or *sources*), *messages*, and *receivers*. Sources send messages across some system of transmission to a receiver.

There is general agreement among scholars that information transmitted in human communication systems is *imperfect, costly,* and *asymmetric,* and that it can be *private* or *public. Imperfect information* simply denotes that there is never enough information to ensure certainty in any choice. Imperfections can stem from three different sources: limits in knowledge (nobody knows enough to provide exactly the right information for the choice); imperfections in the system of transmission of the information; and limits in the cognitive abilities of the receiver to retrieve and understand the relevant information (including deciding exactly what is relevant).

The exchange of information is always _costly_ to both the sender and the receiver. Because the sender incurs a cost of providing information, a rich literature has developed in economics (Stiglitz 2000) and political science (Gilligan and Krehbiel 1987, 1989, 1990) centering on what conditions will lead a sender to provide information to a receiver, and what implications that has for decision making. For example, Gilligan and Krehbiel ask why a committee of Congress would go to the trouble of becoming expert in a subject when the legislative chamber could, based on this knowledge, simply substitute its preferences for the preferences of the committee members (assuming there is a difference). Their logic suggests that there must be some advantage in terms of deference from the chamber to the committee in order to justify this effort.

But information is also costly to a receiver, and this influences how imperfect the information is that he or she uses in a decision. In his classic study applying the principles of economics (and in particular the principles of the then-emerging theory of economics of information), Anthony Downs asked how citizens became informed when information was imperfect and costly:

> When information is costly, no decision maker can afford to know everything that might possibly bear on his decision before he makes it. He must select only a few data points from the vast supply in existence and base his decision solely upon them. This is true even if he can procure data without paying for them, since merely assimilating them requires time and is therefore costly (1957, 145–46).

Most of us are not experts in matters of public policy that require choice. In the case of government in democracies, citizens must become informed about issues without becoming experts. Moreover, within government, elected decision makers must rely in part on subject-matter experts on complex issues. As Downs notes, "democracy is impossible without a shifting of factual analysis onto specialists" (2008, n.p.). That is what we mean about *asymmetric* information. It is clear that if we defer to an expert's knowledge in grappling with a policy problem, we may also inadvertently defer to his or her preferred solution to the problem—that is, the expert may substitute his or her preferences for ours.

Finally, information may be provided either in a *private* or *public* manner. If information is provided in a private manner, then an expert may charge for that information, as would be the case if one consults an accountant or doctor. But some information is free (that is, there is no monetary cost) to the consumer, and these situations are particularly common in politics. If one side in a debate does not supply information, the other side will, gaining the asymmetric information advantage (Jones and Baumgartner 2005b, 9). As Downs notes: "It is in the self-interest of political elites to distribute information" (2008, n.p.). As a consequence, information in politics often will be abundant rather than scarce. In such situations the costs are heavily shifted to the receiver of the information, who must sift through the various sources sending messages and decide what is relevant and what is not.

SEARCH COSTS AND COGNITIVE COSTS

There are elements of the study of information in politics that, unlike the consensual elements detailed above, generate vigorous disagreements. Nowhere is this more evident than in the conceptions of the receiver of information. On the one hand, economists and many political scientists assume that the receiver is rational. Even rational individuals may remain ignorant in politics, because "[i]t is always rational to perform any act if its marginal return is larger than its marginal cost. . . . The marginal return from a "bit" [of information] is the increase in utility income received because the information enabled the decision maker to improve his decision" (Downs 1957, 146). More generally, a rational individual searches for information until the expected returns of the last "bit" of information equal the expected cost of obtaining that information.

But there are, in addition, costs associated with the nature of human cognitive architectures—we refer to these as *cognitive costs* (Jones, Sulkin, and Larsen 2003; Jones and Baumgartner 2005b). Humans have great difficulties in adjusting their choices in a manner that is proportional to the new information they receive (Jones 2001). One need delve no deeper into cognitive structures than to observe the limited natures of attention and short-term memory; our short-term memory allows us to pay attention only to a small number of things at a time. In addition to this cognitive limitation are various mechanisms that retard attending to and acting on information, which we summarize as *cognitive friction* (Jones, Sulkin, and Larsen 2003; Jones and Baumgartner 2005b). As a consequence, we observe a pattern of under- and overreaction to new information. Humans are simply not generally capable of matching expected marginal costs of information to expected marginal returns. The basic architecture of human decision making hardwires us into a pattern of lurching, not to smooth transitions from one decision to the next. We are disproportionate information processors, and the implication of that is that we underattend to issues below some cognitive threshold of urgency and then later we react in surprised alarm to something that may have been there for quite some time, but to which we were not paying sufficient attention. Further, these are not "errors in judgment" or "mistakes," and they certainly are not "anomalies"; these are basic characteristics of human decision making.

Expert Information versus Entropic Information

Different aspects of information have relevance for different parts of the decision process. In determining what solution fits a given problem, we rely heavily on experts (or at least we ought to). We also rely on expert analysis to break apart a given problem to understand its components—indeed, the term "analysis" means the breaking down of a complex problem into its component parts. It is not so clear that experts are as good at prioritizing problems, however. They may have preconceived notions about what problems are important, perhaps due to their training and past experiences as experts. When asked what major problems are facing the United States today, a civil engineer is likely to rank the crumbling transportation infrastructure as a higher priority than is a teacher, who may well rank problems in K–12 education higher than the engineer. The two state-university college professors who authored this book, you will not be surprised to learn, think the decline in public support for higher education ranks very high in the national inventory of serious problems. Our point is that the focused expertise that allows a fuller understanding of the potential solutions to a given problem can render experts inept at making choices across problems.

Some process other than delegation to experts is needed for this. By definition, an expert cannot be expert at everything. And if the question is which of all the potential problems facing the country deserve attention, no one is an expert at that.

When we must choose across the many problems that could demand our attention, we want some other mechanism for acquiring information, and that mechanism ought to cast a wide net to make sure major problems or understandings of those problems are not omitted. This is especially important because in the midst of setting priorities, cognitive costs play a heavy role in problem prioritization. In particular, the inability of humans to pay attention to multiple streams of information simultaneously is critical (Jones 2001). As Herbert Simon often noted, humans are serial processors—that is, they process one stream of information at a time. That means we tend to focus on the problem at hand, ignoring other problems that could be as important—unless we have a mechanism for alerting us to the importance of those other potential issues we should address.

We can state this as a simple principle: in setting priorities, we need diversity, whether we recognize it or not. This "information as diversity" is very different from information as expertise, and each is applicable to different parts of the process of decision making. To distinguish it from expertise, we term this form of information as *entropic information*. A receiver has more information when messages on a variety of topics are produced by multiple nonredundant sources.

Diversity of Sources as a Key Element in the Supply of Information

Different types of problems require different types of information. If the problems we dealt with were "engineering problems" (ones with known and effective solutions—such as building a bridge to solve the problem of crossing a river), then clarity of authority and conciseness of discussion would be values. But in the messy world of complex problems, too much "clarity" can be a sign of too little information, too much orthodoxy, or too little willingness to look at those parts of the problem where the information is unpleasant. Six repetitions of the same argument have less informational value than six statements focused on different elements of the underlying debate. As social problems are complex, a wider range of information provides a better context for decision making than a narrowly focused discussion.

Here we make no attempts to assess the quality of the information that enters politics. We can all see that false information sometimes rules the day.

Rather than look at quality, we want to focus on diversity. How much information is present? More to the point: How diverse is the set of information that is incorporated into the policy-making process? Diversity is not self-correcting, because it allows for the entry of misleading or incorrect information into the process. But no other mechanism is capable of ensuring that information about problem prioritization enters the process. Diversity of information is undesirable when dealing with engineering problems: here we need to grant clear authority to those who know what they are talking about and to suppress other voices. But in complex issues, greater diversity of voice can only lead to a greater appreciation of complexity. And, we can measure diversity in a way that we cannot measure quality.

Unfortunately, it is not always clear which issues are engineering issues and which are not. Different participants may view the same issue in a different light. Is climate change a now-settled scientific issue, so that engineering solutions are the major challenge? Or is it less settled? Even if it is settled, how do we rank its importance among many pressing issues? Is it the preeminent challenge facing the globe, or does it compete for prioritization for scarce resources with other areas?

Information affects the dynamics of politics because it shifts our attention and causes us to change our priorities. News that a given policy works better or worse than was previously understood should not be expected to change our preferences at all. But because we have so many preferences and cannot act simultaneously on all of them, such news can indeed change behavior, particularly the relative place we put each issue on our list of priorities. Among political leaders, lobbyists, and those involved in the policy process, news can alter agendas. What kind of news can do this? It can range from a new study (giving relevant facts about costs or benefits), an advertising campaign (suggesting that a given interest group is going to invest significant resources in a topic), or the actions of a key political player (suggesting that movement on the issue may now be more or less likely). Within a Washington-based policy community, information of many types can cause scores of political leaders simultaneously to alter their understandings of what is "good public policy" and what is not, what is feasible and what is not, and what others will be willing to accept and what they will refuse. So, without changing anyone's preferences, information can change everyone's behaviors.

Information in politics is often inaccurate. It is almost always incomplete. So when we say that information drives politics, it is not necessarily for the best. But we can distinguish between policy debates that are richer and those that are poorer in their informational content. In the environment of a debate surrounding any complex matter of public policy, a wider range of considerations is always a better basis on which to base decisions than a narrower range. The struggle between information and control can be seen as a struggle over the incorporation of many forms of information and the desire to limit information.

Diversity as Information

Do we know more if we listen to more people, or if we listen to fewer? Most are tempted to answer this question as "it depends on the people." We would say that it depends on the problem. Surely we do not want to discuss our medical problems with the local grocer, and we do not normally ask our doctor for car repair advice. While we may consult different experts within a subject domain, we do not normally ask these experts to move beyond the subject domain where they have specialized knowledge.

It is also true that "it depends on the people," but in a sense that is probably opposite to what most of us mean by the phrase. Generally people seek out like-minded individuals in social situations, but they also turn to like-minded people in a broader sense—when they discuss politics or business or religion. Republicans tend to consult different news sources than Democrats. The evidence from psychology indicates that often people act like lawyers, seeking out information to defend a point of view rather than seeking out information for illumination (Kahneman 2011). The modern mass media, with its niches stratified by ideological perspective, make that easy.

Scott Page's 2008 book, *The Difference*, focuses on the value in decision making of having diverse viewpoints at the table. When a group makes a decision, he shows, the quality of the decision is enhanced when the group is more diverse. Diversity of the decision-making body ensures that a variety of perspectives are integrated into the analysis. The idea that in facing complex problems institutions will do better if they can incorporate and institutionalize consideration of more, rather than fewer, dimensions of the issue is exactly our point.

The problem with consulting diverse viewpoints in setting priorities is that at some point we must come to a conclusion, and a cacophony of voices can obviously lead to confusion. We address this issue in other chapters of this book, but for now we simply distinguish between the *supply* of information and its *prioritization*. These are two distinct processes, although it is common in real world decision-making situations for acquisition of information (that is, increasing supply) and prioritization to take place simultaneously. And we note that when it comes to supplying information about priorities, we want to avoid, to paraphrase former defense secretary Donald Rumsfeld, omitting knowable unknowns. For complex or poorly understood problems, more information from the greatest diversity of backgrounds and perspectives is better. This is why we pay attention to the entropy of information sources.

The Trade-off between Diversity and Clarity

In making complex decisions, considering a wider range of dimensions of the situation can lead to a better decision. Consider the purchase of a car. What if the only aspect one considered was how close the dealership was to home? Certainly that consumer would be more likely to have buyer's remorse than the one who also sought out information about safety, cost, fuel economy, comfort, style, and functionality. Also note how much simpler the decision is for the first consumer, and recall how hard it is for many of us to make consumer choices such as buying a car. As the diversity of perspectives used in a choice increases, the decision becomes richer, but more difficult. Diversity is *inversely* related to *ease* of decision making. Unfortunately, difficulty is likely to increase exponentially with the number of perspectives evaluated (since the difficulty of comparing perspectives can quickly become overwhelming). A wide range of perspectives increases the informational richness of a decision, but it makes the decision exponentially harder, hence the trade-off between information and clarity.

Figure 3.1 illustrates this decision-making perspective. A decision maker receives numerous messages from potentially competing sources. The greater the number of divergent sources, the richer the informational environment will be. But the more the information, the harder it is to prioritize the various bits of information that may be relevant to the choice. In order to facilitate choice, one can eliminate information sources, as illustrated in Figure 3.2, a process akin to censorship.

The temptation to impose clarity consists essentially in ignoring sources of information that are deemed "irrelevant." That is, in order to make sense of what could potentially be a cacophony of unrelated signals coming from an overwhelming range of sources, the decision maker may well decide to ignore some of them. This is done both by conscious choice as well as subconscious processes of human cognition, most importantly our limited range of attention. In Figure 3.2, the decision maker ignores all but Source$_2$. In government, this would mean having clear rules of standing, strong norms of who is allowed to participate, and powerful barriers to keep outsiders out of the decision-making environment. Such things are common, for example,

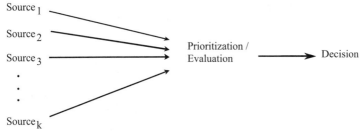

FIGURE 3.1. The Information / Prioritization Problem

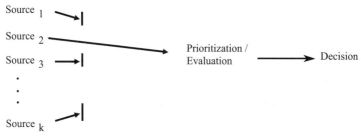

FIGURE 3.2. Facilitating Decision Making by Censorship

in expert-based decision making or within institutions that have strong jurisdictional boundaries around their work, as in certain technical agencies. In management, this would mean listening to only one point of view, ignoring dissident viewpoints. In buying a car, this is ignoring many dimensions and buying the one suggested by the dealer closest to home.

Taken to the extremes, both Figures 3.1 and 3.2 are pathological. With too much information, decision-making capacity can be overwhelmed. With too little, important bits of information are overlooked (though this may not be recognized until later). We cannot suggest any absolutes in how many dimensions of an issue a decision maker should evaluate. Some individuals find themselves stymied by even relatively simple decisions; others seem comfortable juggling significant ambiguity. We can say, however, that the temptation to exclude information can be dangerous, especially in dynamic information environments. As long as the world is complex, our information-gathering mechanisms need some degree of openness. When these are shut down, decision making is simplified, but the quality of the decisions suffers.

Complex public policies differ from engineering problems. Where the problems are well understood, the solutions known, and the decision makers knowledgeable, it is straightforward to gather the relevant information and to exclude the irrelevant. One of the biggest mistakes in political life is to believe that we understand more than we do. This is the temptation of clarity.

Comparing Expert Search and Entropic Search

Expert search is based on intense focus on a single, well-defined problem. It works best with hierarchy and well-defined jurisdictional boundaries. Entropic search is based on a dispersion of attention where problems are ill-defined and complex. It works best in decentralized organizational structures with an element of confusion and overlap in their jurisdictional boundaries.

Complexity in the problem space may or may not be associated with complexity in the solution space. We may think of complexity in the policy or solution space as associated with the number of dimensions that must be addressed to forge a satisfactory solution (Jones and Baumgartner 2005b). If the problem space is reasonably simple, then expert search will be focused on reducing the uncertainty concerning the effects of a policy solution. Figure 3.3 depicts this situation. The policy being evaluated is at the star; it is optimum based on existing knowledge. But its effects are uncertain. The outer semicircle represents the uncertainty associated with the proposed policy. There is some probability that the policy will have very different effects than we expect. The narrower ellipse indicates the uncertainty about the policy's effect after the information about the policy is produced. We still are uncertain about the exact effects of the policy, but the range of that uncertainty is far more tolerable. Expert search often limits the uncertainty about the effect of the policy.

If, however, the problem space is complex and classic expert search directed at reducing the variance of the impacts of the solution is pursued, then the solution may well be suboptimal in the dimensions that are not addressed. This is the classic meaning of "unintended consequences," but ignoring the potential consequences on other dimensions of a problem makes them something less than "unintended." In fact, they are "unattended." Figure 3.4 illustrates this. There the optimum policy is at the star, as in Figure 3.3. But the optimum policy in one dimension is definitely not the optimum policy in the three relevant dimensions. The distance between the point representing the optimum policy solution in three dimensions and the point representing the projection of the optimum solution in one dimension suggests the potential error introduced by relying on expert search in complex problem spaces. Those dimensions that are unattended cannot be maximized, except by dumb luck; therefore, the ability to maximize efficiency in decision

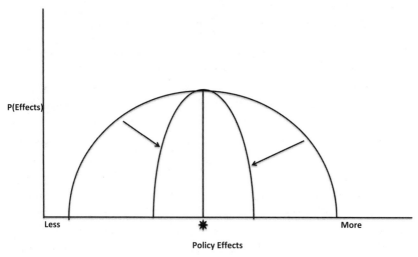

P(Effects)

Less   ✳   **More**

Policy Effects

FIGURE 3.3. Expert Search Focuses on Reducing Uncertainty

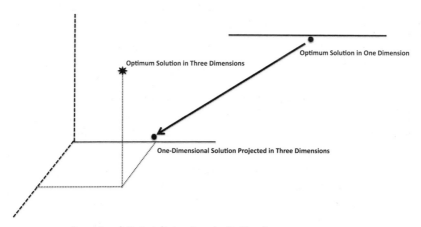

Optimum Solution in Three Dimensions

Optimum Solution in One Dimension

One-Dimensional Solution Projected in Three Dimensions

FIGURE 3.4. Expert Search Projected into a Complex Problem Space

making depends completely on the ability of the system to incorporate all relevant dimensions of consideration into the decision-making process. This is another way to restate the trade-off between complexity and information, as decision making with multiple dimensions is much more difficult to maximize than in cases with one or a few dimensions. This is especially true when one is unsure of the dimensionality of the problem space.[1]

1. And the weights of the various dimensions, a complexity that we ignore in the present exposition.

Measuring the Diversity of Information in Organizations

We have argued that some organizational structures promote entropic-type information acquisition, whereas some others promote expert analysis. In this book we are able to trace the information acquisition process, especially focusing on the U.S. Congress, and its relationship to changes in public policy activities. That requires some summary measures of the two types of information. Our primary focus here is the role of entropic information processes in government, but we also assess the extent of expert search, especially program evaluation and policy analysis.

Our strategy in assessing entropic search is to examine the manner in which the examination of policy issues is divided up among organizational jurisdictions. In particular, we focus on how issues are assigned to congressional committees for study in the hearings process. So the problem is how n objects (the hearings) are assigned to k categories (the committees). This assignment of issues to categories involves more issue diversity when an issue is assigned for study to multiple committees than when it is assigned to one committee. That would assess information diversity for a single issue, but we can add issues and get an overall summary measure.

This kind of diversity of objects across categories can be measured in a number of different ways (Boydstun, Bevan, and Thomas 2012). Two have been common in the study of policy agendas: the Herfindahl index and Shannon's entropy index. The Herfindahl index (or the Herfindahl-Hirshman index, as it is sometimes called) was developed to assess the market concentration of firms, and is often used in antitrust law. In a single industry, sales can be divided across firms in any number of ways, but if all sales are concluded by a few firms there is less diversity in the market for that good or service than if sales were divided among numerous firms. The Hirfendahl index is the sum of the squared proportions of a market (or market share) that firms hold:

(1) $HHI = \Sigma\, p_i^2$

   $i = 1$ to k, where k is the number of categories.

The larger the index, the larger the concentration of market share in a few firms.[2] The index reaches its maximum of 1.0 when one firm monopolizes the market. In political science, the Herfindahl has been used to measure committee jurisdictions in Congress (Hardin 1998; Baumgartner, Jones, and MacLeod 2000). If one has a measure of the proportion of an issue (say, ag-

---

2. An identical index was developed for the study of ecology at about the same time as the Herfindahl index (the late 1940s). It is the Simpson diversity index.

riculture) that falls within the activities of committees, then the higher the index, the purer the jurisdiction; the lower the index, the more dispersed the issue is among competing jurisdictions. This captures the difference between expert and entropic information discussed above. The higher the purity of a jurisdiction, the more likely it will be comprised of subject-matter experts, but it will exclude the diverse voices characteristic of entropic information.

A second measure of diversity that is commonly used is Shannon's entropy index (sometimes the Shannon-Weaver index). Claude Shannon, a mathematician working at Bell Laboratories in the late 1940s, analyzed uncertainty in the transmission of information (Shannon 1948, Shannon and Weaver 1971). If the transmission is very clear, all the information would be in the same category (and the system would have great structure, or low entropy). If the transmission were extremely unclear (noisy, ambiguous, uncertain), then it would be spread across many categories (e.g., it would have low structure, high entropy). Shannon's index, often called Shannon's H, is a measure of diversity:

(2) $Entropy = -\sum p(x_i)\log_k p(x_i)$

where:

x_i is a category,

$p(x_i)$ is the proportion of the items in a given category, and

k is the number of categories.[3]

If all objects are in one category, a situation of perfect structure, then H = 0. If the items are uniformly distributed across all the categories, there is no structure, and entropy is at its highest value, which depends on the number of categories.

Shannon's entropy and the Herfindahl index tap similar aspects of object concentration within categories, since both are based on similar measurements. Each index is a weight of the proportion of cases within a set of categories. The Herfindahl index is the summed proportion within each category weighted by itself (p x p), while the Shannon index is the summed proportion within each category weighted by its logarithm (p x log(p)). As a consequence, the two measures are highly correlated. Entropy does a better job at distinguishing among situations with low levels of concentration than does the Herfindahl, which is sensitive to changes at high levels of

---

3. Because logarithms are undefined at zero, and many categories are likely to have zero entries, the convention is adopted that for P(x) = 0, 0•log(0) = 0. In practice, for ease of calculation, we add a very small fraction to the actual proportions (estimates for P(x)) equal to .000001 when values are zero.

concentration, but distinguishes less well at lower levels (recall that it was designed to assess market concentration). Studies of the effects of diversity suggest that even some individuals who articulate a different point of view from the prevailing line of thought can have an effect. As a consequence, Shannon's H is preferred for assessing the diversity of political information.[4] In the empirical chapters of this book we make extensive use of these indicators of diversity of information, and we often refer to them as entropy. Entropy in information reflects its spread. Typically, when thinking of simple decision problems, we want no entropy, but rather to grant clear authority to those who know the answers. But in government, entropy is a useful indicator of the richness of the information environment, and we treat it as such throughout this book.

Agenda Denial and Information Censorship

Policy jurisdictions never perfectly fit the flow of information. While the tendency to organize for clarity is a major factor in limiting the supply of information, limiting jurisdictional scope of policy-making organizations is also a tactic in the politics of agenda denial. Because farmers used future contracts to limit their losses due to crop failure, the regulation of these derivatives fell traditionally to the Commodities Future Trading Commission (CFTC). In the late 1990s, Commission Chair Brooksley Born began to examine the desirability of regulating over-the-counter derivatives. The Clinton administration's Treasury Department, the chair of the Security and Exchange Commission (SEC), and Federal Reserve Chair Alan Greenspan asked Congress to approve a moratorium on such regulations. Congress did so, Born resigned, and the Commodities Futures Modernization Act of 2000 denied both the CFTC and the SEC jurisdiction over the derivatives industry. Johnson and Kwak (2010) comment, "The financial sector had succeeded in sealing off one of its profit-making engines from the possibility of government interference." This action also stifled the flow of information into the policy process through the mechanism of dedicated bureaucratic agencies. The denial of jurisdiction implies censoring information.

Designing the jurisdictions of government organizations is not a sterile exercise in public administration. Organizational charts matter, because they

---

4. We use a normalized version of entropy when we compare entropy across indicators that feature different numbers of categories. Non-normalized entropy scores are not comparable when one is calculated, for example, across three categories and another across twenty-five (see Boydstun et al. 2012).

filter the flow of information into the policy-making process. Because information is always more complex than organizational forms, the latter can never fit the former. The only alternative is censoring. Where the line is drawn affects whether governments produce too much policy or too little. Shifts in the trade-off are dynamic. The supply of information in public policy, and the trade-offs among information supply, policy expertise, and public authority, color the trace of public policy across time. In the chapters to come, we turn our attention to documenting empirically the relations between information, organizational design, and government from 1947 to present.

PART II

Information and the Growth of Government

We shift now to empirical tests and illustrations of our ideas. We rely in large part on the resources collected through the Policy Agendas Project; however, we begin in Chapter 4 with a historical review of the analytic capacity of government through those agencies specifically charged with policy analysis. These grew into powerful entities in the 1960s and 1970s but were attacked by those seeking to limit the growth in government. We assess the linkages between entropic information and clarity in various ways in the subsequent chapters, with our focus ranging from the development and structure of the congressional committee in Chapter 5 to the rise of new issues in Chapter 6 and the broadening versus thickening of government in Chapter 7. In Chapter 8 we assess a number of "usual suspect" theories from political science and show that the trends we observe are not explained by any of them, nor by all of them in combination. So, we turn now to the evidence.

4

The Rise and Decline of Institutional Information Processing in the Executive and Legislative Branches

It would seem a truism that more complex governments need more extensive mechanisms for processing information—information relevant to the definition of problems, to the design of solutions, to the preferences of major stakeholders, and to the evaluation of the cost/effectiveness of existing programs. Yet as we have seen, more search capacity can lead to the development of more government programs to address the issues uncovered by the search process itself. As a consequence, the development of institutional capacity to acquire and process information is not automatic; rather, it is part of the political struggle. Some seek to oppose what Walter Williams (1998) has called "honest numbers" because they fear an agenda of government growth. Policy analysis, especially the institutionalized capacity to perform it correctly, is clearly part of the political struggle that inevitably surrounds policy decisions in any democracy. Information is politics.

In this chapter we trace the rise, decline, and subsequent stabilizing of systematic information processing in both the executive and legislative branches. We find that the support coalitions underlying building institutional information-processing systems vary across issues and cut across traditional ideological divisions. Traditional conservatives display more hostility toward systematic information gathering and policy analysis when it comes to social programs, but liberals do so when it comes to security policy. As a consequence, increases in information-processing capacity can occur in some policy areas at the same time the capacity in other areas is being cut.

We have argued that governments need two kinds of information: entropic (most relevant to problem search) and expert (most relevant to search for solutions). Moreover, the two types of information processing are best encouraged by different organizational forms. Yet both types of search require substantial organizational capacity and some commitment on the part of political leaders to maintain and enhance these structures over time. Because this commitment is substantial in cost and because it has important policy and ideological implications, political support for systematic information gathering and policy analysis has ebbed and flowed in the federal government since the 1950s.

The late Walter Williams, the preeminent student of the development and use of policy analysis in the federal government, saw the systematic use of policy analysis as a function of both the supply of competent analysis and the demand for systematic information by political leaders (1998, chapter 2). Tracing changes in the willingness and abilities of political leaders to use analysis and the reliability and validity of the information (both real and perceived) goes a long way toward explaining the ebb and flow of the analytic capacity of the federal government.

The Rise and Decline of Search Capacity in the Executive Branch

Systematic policy analysis in the federal government developed first in the executive branch, and in particular the military. With the successes in the Second World War and the challenges of the Cold War, the need for sound information gathering and processing and rigorous policy analysis was self-evident. President Eisenhower proved to be an exceptional manager of government who was comfortable making decisions based on multiple streams of information, which had the effect of reinforcing demand for sound information and analysis (Greenstein 1982; Williams 1998, chapter 3).

While President Kennedy displayed few of the organizational abilities of Eisenhower, his defense secretary, Robert McNamara, institutionalized policy analysis in 1961 when he created a formal policy analysis unit in the Department of Defense. The unit was based on the systems analysis perspective developed at the RAND Corporation, a nonpartisan research organization with extensive connections in the military domain, but which expanded into other areas of policy analysis as well. Based on the successes of the Department of Defense's analytic agency, President Lyndon Johnson, a strong supporter of systematic policy analysis, had the Bureau of the Budget issue a directive establishing policy analytic offices in federal departments and agencies (Williams 1998, 61).

The analytic capacity of the U.S. government increased dramatically from the 1950s through around 1980 as a result of a bipartisan consensus on the necessity of getting the president and the cabinet the best available information on potential problems and opportunities to solve them. Policy makers should have the best decision-making environment possible, and this meant lots of information and the capacity to analyze it. Presidents Nixon, Ford, and Carter all supported the use of sound information in the policy process, relying on its provision by policy analysis professionals (Jones and Williams 2008, chapter 9). Yet each had different organizational capabilities in the use of (and, hence, demand for) systematic information.

In the Nixon years, systematic policy analysis in the executive branch reached its high point (Williams 1998, 31). Of the presidents since Eisenhower, Gerald Ford established the best system for integrating policy analysis into executive decision making, primarily by establishing an organizational framework that allowed relevant information to filter up to the White House level and thorough his open decision-making style (76). Ford was exceptional in his ability to digest complex policy arguments in short memoranda and ask analysts penetrating questions (Williams 2008). Unfortunately, President Carter was unable to establish a policy-making style that allowed full use of systematic information, though he strongly supported systematic analysis.

Support for the system was bipartisan, and its utility remained unquestioned until the Reagan administration. The shift in analytical capacity is associated with a change in attitude toward the information-gathering and analysis capacity of government. Unlike the Republican presidents who went before him, Reagan distrusted analysis and tended to rely more on ideological understandings of the policy process (Williams 2003). He was less interested in having access to data and examining the nature of problems facing government and more interested in imposing solutions suggested by conservative ideas. Williams traces a great deal of this decay in capacity to President Reagan's leadership, whose presidency he termed "anti-analytic" (Williams 1990; Williams 2003). Reagan and many of his advisors distrusted the professional policy analysts, on the grounds that government search and analysis invariably led to the discovery of more problems. The Reagan and subsequent Republican administrations increasingly turned to conservative think tanks for policy advice and cut the funding for domestic policy analysis. "The Department of Health, Education, and Welfare (now Health and Human Services) had around 300 staff members in the Carter administration and supported major social policy experiments over time. Under Reagan, the office suffered a loss of two-thirds of its staff and ceased funding new large-scale projects of this type" (Jones and Williams 2008, 243).

The Reagan-era shift in emphasis away from analytic capacity and toward ideology is perhaps most evident in his adopting of notions of supply-side tax cuts as a panacea for both economic growth and budget control

(Jones and Williams 2008). A major reason that Reagan was successful in his approach was the evident difficulties in the policy analytic model for policy making. By the late Carter years, it was becoming increasingly evident that the ability of government to manage and direct society was, if not failing, at least not producing results at the level that proponents had thought possible. The successes in using policy analysis in government led to unrealistic expectations and unwarranted claims about the ability of government to manage the economy, foreign affairs, and social policy. The Vietnam War ended in failure, discrediting Secretary McNamara and his analytic "whiz kids"; the belief of economists that they could "fine-tune" the economy wrecked on the shoals of the stagflation that followed the OPEC oil embargoes of the 1970s; systematic budgeting developed by experts and directed toward achieving explicit program goals proved elusive; and President Johnson's goal of ending poverty in America proved far more elusive than putting a man on the moon. Thus, while the analysts once had much to tout in terms of their own policy successes, by the late 1970s there were many reasons to discredit this model.[1] This allowed the pendulum to shift away from entropy and complexity to a top-down model of decision making based on hierarchical control, with less concern for analytics, information, and contrasting voices.

The top-down model of policy making reflects a type of political organization that is much admired among many political scientists—the so-called Responsible Party model of governance. These parties offer platforms of policy proposals that they plan to implement should they win an election. Reagan's approach may be seen in part as a move from a problem-solving model of governance to such a Responsible Party model. It is an approach that downplays the role of information in policy making and emphasizes the primacy of preferences, and in particular offers a mechanism for adjusting the preferences of the governors to those of the governed. But it offers no answer for adjusting the course of public policy between elections.

While President Reagan and the new Republicans attracted to his banner were certainly more ideologically driven than Presidents Eisenhower,

---

1. See Baumgartner (2013) for a discussion of discrediting the status quo before one can replace an existing policy paradigm with a rival one. Clearly, success breeds future deference from those who might be interested in challenging an incumbent policy regime. This is why policy failures can have such consequence. In the Reagan era, a large-scale shift occurred affecting the respect and deference that an entire profession—policy analysis—commanded within the halls of government. Ideological motivations were certainly behind this, but it would not have been possible if there had not been clear failures of the cybernetic and policy analytic approach in addressing such issues as the war on poverty, joblessness, and Vietnam. These failures opened a door that had previously been firmly shut.

Nixon, and Ford, what stands out even more starkly is the differences in approach to information. President Nixon used systematic policy analysis to limit the reach of the federal government (by instituting block grants to states and localities, for example) and by thinking through policy designs that would minimize the effects on individual choice (as in the case of his family assistance plan, discussed below). Reagan, on the other hand, was dismissive of analysis, and it tended to be used in this White House to win political arguments (Williams 1998, 31).

Reagan's penchant for accepting propositions that made sense in terms of his own ideological predilections, but which did not survive encounters with the facts, served to undermine the demand for sound analysis (Williams 2003). Most detrimental was his belief in "supply side economics" of the "miracle" variety, which decreed that cuts in tax rates would "pay for themselves" by causing more economic activity that would bring in more tax dollars than had been cut (Jones and Williams 2008). Advisors convinced Reagan that he needed to raise taxes to limit the deficits he was running, but he left his successor with a severe budget problem.

President George H. W. Bush acted to staunch the flow of red ink by negotiating a program of raising taxes and cutting spending with the Democratic Congress, and President Clinton followed in 1993 with a second budget-balancing bill that finally set the nation on the path toward fiscal sustainability. The sanity of economic and budget policies in the Bush and Clinton administrations did not lead to the establishment of decision-making systems in the White House that were capable of integrating systematic analysis into executive choices. Bush was amenable to policy analysis, and appointed strong independent professionals to head his analytical agencies (Williams 1998, 152–53), but his decision-making system was centralized and secret. He was uninterested in domestic policy, and that "benign neglect" left too much decision-making power in the hands of political advisors. Clinton's undisciplined but analytical style carried over into his decisional processes, and as a consequence he also failed to establish a system for the systematic use of policy information. While both Bush and Clinton supported sound analysis, neither took the steps to reestablish analytical capacity in the executive office of the president.

THE BUDGET AS A POLICY PLANNING TOOL

The executive branch began preparing an annual unified budget as a consequence of the Budget and Accounting Act of 1921. That act established the Bureau of the Budget in the Treasury Department, which gave the president the capacity to produce budgets based on sound numbers from what agencies were actually spending and reasoned economic projections. The bureau was moved to Roosevelt's White House in 1939 and was reorganized into the Office of Management and Budget by President Nixon in 1970.

As the executive branch built analytical capacities in agencies and in the executive office of the president, the legislative branch allowed its capacities to deteriorate. This was not deliberate. In the 1950s and 1960s, an informal system of agreements among Appropriations subcommittee chairs and the party leadership acted as "guardians of the purse" (Fenno 1966). The subcommittee chairs consisted disproportionately of Southern Democrats who were not predisposed to increase spending nor to search for new issues that were candidates for legislative action. The system produced budgetary balance though a well-understood set of incremental adjustments produced by interactions among subcommittees and agencies (Wildavsky 1964; Fenno 1966). Passing twelve separate appropriations bills without reconciling any or all of them with existing revenue streams worked well so long as the incrementalist rules and associated bargaining and adjustment processes were well understood by the participants. By the 1970s, the system was severely fraying as newly elected Northern Democrats explored ways of circumventing the Appropriations Committee through increasing entitlements and indexing benefits, both of which were popular with the public but which left the old system of budgetary politics incapable of producing budgets that were adjusted to income streams.

By the mid-1970s the analytical capacities of the executive branch so far exceeded those of the legislative branch that President Nixon felt confident enough to provoke a constitutional crisis over the issue. Empowered by his landslide victory in 1972, Nixon confronted Congress on a variety of fronts. In 1974, Nixon impounded (that is, refused to spend appropriated funds) congressional appropriations for subsidized housing, community development, transportation, farm programs, and clean water (Jones and Williams 2008, 123–24). Presidents had employed the procedure since Jefferson refused to spend appropriations for river gunboats, but until Nixon the procedure had been about defense or had explicitly been authorized by Congress (Kutler 1992). In essence, Nixon suspended programs that were statutorily authorized. Although his goal was clearly to limit the growth of government, Nixon argued that Congress had no mechanism for assuring that revenue streams matched expenditure streams, but the executive branch did. So, he argued, he was forced into his impoundments to ensure a balanced budget.

In the constitutional crisis that followed, the Supreme Court, in *Train v. City of New York*, a case involving appropriations for the newly enacted Clean

Water Act, ruled against the president. While the institutional crisis was averted, the stark institutional difference in the ability to gather and analyze budget information remained. Congress addressed both the impoundment issue and the problem of the lack of a congressional budget in the Congressional Budget and Impoundment Control Act of 1974. The act established a congressional budget procedure and provided for a new analytical agency for the legislative branch: the Congressional Budget Office (CBO). The agency is responsible for budget projections and analysis, including the likely budgetary impacts on specific legislative proposals.

Although Congress was a latecomer compared to the executive branch in providing institutionalized budget analysis, the CBO has performed better overall than the Office of Management and Budget (OMB). In hindsight, the decision to combine the management aspects of budgeting with the analytical components of budget in Nixon's reorganization seems to be the heart of the problem. OMB, as part of the executive branch, can be subject to political pressures that have shown up in the performance of the agency. But the agency has two goals: manage the budget according to the president's program (for which political control is obviously called for), and provide solid econometric, demographic, fiscal, financial, and other estimates of future trends so that the budget can be based on the best analysis. For that last goal, analytic clarity, political oversight and responsiveness to the president are highly detrimental. For most of the history of CBO, its estimates have been more correct than those of OMB (Williams 1998, 214).

OMB directors are political appointees and are responsible for the control aspects of budgeting, but unfortunately the political role has too often spilled into its budget estimates. The idea of supply tax cuts replenishing revenues, an idea supported by Presidents Reagan and George W. Bush, did not affect OMB's estimates of what would occur to deficits if the 2001 and 2003 tax cuts were renewed in 2012. Budget analysts estimated that the renewal would lead to strong upward pressures on the deficit. But the director of OMB at the time, Joshua Bolton, claimed in his comments on the release of the fiscal year 2007 budget that the failure to renew the cuts would lead to problems with "the government's fiscal health" (Jones and Williams 2008, 288), a statement that was not consistent with the thrust of the agency's own analysis.

How did Congress achieve what the president could not? Congress is an essentially partisan institution, but requires bipartisan consensus to achieve many of its goals. Had the leaders of the CBO succumbed to partisan pressure to affect their analytic goals, the rival party could have withdrawn support. So we saw more "honest numbers" coming out of the CBO than from the OMB (Williams 1998), a fact that dramatically altered the balance of power that had swung so heavily toward the executive branch in the period leading to the Nixon impoundments.

The story of the development of policy analysis in the executive branch, then, is one of growth and vigor up until the late 1970s, followed by extended decline. This does not mean that policy analysis and the production of honest numbers is not done in the executive branch; it remains big business. The decline has been steeper in social policy than in other areas. It is especially vibrant where it started: in the Department of Defense and associated security agencies. Data-mining activities at the National Security Agency such as retrieving meta-data on hundreds of millions of phone calls and systematically collecting huge amounts of internet traffic in order to understand the patterns of who is communicating with whom (if not always the content of what is being said) have reached unprecedented levels in recent years. These new activities have spawned a huge interlocking set of bureaucracies and contractors, and even its own special court system (Priest and Arkin 2011). But the system's huge size and extreme secrecy raise a whole set of issues relating to privacy and efficiency in the deployment of national security resources.

ENTROPIC SEARCH IN THE EXECUTIVE BRANCH

Thanks in large part to Williams's work, we have a pretty good idea of the development and subsequent decline of the policy analytic agencies in the executive branch. But we have little understanding of the development of what we term "entropic search." Entropic search, which usually means detecting and prioritizing problems, is best accomplished within an organizational framework characterized by overlapping and even conflicting grants of authority, redundancy, and considerable conflict—in a word, a Madisonian arrangement mimicking the U.S. constitutional system. Yet, there is much resistance on the part of policy makers to these organizational forms, for three reasons. First, our understanding of the role of diversity in the search process is in its infancy, and the appreciation of how organizational arrangements contribute to that process is particularly ill-understood. Indeed, until this book it has not been systematically addressed. Second, it seems so inefficient to build in competing jurisdictional arrangements to accomplish a single goal. And indeed it is. But in the public sector, goals are vague and ends–means relations are often not clear, so entropic search is particularly important there. Finally, the tension between search and control and the lack of any easy way to resolve it are reflected in how policy makers view government organization. Many diagnoses of failures to detect developing problems in the area of national intelligence and in the failure of financial regulatory agencies to detect and correct the housing bubble of 2007–08 emphasize the failure to share information and confusing and conflicting jurisdictions, and turn to hierarchy and jurisdictional clarity as solutions. Put someone in charge and all will be well. Unfortunately, hierarchy under these conditions itself is inefficient at controlling the diverse units responsible for the policy area and in using diversity to detect and prioritize problems.

JURISDICTIONAL CLARITY IN FINANCIAL REGULATION

Because we lack the systematic studies of jurisdictional arrangements and entropic search in executive agencies, we rely on case material and examples. Financial regulation illustrates the tension between hierarchy and jurisdictional clarity, on the one hand, and entropic search on the other. As the business of finance became more complex, so did the regulatory agencies with the responsibility of regulating it. Beginning in the 1970s, the previously staid business of banking became "exciting" (Johnson and Kwak 2010). It had been exciting before the Great Depression of the 1930s, as well. Government responded by the earlier period of excitement with a round of regulatory activity that led to the New Deal's "alphabet soup" of regulatory agencies, and expanded regulatory capacity in the Treasury Department and the Federal Reserve. As banking became exciting again, regulatory authority was divided among the various agencies, the Treasury, and the Federal Reserve. Gradually at first, and then in a wave during the Clinton and G. W. Bush administrations, banking regulations were relaxed and made more "banking friendly." But lots of regulatory activity continued, and regulators faced an increasingly complex environment with (it turned out) much enhanced risk to the economy.

We can anticipate the issues that emerged: the more the overlap, the more the potential information (if the capacity of the agencies to address the complexity was maintained), and the more difficulties the emerging financial companies had with regulators. While each regulatory agency had its own area of jurisdictional superiority, the increasing size and complexity of financial companies meant that many companies were under the jurisdiction of more than one regulator. One of the responses to the inability of financial regulatory agencies to divide up the terrain in a simple manner was to allow companies falling under more than one regulator to choose by which it wanted to be regulated. This particularly bad idea meant that complex financial companies could fall under the regulatory authority of an agency with little expertise in areas where the company was engaging in the riskiest activities. American International Group (AIG), an insurance conglomerate with a massive derivatives business, chose the lax Office of Thrift Supervision as its regulator because it held a savings and loan. This kind of jurisdictional clarity—probably most kinds of jurisdictional clarity—underproduces the information necessary to make sound regulatory decisions. In the search for one kind of clarity, decision-making authority, the system sacrificed information and perspective. At the same time—though this was not inevitable—it chose a solution to regulatory overlap that could be paralleled with allowing a criminal to determine which police officer will "supervise" him or her—a very bad idea.

The existence of overlapping regulatory responsibilities also can counteract what Johnson and Kwak call "cultural capital," in which regulators adopt the mind-sets of the regulated industries. In 2012 the Commodities Futures Trading Commission (CFTC) announced a major settlement against Barclays Bank and the pursuit of several other major financial institutions in the United States regarding the manipulation of the London Interbank Overnight Rate (LIBOR). LIBOR is the unsecured rate that banks charge one another for overnight borrowing—it is necessary to clear unbalanced accounts when withdrawals at a particular bank exceed liquid assets. The banks' regulators were uninvolved in the settlement, due perhaps to the cultural capital issue. The CFTC could have become involved in a bank regulatory issue because of its role in regulating currency futures, which was authorized in the Dodd-Frank Wall Street Reform and Consumer Protection Act of 2010.[2]

The financial regulatory example illustrates another point. Regulatory complexity is, in large part, a consequence of increasing financial complexity and the clear and present danger of an unregulated financial system. Simplifying jurisdictions may increase clarity, but it does so at great cost to entropic search.

Congress

Policy analysis was born in the executive branch and did not migrate to the legislative branch until much later. The 1970 amendments to the Legislative

---

2. The bank violations involved the banking division within a bank (responsible for reporting overnight rates) setting rates at the request of currency futures traders in the bank's trading division—a violation of the "firewall" that was supposed to separate the two divisions. As a consequence, CFTC was able to assert jurisdiction.

Reorganization Act of 1946 provided the major impetus. These amendments began a decade-long period of intense activity in building the analytic capacity of the legislative branch. In the early 1970s, Congress was a group of legislators often operating in committees that got things done through norms of specialization and reciprocity, a system formalized in the "gains from trade" models of legislatures (Shepsle and Weingast 1981, 1987). By the end of the decade, Congress was not just a legislature but a bureaucracy as well—or rather a set of interacting bureaucracies—with much improved committee staffs and a set of analytical agencies as capable as any fielded by the executive branch (Williams 1998, 210). By 2011, the congressional bureaucracy consisted of some 30,000 employees, with the Senate employing 7,000, the House employing 10,600, and the remaining 13,000 employed by the analytical bureaucracies and other support agencies such as the Library of Congress (U.S. Office of Personnel Management, Federal Employment Statistics, Table 9; http://archive.opm.gov/feddata/html/2011/December/table9.asp#).

THE ANALYTICAL BUREAUCRACIES

The first of Congress's analytical bureaucracies did not begin life as an arm of the legislative branch.[3] The Budget and Accounting Act of 1921 created the General Accounting Office (GAO; the General Accountability Office since 2004). The act made GAO independent of the executive branch and gave it authority to investigate how government spent its funds. During the early part of its existence, GAO focused on auditing processes, basically ensuring that government funds were being legally spent. After the Second World War, the agency instituted more comprehensive audits focusing on the efficiency in government operations, and concentrated on hiring accountants during the 1950s and 1960s.

Lines between comprehensive audits and more extensive policy analysis were hard to draw. With President Lyndon Johnson's appointment of Elmer Staats to the position of comptroller general (the title of the director of GAO), the agency began to move toward such policy analysis, while at the same time increasing its attention to requests from Congress from around 10 percent when Staats took over as comptroller in 1966 to 40 percent at the end of his fifteen-year term in 1981 (Krusten 2001). The 1967 amendments to the Economic Opportunity Act of 1964 explicitly authorized GAO to engage in program evaluation. The 1970 amendments to the Legislative Reorganization

3. This brief history of GAO relies heavily on Krusten (2001). We are indebted to Michelle Wolfe for providing the graphical analyses of GAO reports.

FIGURE 4.1. Total GAO Reports Issued and Those Concerned with Auditing and Financial Management
Source: Calculated from http://www.gao.gov/browse/date/week; website accessed 6/20/2013
Note: The figure shows the dramatic increase in GAO reports following the 1970 Amendments to the Legislative Reorganization Act and its subsequent more-or-less stable path. Audits and financial management are tabulated separately to ensure that the counts do not solely reflect a shift from audits to policy analysis but rather represent an increase in total activity.

Act and the Congressional Budget Control and Impoundment Act of 1974 made that authorization a general mandate.

This mandate shift along with increases in budget allocations allowed GAO to vastly expand its policy analytic capacities. Figure 4.1, a count of GAO reports tabulated from the agency's Web site, gives some indication of just how extensive this new role became.[4] In 1966, the agency issued a total of thirty-seven reports; two years after its mandate to investigate antipoverty programs it issued one hundred. In 1970, GAO produced almost seven hundred reports, and by 1973 it produced over sixteen hundred.

OTHER ANALYTIC AGENCIES

Congress also increased its information-processing capacities by a series of actions during the 1970s. The 1970 amendments to the Legislative Reorganization Act of 1946 transformed the Legislative Reference Service, authorized by the original act into the Congressional Research Service (CRS). The amendments expand its authority from a primarily librarian service to doing research and analysis to assist Congress in the legislative process (Brudnick 2001). The 1970 amendments instructed CRS to "advise and assist

---

4. The number of reports is somewhat deceptive. More recently, within each report the GAO can make multiple recommendations to multiple agencies. But we judge that the early part of the series adequately represents the shift in activity in the agency beginning in 1970.

any committee" of Congress in the evaluation of legislative proposals, determine the advisability of enacting the proposals and estimating the probable effects of such proposals, and evaluate alternative methods for accomplishing the results (Williams 1998, 230). CRS's mandate is noteworthy because it offers committees and their partisan staffs a different perspective on legislative proposals—a contribution to entropic search.

In 1972, Congress created the Office of Technology Assessment (OTA) as a third analytic agency, with the mandate to aid Congress in the "identification and consideration of existing and probable impacts of technological innovation" (Technology Assessment Act of 1972; Public Law 92-484). In 1975, OTA issued ten reports; by 1995 (its last year of existence) it issued sixty-five, on topics as diverse as the role of technology in the development of metropolitan regions and the effectiveness of osteoporosis screening and hormone replacement therapy (OTA Legacy; http://www.princeton .edu/~ota/; publication counts from http://www.princeton.edu/~ota/ns20 /pubs_f.html).

In 1974, the Congressional Budget Control Act created the CBO and increased the authority of GAO. The act emerged from the constitutional crisis provoked by President Nixon's impoundment of congressionally authorized funds. Congress created CBO in large part to gain analytical independence from the executive branch's budgetary estimates. At the outset, the agency was beset by partisan expectations and conflict with the newly created budget committees, but the agency performed exceptionally well and gained great credence, with budget estimates that were more accurate than those of the Office of Management and Budget (Williams 1998, 220).

INTERACTIONS BETWEEN EXECUTIVE AND CONGRESSIONAL POLICY ANALYSIS

As we noted above, Williams (1998) distinguished between the demand by policy makers for sound policy analysis and the supply of such analysis. Supply factors include not just the availability of analysts but also the ability of analysts to present information and analysis in an unbiased and nonpartisan manner. This is especially true in Congress, where partisan polarization increased throughout the period of our study. In the 1970s and 1980s, Republicans and Democrats sparred over the composition of analytical agencies, especially the directorships of CBO and GAO, but both parties shared commitments to the process. Good policy required good information.

During the 1970s, policy debates centered on issues of how to develop or modify policies in a manner more conducive to the parties' fundamental policy premises. Republicans sought to build policy on a market basis and urged that policies be decentralized to the states and localities with great discretion at that level. Democrats preferred policies to be implemented with strong central direction.

For some issues the debate could be solved through good policy analysis. We cite two examples. The first is the Nixon administration's advocacy, through the urging of presidential domestic policy advisor Daniel Patrick Moynihan, that welfare programs be aggregated from a mixture of income and services transfers based on categorical determinations of eligibility to a guaranteed income for all (Moynihan 1973). The plan was based on conservative ideas. Milton Friedman proposed the basic proposal for a negative income tax in 1956, in which rates of transfer decreased as the income of recipients increased, but at less than a 1:1 basis (Williams 1998, 95). The Nixon proposal envisioned a 50 percent tax rate, in which for every dollar a recipient earned, the transfer would be reduced by 50 cents. Several policy analysts had proposed the idea to President Johnson as early as 1965, but he rejected the proposal. Major reasons included the lack of a single influential advocate and the lack of knowledge about the work disincentive effects of such a program (97).

The lack of sound research led to the largest-scale social experiment to date: the New Jersey Negative Income Tax study, initiated in 1967. It was designed explicitly to test the work disincentive effects of various forms of the policy on real populations using a classic experimental design. The study played a role in the Nixon administration's Family Assistance Program (FAP), which was basically a negative income tax. Also critical was the role of Moynihan and the steeply increasing welfare costs that seemed both ineffective and uncontrollable (106).

Nixon's FAP proposal was subjected to lengthy hearings and sophisticated analyses by Ways and Means committee staff and was adopted by the House in 1971 as H.R. 1. But the bill was defeated in the Senate Finance Committee. Both Williams (1998) and Moynihan (1973) attributed that defeat in part to the lack of analytical capacity in Senate Finance at the time. The lack of analytical capacity led to serious misrepresentations of the proposal, misrepresentations that Moynihan thought unsustainable if Senate Finance's analytical capacity had been on a par with House Ways and Means. An important part of the story of the failure of Nixon's FAP is the disjuncture between an executive branch that had fully competent capacity and strong support from the president and the lack of such capacity in Congress, especially in the Senate.

THE DECLINE OF CONGRESSIONAL
POLICY ANALYTIC CAPACITY

President Reagan brought a new model of policy making to the executive branch, one less reliant on information and analysis and more directed at undermining the foundations of the social service state that developed following the Great Depression. One did not need program evaluation if the whole set of domestic policy premises were to be questioned.

During the Reagan years, the legislative branch continued to hew to its bipartisan commitment to its analytical capacities. The House remained solidly in Democratic hands, but the Senate was controlled by Republicans from 1981 to 1987. The staffs of the analytical bureaucracies, generally growing in the 1970s, stabilized in the 1980s, and the committee staffs of both House and Senate were stable (Peterson 2008; Schuman 2010; Schuman and Green 2012). Yet during the period a strong undercurrent questioning the commitment to this system developed in the House of Representatives under the insurgent leadership of Newt Gingrich (Theriault 2013). Gingrich advocated an approach based on stronger ideological premises, challenging the governing consensus and attacking the compromises that the existing Republican leaders had forged, including the commitment to analysis in program development.

When Republicans won control of both House and Senate, and Gingrich was elected Speaker, a first item of business was eviscerating the budgets of the analytical agencies, the committees, and even the personal staffs of members. Congress eliminated the Office of Technology Assessment, cut the staff of GAO by 27 percent (on top of a 17 percent decline from GAO's peak staffing in 1991), and cut the House committee staff by almost 40 percent (Peterson 2008; Schuman 2010).

Williams's (1998, 211) interviews with members of the Washington policy analysis community indicated some support for the measures. Some thought OTA was redundant and that GAO needed some judicious downsizing. GAO had not played the nonpartisan role as adeptly as CBO and CRS and had already suffered cuts in the Democratic Congress of 1993–94. Respondents uniformly saw CRS as the best of the congressional analytic agencies.

A desire on the part of the new Republican majority to display frugality was behind the demand to cut Congress's analytical capacities, but it also is indicative of the loss of confidence in the role of information processing in the legislative branch. Staffing of the analytical agencies and congressional committees never recovered (Peterson 2008; Coburn 2011), and this is presently affecting the ability of the analytical agencies to engage in expert search. Recent reports by the Sunlight Foundation argue that staffing cuts and low pay have limited Congress's "ability to engage in reasoned decision-making, placing it at the mercy of special interests." Congress has "weakened its institutional knowledge base and diminished its capacity to understand current events through a dramatic reduction in one of its most valuable resources: experienced staff" (Schulman and Green 2012, 1). A report by Senator Tom Coburn (2011) is similarly critical of these cuts, and notes that leadership and personal staff have increased since 2000, but not committee staff. Coburn argues for more resources for GAO to substitute for what he sees as a poor job of committee work in the modern Congress. Coburn's report is noteworthy because he is in effect calling for a return to the vibrant information-processing commitments of Congress in the past, arguing that to cut programs requires good information to make them more efficient. More than that, while he focuses on GAO, his plea is general, basically a call for rebuilding the institutional capacity for policy analysis in the legislative branch. Senator Coburn's conservative credentials (and his successful sponsorship of legislation to eliminate political science funding from the National Science Foundation in 2012) make clear that ideology is not the only driving force in the struggle between information and complexity. The search for clarity and control can generate cuts to the analytic infrastructure of government that even ideological conservatives such as Senator Coburn recognize.

While the analytic agencies are critical to Congress's capacity for sound information processing, much of that capacity is located in the committee structure. The Legislative Reorganization Act of 1946 anticipated nonpartisan committee staffs, but by the early 1950s committee staffs had been divided into majority and minority components (Weiss 1989, 414).

Weiss's interviews in the 1980s with committee staff on the use of policy analysis in the legislature indicated that partisanship and fragmented committee jurisdictions tended to undermine analysis. Partisanship, according to staff, undermined the nonpartisan traditions of policy analysis, while fragmented jurisdictions undermined the ability of a committee to look holistically at a problem. On the other hand, Williams (1998) argues that policy analysis is consistent with partisanship. His emphasis on "honest numbers" stresses the need for the analysis to be dispassionate, but the use of the analysis can quite clearly be partisan, especially in the evaluation of policy solutions. It is not clear that holistic committee analysis is critical to the process of information processing, especially with the rise of Congress's analytical agencies. Many times it is important for committees to offer partial analyses based on different points of view—entropic search. The right

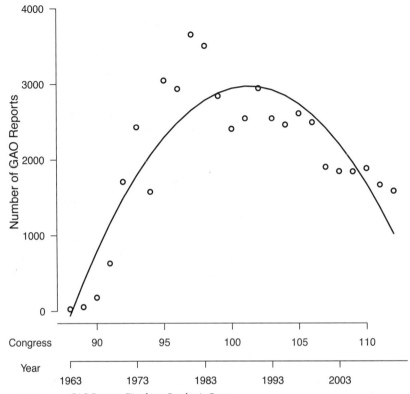

FIGURE 4.2. GAO Reports, Fitted to a Quadratic Curve

Source: Calculated from http://www.gao.gov/browse/date/week; website accessed 6/20/2013

Note: The quadratic curve describes the rise and decline of policy analytic capacity in GAO. Quadratic curves describe trends that increase and then decrease regularly, as did the policy analytic capacity of the legislative branch during the period. Details of the fit may be found in the appendix to the chapter.

question for the committee system as an information-processing system is not so much whether a single committee views a problem holistically but whether the entire committee system is capable of doing so.

ANOTHER LOOK AT THE RISE AND DECLINE OF POLICY ANALYSIS IN CONGRESS

Before we turn to entropic search in the legislative branch, we offer a different perspective on GAO reports. GAO is the most important of the legislative analytical agencies in sheer size and activity, and unlike CRS its reports are all public. As a consequence, we can trace them through time. Figure 4.1 offered simple counts of reports. Now Figure 4.2 offers a different perspective on the same data. In Figure 4.2, we present the data fitted to a quadratic curve, and the data are limited to the period between 1963 and 2009, graphed by Congresses. Curve fitting allows us to study general trends in the data without being distracted by the variability common in any series. Linear fits pick up long-run increases (or decreases) in time series, while quadratic curves are useful in summarizing time trends that increase and then decrease reasonably regularly. The trend line clearly picks up the increase in reports as GAO moved from auditing to policy analysis, a trend that peaked in the 97th (1981–83) and 98th (1983–85) Congresses. A period of stability at the top of the quadratic curve ensued, followed by a steady decline in the number of reports issued. Senator Coburn (2011, 21) attributes this to long-running cuts imposed by Congress on the agency. Budget cuts to the analytic agencies and to the committee staffs indicate more than any other single measure the loss of commitment in Congress to building an institutionalized policy analytic and information-processing capacity. The result is the curve of Figure 4.2. We will see this curve again many times in the coming chapters. As we shall see, it seems to be a characteristic description of much that happened in post-1950s U.S. public policy.

Entropic Search in Congress

Entropic search means incorporating diverse viewpoints into a decision-making process. In the coming chapters, we explore in detail the central role that such search processes have played in the development of public policy in postwar America. Here we examine the politics that generated entropic search and subsequently limited it in Congress.

Just like the use of policy analysis in decision making, entropic search can be seen as a function of both the demand for and the potential supply of such search. But there is one major exception: entropic search is almost never discussed directly in political disagreements; rather it is a side consequence of these discussions. Public officials discuss the organization of jurisdictions, the need for control and the confusion inherent in overlapping responsibilities, but they almost never grasp that such arrangements can facilitate information processing. In the case of Congress, the fights were about breaking up the old oligarchies of Southern Democratic committee chairs and the desire to strengthen party government in Congress. As we shall see, the political forces in the legislative branch affecting search pushed in two different directions. On the one hand, strengthening party leadership to counteract the power of committee chairs, as the reform-minded Democrats did in the early and mid-1970s and the Republicans did later, had the potential of undermining entropic search. On the other hand, the committee-based reforms, such as the subcommittee bill of rights and the addition of professional staff, had the potential of increasing entropic search. How these two forces played out after 1970 dictated the course of entropic search in Congress.

The story of congressional reform is often told as a series of attacks by more liberal Democrats on the entrenched committee system that dominated the legislative branch in the early postwar period. The idealized system of domination by strong, long-serving Southern Democratic committee chairs (Zelizer 2004) characterizes the House of Representatives nicely, but is less descriptive of the Senate. Sinclair (1989) shows that the Senate committee system was much less dominated by conservatives. Decision making in the smaller Senate was less reliant on committees and was more collegial and governed by well-recognized norms of behavior (Matthews 1960). These norms, in part, were maintained by limiting the scope of the debate, especially when it came to civil rights. As the social base of the Senate shifted beginning with the huge Democratic cohort of 1958, the norms seemed antiquated, and the Senate experienced a reform effort as well.

The whole reform process was messy and complex and did not change the operation of the legislature overnight. Zelizer (2004, 3) writes that "reform is a thoroughly *historical* process that is messy, slow, and involves multiple institutions" (see also Polsby 2004). In part, the reform process was a response to changes in government scope and size since the New Deal; in part it was a response to the incoming liberal Democratic cohorts of 1958, 1964, and 1974.

Liberal Democrats chaffed at the domination of the "conservative coalition," an alliance between conservative Democrats and Republicans, which blocked the enactment of more progressive laws. The House manifested itself as "committee government," which reached its zenith in the 1960s. The standard diagnosis by both liberal reformers and by many political scientists was that parties were too weak and committees were too strong, and the latter needed strengthening while the party caucuses needed more authority over the lawmaking process (Rhode 1991, 6–8).

Rhode (20–28) detects three distinct reform tracks: limiting the power of committee chairmen, strengthening the power of the Democratic Party and its leadership, and increasing the power of the rank and file member to hold leaders accountable. We will not go into detail about these reforms, as they are well-described elsewhere (Rhode 1991; Sinclair 1995).

From the perspective of entropic search, the strength of committees in the prereform Congress was not the major problem; rather, it had to do with the exclusivity of jurisdictions, the unilateral power of committee chairs, and the norm of deference to committees. From that perspective, the committee-based reforms increased the capacity of the institution to conduct entropic search. Yet, as Rhode (1991, 12) notes, the prevailing thinking among political scientists at the time of the reforms was to highlight decentralization and inefficiencies associated with fragmentation that detracted from the strong party leadership that was the standard for good legislative organization at the time. A major concern was the inability of the legislative political parties to put forward and implement a coherent legislative program because of the dominance of "subcommittee government" (Davidson 1981) after the reforms. The discomfort with the decentralizing and fragmenting effects of the reforms highlights the trade-off between entropic search and coherent implementation that we have continually stressed in this book. It is interesting that consensus of the political science experts on Congress was to decry the decentralization without recognizing its value in opening up the process to diverse voices.

As Adler (2002) shows, the resistance to the reforms was strong and in many ways successful. The reforms proved to be more successful in the "fostering of the majority party's ability to enact a party program" (Rhode 1991, 14). Since the 1970s, parties in Congress have become increasingly polarized, with little cross-partisanship evident in more recent Congresses. The proportion of party votes in the 112th Congress (2011–13), in which a majority of one party opposed a majority of the other, was almost 75 percent, the highest since the 58th Congress (1903–05), during the strong speakership of the legendary "Boss" Joseph Cannon (Cooper 2013).

The reforms of the committee system and the Democratic Party certainly did not stall the increasing partisanship in Congress, but they cannot be held accountable for it. Beginning in the late 1970s, the Republican minority in the House of Representatives became increasingly assertive in attacking the majority Democrats. This led to more leadership control of the legislative process to forestall legislative tactics employed by the minority party designed to stall action or to embarrass the majority, such as offering amendments designed to cause the majority to take uncomfortable public positions. Republican legislative successes in the Senate in the 1980s cumulated in the landslide Republican victory of 1994. Reforms of the new Republican majority were directed at limiting the power of committees (including a strict term limit for them) and strengthening the power of the Speaker, and these reforms were more successful than the earlier Democratic committee reforms (Adler 2002). At the same time, the realignment of the South led to a more homogenous Republican caucus as Southern conservatives replaced more moderate Eastern Republicans. Similar forces were making the Democrats more homogenous, but the legislative Democrats have remained more heterogeneous in policy preferences than the Republicans. In the 112th and 113th Congresses, this has resulted in tension between Speaker John Boehner and his caucus.

For our purposes, the important question is not how strong or weak the party leadership is with respect to the caucus but how these dynamics influence the capacity of Congress to engage in policy search. It matters little in this regard whether the committees are subject to a strong leadership or to a caucus of homogenous policy preferences; in either case, the demand for such search is likely to be attenuated. We explore these dynamics empirically in the next chapter and document important increases in jurisdictional entropy across the committee structure through the postwar period until the mid-1970s, and a stagnation since then.

EXPLANATIONS

How are we to explain the changing patterns of search and information processing in Congress? Although there are many accounts of changing patterns of political coalitions and governance, surprisingly little of the theoretical work on Congress has been devoted to dynamics. If there is a standard model of change, it is an electorally driven one based on changes in the preferences of members, the partisan composition of the chambers, and the size of the partisan coalitions—because of supermajority requirements (Brady and Volden 1998). But such explanations do a poor job of explaining issue prioritization, the decisions of policy makers to work on some issues and not others in an environment where attention is limited (Jones and Baumgartner 2005b). They are also of limited utility in understanding legislative information processing more generally. Finally, the standard model treats institutions as fixed, or changing only occasionally in disjoint shifts. We show in later chapters that there is a gradualist evolutionary component to legislative entropic search processes as well as disjoint shifts that are only partially explained by elections.

We suggest that two elements are critical in explanations. The first is that developments in the structure and organization of Congress have been strongly influenced by developments in public policy and in the policy communities drawn to Washington as government has grown. The reforms in Congress and changes in the norms of behavior did not occur in a vacuum; they followed the great expansions of government in the 1960s. Sinclair (1989, 51) writes: "The combination of the expansion of the issue agenda, the explosive growth of interest groups, and the increased role of the media produced a new Washington policy community, one that rewards Senators differently than did the old policy system." These changes in the operation of the legislative body also affected the character of the policy community, and of course continue to do so.

In more recent times, the increasing partisanship, the "arms race" for campaign contributions among legislators, and the decline of committee staff and nonpartisan analysts in the analytical bureaucracies have led to an increasingly assertive interest-group environment and a tendency for more and more issues to be drawn into the partisan conflict. Studying roll-call votes by Policy Agendas Project's content codes, and dividing their period of study into two parts: 1965–80, and 1981–2004, Jochim and Jones (2013) found three distinct patterns. Some issues, such as labor relations and macroeconomics, were polarized in both periods. Some, such as agriculture, were not polarized in the early period and were not in the later period. But some moved from unpolarized to polarized, and these included such areas as education and health care. Party polarization did not occur across all issues at once; rather, it infected issues sequentially.

At the subsystem level, a somewhat similar pattern can be detected. The operations of problem search and solution recommendation continue, but they have been affected by changes in the partisan composition of Congress. Workman (2012b) has intensively analyzed the interaction between the activities of congressional committees and the rule-making activities of executive agencies. He finds evidence of shared responsibility for defining and acting on problems, a process he terms a "dual dynamic." However, the operation of the dynamic shifts with changes in the partisan composition of Congress. When the control of Congress shifted from Democratic to Republican in 1995, problem search and rule making changed little overall, but the issues about which search was more aggressive changed. Executive agencies whose rule making within the Policy Agendas codes for business and finance and the environment became more active, while transportation, public lands and water, and education lost favor.

The second critical point is that the changes in Congress, the executive branch, and the interest-group system have generally not been abrupt, shifted by elections, but have been more gradual and evolutionary. Elections do influence this evolutionary path, but typically do not do so in a disjoint fashion. Dodd's (2012, chapters 5 and 6) theory of congressional cycles stands out as the major attempt to understand congressional change in both a broader historical context and in terms of the interactions of the motives of members and the development of structure and processes in the legislative branch itself. Policy making plays a key role in the mix as well, because policy change is the raison d'être for seeking power in the first place, as well as the mechanism for getting reelected. The cycles are complex and evolutionary, as they consist mostly of smooth adjustments but are subject to occasional disjoint shifts as well. Dodd sees the resulting cycles as "an unintended consequence of the legislators' quest for power" (194).

Dodd's cycle theory is important because it gives us a sound theoretical basis for expecting a mix of complex evolutionary changes in the structure and organization of Congress and the potential for disjoint shifts that may or may not be associated with elections. They are clearly important, but, unlike the role of elections in the standard model, in Dodd's approach they are one of a mix of interacting factors that lead to patterns of change.

THE POLITICS OF DEREGULATION
AND THE REFORMED CONGRESS

In the mid- to late 1970s, the U.S. government broadly deregulated many industries previously governed by specialized regulatory subsystems, including air travel, communications, trucking, financial securities, and railroads (Derthick and Quirk 1985). All of these actions were aimed at removing barriers to competition. Why did so many regulatory subsystems collapse at about the same time? Shifts in electoral majorities cannot explain the actions, as Congress passed many of the major acts at the absolute nadir of Republican fortunes—after the very large Watergate class of Democrats joined an already Democratic Congress in 1975. Surely Democrats were more inclined to try to protect the unionized jobs that were associated with transportation and communication in particular.

Several features of policy making in Congress came together to promote deregulation. First was the new role of the Senate as it moved from a body dominated by seniority and deference to one more integrated into the developing Washington policy community in providing a stepping-stone to the presidency. Also important was the expanded jurisdictions of committees and subcommittees that occurred with the 1970s reforms. Finally, the ambitions of Senator Ted Kennedy play prominently in the story. As the chairman of the Subcommittee on Administrative Practices and Procedures, Kennedy held a series of hearings on deregulation. The prominence of Kennedy and media coverage of the hearings "raised the profile of what had previously been a largely academic issue to pro-consumer status" (McCarthy 2009). The Subcommittee on Administrative Practices and Procedures held no jurisdiction over any of the regulated industries and could not write legislation concerning airline transportation, which was Kennedy's main target. But the elastic interpretations of committee and subcommittee jurisdictions with respect to nonlegislative (oversight) hearings and the enhanced resources from the reforms allowed Kennedy to move aggressively to investigate the issue and engage in classic conflict expansion (Baumgartner, and Talbert 1993; Talbert, Jones, and Baumgartner 1995; Jones, Baumgartner, Jones, and Mac-Cleod 2000). Kennedy successfully swapped the primary understanding of the issue from one of jobs and protecting unions to one of consumer rights, illustrating the notion that as conflict expands and an issue moves from subsystem to macropolitics, there is a strong tendency for the problem to be understood in terms of different attributes (Jones and Baumgartner 2005b; Baumgartner and Jones 2009). Senator Howard Cannon, who chaired the Aviation subcommittee and did have legislative jurisdiction over the issue, was a strong proponent of the regulatory structure supported by airlines and by unions. But he was persuaded to cosponsor the Airline Deregulation Act with Kennedy, which President Carter signed in 1978.

Deregulation is a story of jurisdictional fragmentation and competition, of new venues offering institutional representation for new ideas, of the changing role of Congress in policy making, and of the interactions of member goals with the structure and process of Congress. It is a story of the spillovers among subsystems and the inability to draw tight boundaries to limit change as major new issues reach government (Baumgartner and Jones 1994). If Congress had not been in a reform stage of its cyclical behavior, it is unlikely that such broad regulatory reform could have been accomplished (Dodd 2012).

Figure 4.3 gives an indication of the power of these interacting forces. It graphs the number of hearings coded by the Policy Agendas Project as focusing on airlines, trucking, or railroads, the major subjects of the deregulatory movement. A clear peak occurs in 1979, but the momentum built for several years before, beginning in the late 1960s, as committees and subcommittees competed for part of the deregulatory action. The graph also shows how the subsystems became linked via the consumer movement. All three series had peaks in the late 1970s. After that, their trajectories deviated. Congress lost interest in trucking and railroads but maintained vigorous oversight interest in airlines (much of this, however, is due to safety issues, which are included in the subtopics).

But there is also a powerful backstory to deregulation. It involves the incorporation of information and analysis into the decision process. While it is true that airline deregulation may not have been possible without Senator Kennedy's entrepreneurship, it is also true that it would not have been possible without the reams of economic reports, articles, and analyses that

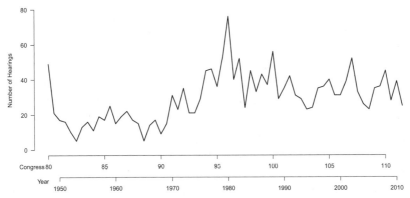

FIGURE 4.3. The Number of Hearings Focusing on Air, Rail, or Trucking Transportation
Source: Policy Agendas Project

showed the benefits of deregulation for consumers. Finally, the role of staff in summarizing these ideas and developing them to make them politically feasible cannot be underestimated. In deregulation, the politics of policy analysis and of entropic search come together at the apogee of both.

The Importance of Institutionalized Analytic Capacity

In this chapter, we have examined developments in the two critical components of information processing in government that have been the primary subjects of this book: policy analysis, which is primarily devoted to systematic data-based study of policy solutions and to specific problems, and entropic search, which involves the incorporation of diverse viewpoints and ideas in the definition of problems and the generation of potential solutions. We have seen that since the Second World War, the institutionalization of these two kinds of search in the U.S. federal government have ebbed and flowed at different times in the executive and legislative branches. Systematic, institutionalized policy analysis developed in the Department of Defense and spread in the Lyndon Johnson administration to the domestic agencies. Republican Presidents Nixon and Ford had penchants for analytic policy thinking and employed analysis to limit excesses in established programs, consolidate them, and move responsibilities to state governments. The analytic capacities of the executive branch reached an apogee in the late 1970s. The Reagan administration brought a distrust of policy analysis, and the incoming Republican administration felt that the institutionalization of policy analysis constituted part of the subsystem government they associated with the development of a big intrusive state. As a consequence, the analytic agencies suffered and essentially were not fully restored even in administrations that were favorably inclined to analysis (including G. H. W. Bush, Clinton, and Obama).

Developments in the legislative branch were stimulated, in part, by the successes of policy analysis in the executive branch and by the response to changes in the composition of Congress and the policy goals of members. The growth of GAO and the additions of CBO and OTA indicated congressional determination to build the policy analytic capacity of the branch, as did the bolstering of committee and subcommittee analytic capacities beginning with the 1970 amendments to the Legislative Reorganization Act. Simultaneously, the legislative reforms in the House directed at undermining the power of committee chairs led to an increase in the capacity of the committee system to conduct entropic search. The entire process became more open to the increasing demands on government resulting from the intense activity of the Great Society and the early Nixon years. Indeed Roger Davidson (1981) recognized exactly this in his "Subcommittee Government: New Channels for Policymaking." But most congressional observers decried the decentralization and fragmentation as a detriment to coherent policy making. But coherent policy is an incoherent goal if you do not know what you are doing. And in fact, many times the coherent goal behind greater jurisdictional clarity has been to silence those voices who pose uncomfortable questions, demand more attention to unresolved aspects to public policy failures, or generate information that might be used to create support for more aggressive policy response. Cutting government is a coherent goal, and it is often done by cutting information. But these strategies work only for a while because information is indeed valuable for governments seeking to solve social problems; indeed, it is critical, as all government leaders recognize.

In any case, the reforms themselves carried more long-term incentives for centralized party action than was recognized at the time (Rhode 1991). The late 1970s instituted a long-run period of increased partisan polarization and legislative organization far more centralized than before. When the Republicans gained control of Congress in 1995, they moved quickly to limit the capacities of the analytic agencies and reign in the power of committees. The theory underlying this move was based less on performance and more on a desire to show frugality and the desire of Republicans to bring party member preferences more to the fore of policy making. By cutting down on policy expertise and strengthening the role of the Speaker and the Republican caucus, Republicans ensured that ideology would play a more important role in the policy process.

The result by the Obama administration was a Congress that hewed much more closely to the Responsible Party model than before. But in such a model there is a role only for party programs, presumably based on the preferences of party members. There is no explicit role (nor even an understood but unarticulated role) for analysis and information. And the lack of commitment to the development and maintenance of such capacity in the modern Congress shows in the data (Coburn 2011).

This chapter has focused on documenting long-run trends in the politics of information and policy analysis within the U.S. government since the Second World War. In the next chapters, we turn to make use of the resources of the Policy Agendas Project. We focus next on the jurisdictional structures of the congressional committee system, in Chapter 5.

5

From Clarity to Complexity in Congress

Even in today's polarized era, the congressional committee system remains the lynchpin of congressional lawmaking. Committees examine potential problems, hear evidence about potential legislation, mark up legislative proposals, forward those proposals for votes on the floor of the chamber, and oversee the agencies implementing the nation's laws. While there are other avenues of access for information and ideas to enter the legislative process, including especially the General Accounting Office, the Congressional Budget Office, the Congressional Research Service, and the staffs of individual members, committees remain the major institution for bringing information to bear on lawmaking matters. At its best, the committee system reflects diverse policy viewpoints from the numerous perspectives relevant in Congress. As we will see through a comprehensive analysis of all congressional hearings in the postwar period, the committee system reflects the struggle between organizational clarity and entropic search quite well. And, as in the last chapter, we will see that the U.S. Congress was on a path of increasing entropy in its organizational structure from 1950 to about 1980, when the trend was abruptly halted. We can measure the diversity versus clarity of the committee structure very precisely using the Policy Agendas Project, so our analysis in this chapter is highly detailed, but also reflects the broader trends in government that we discussed in the previous chapter and will continue to explore in Chapter 6 as well.

Since Woodrow Wilson, scholars and practitioners alike have understood that the division of labor through the committee system is fundamental to how Congress works. Scott Adler and John Wilkerson (2012) have recently shown that committee members are encouraged to devote years of work to become specialists and experts in their issue domains because they know that, every few years, they will have the opportunity to write important legislation, and they can expect their colleagues on other committees largely to accept the proposals that they put forward. Previous scholars, from Woodrow Wilson (1885) to Richard Fenno (1973), Kenneth Shepsle (1978), and Keith Krehbiel (1991), have focused on the committee structure as the fundamental organizing principle, along with parties, that makes Congress function. David King (1997) and E. Scott Adler (2002) have provided book-length treatments of the problem of "turf wars" among congressional committees and the difficulty in changing these jealously guarded jurisdictional territories. Clearly, the allocation of a particular issue to a particular set of members does not always come without tension. We focus on the tensions inherent in establishing and maintaining clear jurisdictional control in this chapter because it illustrates the same type of tension as affects government more broadly: that between control and information.

The committee system puts in clear contrast the dual goals of any division of labor in Congress: how to ensure that the parts serve the interests of the whole, while increasing efficiency. On the one hand, there is a danger that by giving deference to specialists, nonexperts may not get what they want. On the other, without deference there is no incentive to specialize, and the body loses all the gains that come from a division of labor. This tension is fundamental to the literature on congressional organization and is key to understanding how Congress works. Members expect to be paid back in deference for the years of work they put into the routine oversight of a relatively small part of public policy. On the other hand, they do not want to approve legislation that they believe reflects views of self-selected committee members, not their own nor that of the chamber as a whole. They want to gain something in exchange for the knowledge from becoming a specialist on one topic and by which they lose influence on all other policy domains.

The tension in Congress between allocating power to a subset of the whole, which may or may not then reflect the opinion of the majority, is similar to the broader dilemma in government of assigning authority to a single institution with instructions to "solve" the policy problem. If we understood perfectly the nature of the problem and the best solutions to it, then clear administrative control would be the obvious choice. But if we do not quite understand the causes of the social problem we want government to solve, or if different politically relevant actors disagree on whether the condition is even worth any government attention, as is common, then we may not want monopolistic control by any single group of experts. Any single group, agency, or committee may approach the issue from a particular perspective. If a multiplicity of perspectives is important, then clarity is a danger, as it can lead to "tunnel vision," or a self-defined organizational mission that incorporates this but not that element of the issue. Looking into some detail at the structure of congressional committees provides a rich empirical grounding for a broader consideration of the tension between clarity and control, on the one hand, and breadth of perspectives, on the other. In creating clarity, one must give up breadth. And in incorporating a greater range of perspectives, one necessarily gives up some clarity.

Woodrow Wilson (1885) described the power of committees and is often quoted for his description of "Congress at work" being "Congress in committee-rooms." But it is worth reviewing in greater detail his analysis. In fact, he complained bitterly of the excessive powers of committees. Even in the 1880s, the division of labor had become so powerful, and the norms of deference strong enough, that he wrote that House committees not only wrote the legislation but also largely dictated out to the floor the outcomes to be adopted. He illustrates the fear that the committees serve their own interests, not those of the broader congressional majority. This concern is at the core of the tension between clarity, needed for an efficient division of labor, and the potential that a broader range of perspectives will be excluded as committee members gain too much power:

> The House sits, not for serious discussion, but to sanction the conclusions of its Committees as rapidly as possible. It legislates in its committee-rooms; not by the determinations of majorities, but by the resolutions of specially-commissioned minorities; so that it is not far from the truth to say that Congress in session is Congress on public exhibition, whilst Congress in its committee-rooms is Congress at work (1885, 79).

Wilson complained about the secretive process by which most bills are defeated, not by open debate but by committees simply refusing to bring them forward:

> The fate of bills committed is generally not uncertain. As a rule, a bill committed is a bill doomed. When it goes from the clerk's desk to a committee-room it crosses a parliamentary bridge of sighs to dim dungeons of silence whence it will never return. The means and time of its death are unknown, but its friends never see it again (69).

Wilson continues:

> Of course it goes without saying that the practical effect of this Committee organization of the House is to consign to each of the Standing Committees the entire direction of legislation upon those subjects which properly come to its consideration. As to those subjects it is entitled to the initiative, and

all legislative action with regard to them is under its overruling guidance. It gives shape and course to the determinations of the House. In one respect, however, its initiative is limited. Even a Standing Committee cannot report a bill whose subject-matter has not been referred to it by the House, "by the rules or otherwise"; it cannot volunteer advice on questions upon which its advice has not been asked. But this is not a serious, not even an operative, limitation upon its functions of suggestion and leadership; for it is a very simple matter to get referred to it any subject it wishes to introduce to the attention of the House. Its chairman, or one of its leading members, frames a bill covering the point upon which the Committee wishes to suggest legisla tion; brings it in, in his capacity as a private member, on Monday, when the call of States is made; has it referred to his Committee; and thus secures an opportunity for the making of the desired report (70–71).

For over 125 years the structure of the committee system has been a key organizational facet of legislative life. However, while Wilson's comments about the power of legislative gate-keepers such as hostile committee chairs remain pertinent today, there is another problem to which he only alludes indirectly. That is competition among committees to "volunteer advice" on matters that might also be claimed by another committee. Further, this problem has become vastly more complicated since the time that Wilson wrote.

Congress once had a largely ad hoc system of committee jurisdictions (Deering and Smith 1997), but since the Legislative Reorganization Act of 1946 it has had a relatively fixed system. In the House, the number of committees was reduced from forty-four to nineteen, and these standing committees have remained largely in place since then. Since 1947, a few committees have been newly established (e.g., Science and Astronautics, created in 1958, now called Science and Technology), many have had small changes to their names, and a few have been abolished, but overall the structure has remained remarkably similar over the entire postwar period. This has occurred at a time when the functions of the U.S. government have expanded vastly. The growth of government has led, inevitably, to an important change in the structure of government: each unit of government has grown more intertwined with other units.

As government has become larger and more complex, the legislative system responsible for writing legislation and overseeing the activities of an increasingly diverse executive bureaucracy has as a consequence become more complex. It could cope with diversity by one of two mechanisms. It could either expand the committee system, an option severely constrained by the Legislative Reorganization Act of 1946, or it could assign duties in a manner that causes overlaps and potential jurisdictional confusion. The House's 1973 Subcommittee Bill of Rights expanded the ability of subcommittees to act independently of their parent committees, and therefore probably ampli-fied the jurisdictional overlap problem. In a simple system of government, legislative committee duties can be clear and direct. In a complex system, legislative committee duties cannot be assigned with clarity.

As a consequence, the clarity of congressional committee jurisdiction has declined as the range of activities of government has increased. In this chapter we measure the range of jurisdictional coverage of each committee by looking at its hearings. We do so by examining the nineteen major topics of the Policy Agendas Project, showing not only the growth in the spread of activities across topics by the typical committee but also the increased range of committees claiming some degree of control over each topic area. These are mirror images of each other, and both are consequences of the increas-ing complexity of the growing body of federal legislation and the agencies responsible for implementing it.

The committee system in Congress is a useful lens into the broader theme of conflict between clarity and control because it illustrates the tension be-tween a desire for clear lines of jurisdictional control and the need to con-sider multiple aspects of a single issue. The congressional committee system has resisted large-scale change over the entire postwar period, largely because the organization of congressional life is so tightly bound to the system of com-mittees that members of Congress jealously guard their existing power ar-rangements.[1] And yet, given the rise in the number of issues of concern to the U.S. government (see Jones and Baumgartner 2005b and Chapter 6 in this book), an unchanging structure of Congress implies a significant shift in other ways. Each committee does more, and each issue has a greater chance of fall-ing into multiple jurisdictions. These are not pathologies but are reflections of the growth of government. A division of labor with more issues is inevitably messier than one with fewer issues, given a set number of divisions. And this is exactly what we see. We also see periodic and short-lived efforts to "clean up" or rationalize the system, as the contradictions between information and control rise up periodically. In this sense, the committee structure illustrates our larger themes, which is why we explore these issues in detail here.

This chapter highlights a second straightforward element of congressio-nal organization and behavior, yet one often overlooked by political scien-

---

1. There have been significant reforms, especially with the creation of multiple refer-rals and the "subcommittee bill of rights." These were significant reforms and decentralized power from the committee chairs to a larger number of individual subcommittees. But little has changed in the overall design that Congress work through a set of about nineteen stand-ing committees in the House and a similar design in the Senate.

tists and "beltway" commentators as well. Congress is not an entirely independent actor in the construction of its internal governance structures. It is hostage in part to the law and executive branch bureaucracies it has created in the past. As legislation has grown, it has become more complex. Whereas once most statutes had a single title, today most laws have multiple titles. More importantly, these multiple titles often affect different sections of the U.S. Code, which is the authoritative topical arrangement of the laws passed (Whyman and Jones 2012). As the corpus of law has become more complex, the agencies responsible for implementing them have become both more numerous and more diverse. Congressional committees, grappling with the complexities of law and bureaucracy, similarly become more complex. Whatever Congress is doing is deeply embedded in a large and complex administrative state (Redford 1969; Dodd and Schott 1979; Workman 2012b).

Dividing Up the Work: Committee Jurisdictions in Congress

The organization of congressional work through a system of committees both allows the body to manage its considerable workload and gives differential influence to those members with seats on the relevant committee. If the goal has been to encourage legislative specialization so that all can gain from the division of work across all members, this must be followed by a willingness of nonexperts to defer to those who may have spent decades in learning the details of federal law, agency activity, and the policy problems in that small domain of politics that corresponds to their own areas of legislative specialization. This bargain is a difficult one in two ways. First, it creates the possibility that the specialists will have different preferences than other members of the chamber; this is a particularly real threat because members may seek to gain assignment on committees with jurisdiction over issues particularly important to their own constituencies. Second, it means that members must agree not to assert themselves in areas where they do not have expertise. The giant legislative logroll is then a bargain that comes with significant benefits to generate expertise, but also significant costs in terms of lack of influence in areas of public policy that fall outside of one's own area of jurisdiction. Because of these inherent tensions, the system is constantly being pressured on the one hand to keep things clear, but on the other to allow flexibility if members feel their interests are not represented by those on the relevant committee.

Committee specialization additionally can run afoul of the demands of legislative party leaders to manage the work flow, to bring to the chamber floor essential legislative matters, and to promote a legislative program. As a consequence, the history of Congress can be seen as a struggle between the

centripetal forces of party leadership and the centrifugal forces of committee specialization. Wilson's *Congressional Government* was written in a time
of strong committees; similarly in the 1950s and 1960s, the House's "college
of cardinals" managed legislation and budgets with the Speaker oftentimes
brokering deals among them. After 1995, Speaker Newt Gingrich worked to
bring the committee structure more in line with party goals—centripetal
control at work.

In effect, two intertwined processes characterize congressional organization: one, the struggle between central control and the power of specialized information; the other the struggle to keep lines of authority between
committees clear and distinct. Each involves attempts to suppress attributes
of issues to simplify them (otherwise control is not possible). With simplification comes control; with complexity comes information.

With an ever-increasing set of policy issues on the federal agenda, but a
relatively set number of congressional committees, it is clear that strains and
ambiguities must be common. The U.S. Senate provides this description of
the difficulties in establishing clear boundaries:

> Senate Rule XXV establishes standing committees, determines their mem-
> bership, and fixes their jurisdictions. Setting jurisdictional boundaries among
> committees has always proved troublesome. While some jurisdictions apply
> to oversight of specific executive agencies or precisely defined functions,
> others are not so obviously described. As a result, a half-dozen or more com-
> mittees may claim jurisdiction in such broad policy areas as the national
> economy or environmental protection (U.S. Senate 2011).

In the 112th Congress (2011–12), the House and Senate panels were organized as described in Table 5.1, in a pattern that has been largely maintained
for many decades.

The House committee system includes twenty regular standing committees ranging from the prestigious Ways and Means and Rules committees
through the policy-focused Agriculture, Veterans Affairs, and others, and
also includes three joint or select committees. The Senate system is slightly
smaller, but the general idea of the division of labor into a small number of
overarching tax- and budget-focused committees, a larger number of policy-
focused ones, and a few select or special committees is generally consistent
with that of the House. There are only so many ways to divide up the policy
space, after all. While each Congress is free to revise the formal rules determining the relative jurisdictions of the various committees, in practice
substantial reforms are rare and each committee jealously protects its turf
from the encroachments of others.

TABLE 5.1. Standing and Major Select Committees of the 112th Congress (2011–12)

House of Representatives	Senate
Agriculture	Agriculture, Nutrition, and Forestry
Appropriations	Appropriations
Armed Services	Armed Services
Budget	Banking, Housing, and Urban Affairs
Education and the Workforce	Budget
Energy and Commerce	Commerce, Science, and Transportation
Ethics	Energy and Natural Resources
Financial Services	Environment and Public Works
Foreign Affairs	Finance
Homeland Security	Foreign Relations
House Administration	Health, Education, Labor, and Pensions
Judiciary	Homeland Security and Governmental Affairs
Natural Resources	Judiciary
Oversight and Government Reform	Rules and Administration
Rules	Small Business and Entrepreneurship
Science, Space, and Technology	Veterans Affairs
Small Business	Indian Affairs
Transportation and Infrastructure	Select Ethics
Veterans Affairs	Select Intelligence
Ways and Means	Special Aging
Joint Economic	
Joint Taxation	
Permanent Select Committee on Intelligence	

Source: House.gov and Senate.gov, downloaded April 20, 2011.

The continuity of the formal jurisdictions of the committees of the House and Senate is great enough that in the Policy Agendas Project we have established a "master list" of committees that assigns the same numeric code to the various committees from 1947 to present. That is, in our system, the House Agriculture Committee receives code 102 and in each Congress since 1947 we have been able to identify one, and only one, committee that receives this jurisdiction. In a few cases (Agriculture, Appropriations . . .), even the name has remained constant over that time period, whereas in others there have been slight name changes, but the jurisdiction of the committee has remained substantially the same (for example, the House Armed Services Committee was entitled the National Security Committee from 1995 to 1998). In other cases, some more substantial revisions are clear from the names of the committee, as in the case of the current House Committee on Financial Services. From 1947 to 1975 it was known as the Banking and Currency Committee; then as Banking, Currency, and Housing (1975–77); Banking, Finance, and Urban Affairs (1978–94); and Financial Services

(2005–present). There are a few cases where committees have been disbanded or had only brief but very important existences. But the vast bulk of the work in Congress since the Second World War has been conducted within a relatively stable set of committees that have not changed too much over time. The relative consistency of the committee jurisdiction system is apparent from the fact that we can produce tables that present the number of hearings held in our consistently defined set of committees over time. (See the appendix to this chapter for these tables.) The first table presents the House of Representatives and the second shows the Senate.[2]

Tables 5.A1 and 5.A2 reflect an overview of every hearing held in the House and Senate from 1947 to 2006.[3] We can see significant shifts in the total number of hearings (over 2,400 hearings in the House in the 101st Congress, only about one-third that number at other times) and also changes in the levels of activity of individual committees over time. Looking across any individual row shows whether the committee had an uninterrupted existence; a series of blanks in a row means a committee was abolished or had not yet come into existence. We see only a small number of committees that disappear (in the House: Un-American Activities, District of Columbia, Fisheries, and Post Office; for the Senate: District of Columbia and Post Office). Similarly, a few committees are created: House, Homeland Security; Senate, Budget and Veterans Affairs. Both bodies have the authority, at any time, to rearrange the jurisdictions of their standing committees, and they do so on a regular, if limited, basis. Generally, however, the overall structure remains remarkably similar over time. Tables 5.A1 and 5.A2 are not full of blanks indicating that the committee in question did not yet exist or had already been abolished, and the "all others" category typically is relatively small. This indicates the relative immutability of the structure of committees in Congress.

Assessing Clarity and Overlap

Given that there has been a relatively (though not completely) set committee system, but that the federal government has become involved in an increas-

2. The committee codebook is available at the policy agendas Web site. Whereas committees have been relatively stable, large changes have occurred in the subcommittees. Our list of committees and subcommittees is sixty-seven pages long, largely because of the great number of shifts in the organization of the subcommittees. The codebook lists each committee assigned to our consistently defined committees for each Congress as well as the subcommittees in each.

3. A small number of hearings were jointly held by more than one committee, but the data presented in Tables 5.A1 and 5.A2 reflect only the lead committee.

ing number of areas of activity, the clarity of the committee jurisdictions must have declined. That is, with a set number of committees overseeing an increasing number of activities, each committee must have seen its own "spread" of activity increase. And similarly, for any given topic of congressional interest, the clarity of the jurisdictional authority must have declined. While any single committee leader would like to assert control over "his" or "her" issue, excluding "extraneous" considerations and maintaining sole control over the issues within his or her jurisdictions, problems and new developments may cause others to disagree. When conflict arises, the simplest route is not necessarily to convince the authors of the status quo policy that they were wrong but rather to find another ally within government to expand their jurisdiction to claim some aspect of the issue as falling within their purview. Efforts to restrict encroachments by others often focus on defining the issue in a restrictive manner, one that is clearly germane only to the committee that previously had control. By contrast, efforts to justify change often stress additional dimensions of the issue that are currently absent from the status quo perspective. The latter strategy is considerably easier when laws are not being considered—that is, when a committee or subcommittee is attempting to raise the visibility of an issue or call attention to lapses in executive agency behavior (Talbert, Jones, and Baumgartner 1995).

In previous writing (Baumgartner and Jones 1991) we discussed at length the demise of the once-powerful Joint Committee on Atomic Energy (JCAE). With a virtual monopoly on all things nuclear, and with a restricted membership covering both House and Senate members, the committee presided over a dramatic expansion of the nuclear power industry from its beginnings through the 1960s. When concerns arose about nuclear proliferation, worker safety, waste disposal, and movements to oppose the installation of new plants in particular communities, the JCAE gave little ground. Change occurred when the committee was dismantled and its jurisdiction was split up among other rival committees that reflected better members' concerns about other elements of the nuclear industry, including environmental perspectives. The story of the JCAE in a way encapsulates the struggle between information and control. During the period in which it prospered, the JCAE accepted only a certain view on civilian or military nuclear power: that it was fundamental to our national security and economic progress. For a while this paradigm was successful and the committee could ignore those who disagreed and downplay the concerns that they raised. As events unfolded revealing greater safety problems, especially on the civilian nuclear industry, the censorship of these views was no longer acceptable to the broader chamber, and the committee was seen to be increasingly out of touch or extreme. The committee was disbanded and a wider range of actors exerted influence over various parts of the issue. Clarity was gone. Control was weakened. Information, in the sense of institutionalized attention to many aspects of the issue, multiplied.

HYPOTHETICAL SIMPLICITY AND DIVERSITY OF CONTROL

As we indicated in Chapter 3, we measure information supply using Shannon's entropy index. We can use this basic idea to bring attention to the importance of the spread of ideas: where information comes from. A system with many perspectives on the same issue has a highly *entropic information* system. One with only a monopoly perspective has a system of *expert information*. Shannon was working on the transmission across noisy telephone wires. If a message came across the wire, and the receiver observed it, what is the likelihood that the message was reflective of what was sent? A condition of low entropy would do that, because it would provide great redundancy in the messages that hypothetically could have come across the wires. In the processing of policy information, the experts agree, and therefore send redundant messages. Low entropy is what one wants in a condition where there are experts, or where there is one true answer.

High entropy, on the other hand, captures diversity in the messages. This can be positive in those cases where no consensus exists on the nature of the problem: addressing it from multiple perspectives can therefore be helpful. Since Shannon was truly dealing with an engineering problem, he wanted a measure of clarity, and maximizing clarity is the goal of those who work on the technical aspects of information transmission. But the indicator he devised—a measure of entropy—is equally adept when we want to measure the spread of attention across multiple categories—what we have called "entropic information"—as the concentration of attention on a single topic. The same measure he used to measure clarity can be used to measure the full range on the scale from clarity to complexity, and that is what we do here.

We can calculate entropy for any single agency or congressional committee, and this entropy may vary across congressional sessions. But we can also sum up the committee entropies and get a sense of the entropic information available within the entire legislature. Table 5.2 shows how this is done.

The entries in the table, the P(NK), indicate the proportion of hearings held by Committee N on Issue K. So, for example, Issue A is divided up among the committees, each of whom may be holding hearings on the policy. This may happen because different committees have different aspects of

TABLE 5.2. Committee Jurisdictions and Information

	Issue A	Issue B	...	Issue K	Committee Entropy
Committee 1	P(1A)	P(1B)		P(1K)	$-\Sigma_Y P(1Y) \cdot \log(p(1Y))$
Committee 2	P(2A)	P(2B)		P(2K)	
...					
...					
...					
Committee N	P(NA)	P(NB)		P(NK)	$-\Sigma_Y P(NY) \cdot \log(p(NY))$
Issue Entropy	$-\Sigma_X P(XA) \cdot \log(p(XA))$	...	...	$-\Sigma_X P(XA) \cdot \log(p(XA))$	

the policy assigned to them, or because some committee chairs hold hearings in areas of unclear or undefined jurisdictions. Summing across a row gives the estimated committee entropy for a committee.

Similarly, one may calculate an entropy score for an issue, which indicates how the issue is divided up among committees. The sum on the corner of the matrix (summing either rows or columns) gives the entropy index for the year or for Congress.

Let us illustrate by using a hypothetical example. Table 5.3 lays out a hypothetical committee system with K committees dealing with N distinct issues.[4] The numbers in the cells indicate the number of hearings conducted by a committee on an issue.

Looking down the columns shows, for any issue, how many committees get involved. Looking across the rows shows the relative concentration of attention for a given committee. In this example, Committee A has exclusive jurisdiction over Issue 1, and it does nothing but deal with that issue. Further, except for another committee that has one hearing, this committee has exclusive control over its issue. Committee A is a model of jurisdictional clarity, and provides strong expert signals to other legislators.

Contrast this situation with Committee B. It also focuses exclusively on just a single issue, but it does not have a monopoly. Committee C also has significant interests there. Finally, Committee K is an all-purpose committee that delves into virtually all areas of public policy. It has no concentration whatsoever. It has very high entropy.

The two right-hand columns of the table summarize the spread of attention for each committee. The number of issues on which a committee is active is a simple indicator of spread. We can also calculate an index of entropy to distinguish between those committees with highly focused attention and

---

4. This discussion relies substantially on Baumgartner, Jones, and MacLeod (2000), which provides greater detail.

TABLE 5.3. A Hypothetical Committee System

	Issue 1	Issue 2	Issue 3	...	Issue N	Number of Issues with Hearings	Committee Entropy
Committee A	10	0	0	...	0	1	Low
Committee B	0	10	0	...	0	1	Low
Committee C	0	5	5	...	0	2	Medium
...							
Committee K	1	1	1	...	1	N	High
Number of Committees Holding Hearings	2	3	3				
Issue Entropy	Low	Medium	High	...			

those that are involved in a great number of distinct issues. Similarly for each policy issue, the two rows at the bottom of the table summarize how many different committees are involved and how broadly spread this attention is across all committees. As we noted above, we can take the average of these entropy scores, either by issue or by committee, for any given year or two-year Congress to assess the overall clarity of the committee system as a whole and use these averages to trace information supply across a period of years.

Congress has some committees, such as Appropriations and Government Oversight, that do not have policy-specific jurisdictions. Others, like Agriculture or Veterans Affairs, have clearly defined and relatively narrow jurisdictions. Tables 5.2 and 5.3 simply provide a vocabulary and a set of indicators to quantify the question of clarity. As we will show, clarity differs substantially by issue, by committee, and over time.

We assess clarity by calculating an entropy score. Entropy is a measure of how widely dispersed something is. An ice cube sitting in a glass of water has low entropy; the cube is tightly contained in its own space, and the water is on the outside. But as the temperature of the water in the glass causes the ice cube to melt, entropy gradually increases until the ice is completely melted and entropy is at its maximum. At that point, there is no longer any difference between the ice and the surrounding water; the material has become completely homogeneous. Many physical processes have the characteristic of moving naturally toward their maximum entropy, or a homogeneous state, unless some energy is used to keep them in a structure. In politics, there is no second law of thermodynamics, so no reason why things would *naturally* move from order to disorder. But when we look at a number of social processes, we see a struggle between order and disorder nonetheless. Just as in the physical world, it takes energy to maintain structure. Institutions must fight to protect their turfs from the encroachment of others. Leaders must continually convey the sense of organizational mission, lest it drift into a large number of ancillary activities. And the definition of given social problems must be maintained in the face of others presenting alternative perspectives.

AN EMPIRICAL CONSIDERATION

Figure 5.1 gives four examples of committees that have narrow and broad spans in their respective jurisdictions in one year.

In 1975 the House Committee on Natural Resources (called the Committee on Public Lands at the time) held forty-six hearings, of which thirty-two were coded by agendas project coders as in topic 21, public lands issues. An additional eleven hearings were coded as energy, primarily about oil production, nuclear power, and pipelines located on public lands (agendas project coding rules focus on the primary purpose of the hearing and are independent of congressional rules of jurisdiction). The committee has a very narrow span of attention, making no claims for jurisdiction in the bulk of the nineteen topic areas defined by the project. Its entropy score is a very low 0.29. The figure also gives similar data for the House Agriculture Committee, also relatively narrow in its reach, but with somewhat more spread and an entropy score of 0.45.

Compare these two committees with the two on the next page: House Appropriations and House Commerce. These two committees have broad mandates, virtually across the full range of government. Commerce gets an entropy score of 0.73 and Appropriations gets that of 0.85. The entropy score clearly reflects the relative narrowness or breadth of the activities of the committees.

There is no reason why the jurisdictions laid out in House Rule X and Senate Rule XXV should be expected to correspond to the topics used in the Policy Agendas Project. The Agriculture Committee, for example, has jurisdiction over food stamps issues, which are coded in the agendas project as social welfare issues, not agriculture. House Interior's jurisdiction over energy resources on public lands makes sense, though in the agendas project we call those issues energy issues, not public lands issues. So our point here is not that the congressional system is faulty because it draws jurisdictional lines in ways that do not correspond to the nineteen major topics of the agendas project codebook. Rather, we simply need a consistent way to compare the committees to one another, and to compare them over time. The following analysis does that.

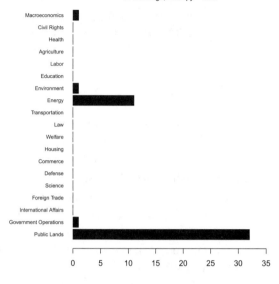

Natural Resources

46 Hearings, Entropy = 0.29

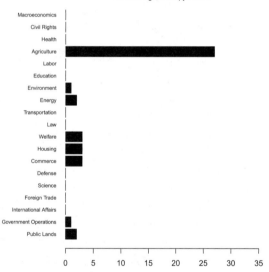

Agriculture

42 Hearings, Entropy = 0.45

FIGURE 5.1. House Committees with Broad and Narrow Scope, 1975

Source: Policy Agendas Project

Note: The figure shows the number of hearings held in four House committees in 1975, across the nineteen topics of the Policy Agendas Project. The Natural Resources Committee held forty-six hearings, virtually all of which were in the areas of public lands management or energy (often mineral or oil resources on public lands); the Agriculture Committee similarly held the vast bulk of its forty-two hearings on agri-

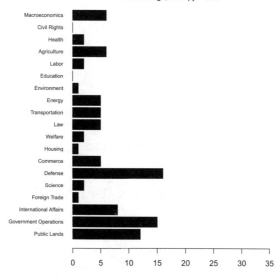

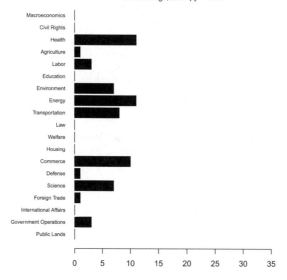

culture. By contrast, the Appropriations and Commerce Committees show broad spans of attention. The entropy score associated with each is a single indicator of this spread; low scores on entropy show high concentration of attention, and higher scores show greater spread.

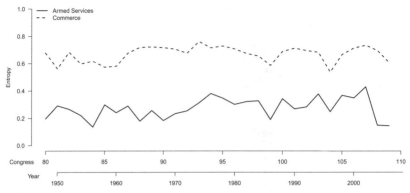

FIGURE 5.2. The Consistency of Committee Entropy over Time
Source: Policy Agendas Project
Note: The jurisdictions of various congressional committees differ by their range. While there have been changes in the overall structure of clarity, for any given committee, the differences remain stark and relatively consistent over time. Commerce has always had a very broad reach; armed services, always a much narrower one.

The differences shown in Figure 5.1 relate to the fundamental mission of the prestigious Appropriations Committee as compared to the more policy-focused committees. Certain committees have relatively narrow jurisdictions while others, such as Ways and Means or Appropriations in the House or Finance in the Senate, seem to be almost unconstrained in their activities. One major reason that the prestige committees are attractive is because of the great range of their activities. The range of activity of a given committee across issues is shown as an entropy score in Figure 5.1. And we can see that, over time, individual committees remain quite different from one another, as Figure 5.2 shows.

In the U.S. Senate, the Commerce Committee has always had a relatively high entropy score, as, like Appropriations in the House, it delves into a great range of activities that affect its mandate, the entire U.S. economy. By contrast, the Armed Services Committee has maintained a narrow reach, as would be expected, throughout the entire postwar period. Generally, individual committees maintain their distinct patterns of entropy.

Another way to look at the relative clarity or muddiness of the congressional committee structure is to ask, for any given issue or topic domain, how many committees claim jurisdiction. Certain topics, such as agriculture or education questions, are likely to fall squarely within the jurisdiction of one, and only one, committee, whereas others, such as domestic commerce, energy, or social welfare, may find a larger number of committees showing interest. Figure 5.3 gives four examples of narrow and broad spreads of attention across particular issues.

Figure 5.3 uses the same format as Figure 5.1, but it shows how many committees are active in each policy domain, rather than looking at how many domains a given committee is involved in. We call this "topic entropy," or the spread of committees involved in a given topic. It is clear, and comes as no surprise, that when talking about agriculture issues, the bulk of the action will be in the Agriculture Committee, with some additional attention coming from Appropriations. Similarly, education issues are virtually all dealt with in the Committee on Education and Labor, with a rare few in Committees on Science or Veterans Affairs. By contrast, government operations and energy issues emerge in a number of committees. Many policy topics are far from the jurisdictional clarity that we read about in textbooks on Congress and which are illustrated by the examples of agriculture and education.

Just as we looked in Figure 5.2 at the relative stability of the committee entropy scores we identified in Figure 5.1, we can look in Figure 5.4 at the stability of the number of committees involved in each policy domain.

Figure 5.4 shows two examples that illustrate the degree of the differences we laid out in Figure 5.3, between those areas with relatively few committees involved and those with many committees claiming some degree of jurisdiction are stable over time. The category of Government Operations has always been subject to many different congressional masters, with an entropy score in each successive Congress since 1948 somewhere in the neighborhood of 0.8. Transportation issues are typically dealt with only in the Transportation Committee and sometimes in Appropriations or one or two others; its entropy score has consistently been closer to 0.4. So we can see through these examples that the committees differ significantly from one to another in the range of their activities, that the policy domains of the agendas project also differ in the number of committees that become active, and that these differences are relatively stable aspects of the institutional functioning of the U.S. Congress.

The Dynamics of Committee Complexity

With these definitions and examples out of the way, we can proceed to look at trends over time: With the rise in so many new issues, but a relatively set number of congressional committees, what trends are apparent in overall levels of entropy?

Let us call the jurisdictional spread of a single committee across our topics "committee entropy" and the number of committees involved on a particular policy topic "topic entropy." (We called this "issue entropy" earlier; we switch to the term "topic entropy" to denote that we are applying the

Agriculture

40 Hearings, Entropy = 0.36

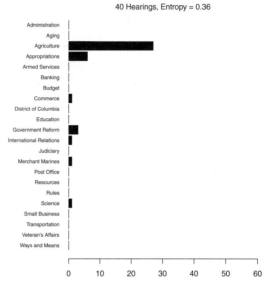

Education

25 Hearings, Entropy = 0.11

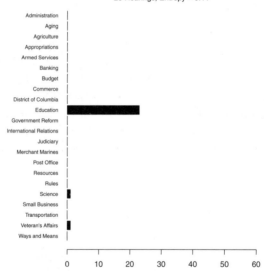

FIGURE 5.3. Policy Domains with Clear and Divided Committee Control, 1975
Source: Policy Agendas Project
Note: The figure illustrates that some policy domains have very clear committee structures, whereas other topics have jurisdictions that span across many committees. Hearings on the topics of agriculture and education, shown on the left, are almost always in the corresponding committee of jurisdiction. On the other hand, government operations and energy, shown on the right, saw hearings in

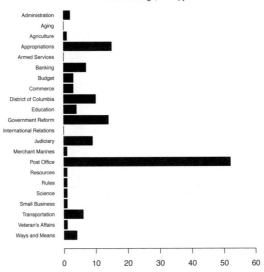

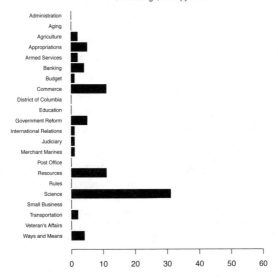

many different committees. Entropy when measured by topic captures the degree to which one or a few committees are active in that domain (low entropy), or attention can come from a large number of committees (high entropy).

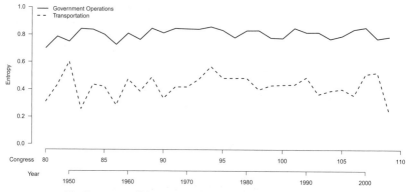

FIGURE 5.4. The Consistency of Topic Entropy over Time

Source: Policy Agendas Project

Note: Certain topics have always been subject to more clearly defined congressional committee jurisdictions, whereas others have consistently been spread across many committees. The figure shows the cases of transportation, which has always been subject to hearings in only a small number of committees, and government operations, where many committees have consistently been involved. This is clear as the entropy scores remain distinct and relatively stable when calculated separately for each two-year Congress.

Policy Agendas Project topic coding system.) Having measured both concepts for every topic and every committee in each year from 1948 to 2006, we can build a general index of the clarity of the jurisdictional system over time. Maximum jurisdictional clarity, as we saw in Table 5.3, was reached if each committee focused on just one issue and if each policy topic domain had just one committee of jurisdiction. Maximum committee entropy occurred in the situation where there was no structure at all: committees had no particular constraints, and topics found all committees equally involved. Figure 5.5 shows our measures of topic and committee entropy separately for the House and the Senate.

Because the four lines in Figure 5.5 are so similar, we have also calculated an entropy index, which is the result of a principal components factor analysis of the four series in the figure. The first factor explains 89.91 percent of the variance, and the four series have the following factor loadings: 0.95, 0.96, 0.96, and 0.92. The resulting index can be thought of as a weighted average of the four individual measures, and the four contributing measures are so highly correlated with each other (these correlations range from 0.78 to 0.92) that it makes little difference which one we might use. The index is based on the greatest amount of information, however, so we present that in the darker line in the figure. Whereas the individual entropy measures range from zero to one, the index is scaled so that it has an average of zero and a standard deviation of one; this is made clear on the left-hand axis.

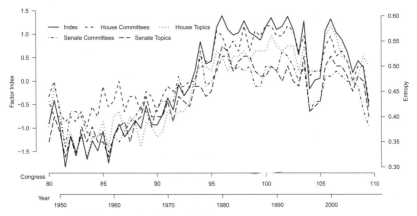

FIGURE 5.5. Four Measures and an Index of Entropy

Source: Policy Agendas Project

Note: The figure shows that no matter which way we calculate entropy (by topic or by committee), and whether we look at the House or the Senate, we observe a strong trend toward greater diversity over time. As there are more hearings in the first year of a Congress than in the second, the annual data show a saw-tooth pattern of greater spread in the first year. Calculating the data by two-year Congress shows the same trend, but without the annual fluctuations.

Committee jurisdictions to a large extent mimic the structure of law and bureaucracy, so by examining the dynamic interplay between changes in the size of government and the nature of legislative jurisdictions, we can begin to map these interdependencies. Figure 5.5 makes clear that we can think of three periods of development in congressional committee organization. The early postwar years were a period of jurisdictional stability, with little added committee complexity. Beginning in the late 1950s, and lasting for about a quarter of a century, we see a dramatic transformation. The index of entropy goes from less than −1 to more than +1 on our scale, corresponding to a huge decline in the clarity of committee jurisdictions. Finally, from about 1980, the line stops increasing. Recent years fluctuate considerably as congressional leaders have attempted to clarify the committee system—note the big but temporary drop in the index of entropy in the 104th Congress (1995–97), when Republican Speaker Newt Gingrich centralized the committee structure and weakened the power of the committee chairs. Because reforms seem to have but a temporary effect, the index of entropy remains at roughly the same level in recent years as it has since about 1980. This level is much higher than it was in the early postwar years, but it has not increased since the late 1970s.[5]

5. Figures 5.2 and 5.4 show relative consistency in the entropy scores for individual committees and issues over time, but Figure 5.5 clearly shows a dramatic increase in entropy from

Why is this the case? Because entropy is an indicator of the diversity of information being addressed by Congress; the cessation of the rise in the index is most likely a consequence of changes in the aggressiveness of the search behavior of Congress. Congress, through its committees, became less interested in pursuing the complex ramifications of problems and more interested in consolidation and expertise.

If so, then why did the index reach an apogee and stabilize, seemingly resilient in the face of attempts to reform and centralize committees? The simple answer is that the complexity of the federal government grew substantially during the period, and for clarity to increase rather than stabilize Congress would have to refuse to oversee the panoply of agencies and programs it created.

From Clarity to Complexity

In this chapter we have presented detailed calculations about the clarity of the congressional committee system from 1948 to 2006. From a position of relative clarity in the early postwar period, things have gotten more complicated. Steadily from the late 1950s to 1980, jurisdictions increasingly began to overlap. For any given issue, more committees were involved. For any given committee, chairs found a way to reach into a greater number of issues. The committee system by the late 1970s had been transformed substantially so that overlap and breadth of jurisdiction were much greater, as compared to the earlier period. Significant reforms decentralizing power to subcommittees in the mid 1970s were an important part of this. However, our evidence shows no single year or particular reform that generated this transformation. Rather, it was steady, indicating a general shift occurring over an entire generation as the scope of government became much broader but the number of committees remained relatively stable.

This was no simple secular trend, and since the 1980s, there has been almost a complete cessation of this growth. While the entropy index we cre-

---

1950 to 1980. Our point in showing the data in Figures 5.2 and 5.4 is to illustrate the dramatic differences among issues and committees: some have greater clarity than others, and they always have. When we combine all the issues and all the committees together, as in Figure 5.5, however, small increases in each committee and in each issue add up to create a very large overall increase in entropy. If, for example, we calculate the entropy score for each of the standing committees and present them in the form of a stacked-line graph, we see that the increase in the overall score stems from small increases in virtually all the individual series, not any particular committee driving the overall trend. Rather, it is related to small increases throughout the entire system.

ated has become less stable from year to year, it has neither grown nor declined. From a purely organizational perspective, the gains from creating specialized agencies in government or committees in Congress that have exclusive control over issues are great. In fact, the value of division of labor is so great it makes one wonder why we have such a complicated, convoluted, confusing, overlapping, inefficient, and frustrating system of committees or institutions of government. It seems simple enough: division of labor suggests that one committee should deal with education, another with poverty, another with defense, and each should keep out of the work of the others. In exchange, the system gains from the expertise that such specialized institutions can gain, and the clarity of authority makes it easy to understand just who is in charge. But this does not characterize the interaction between issues and committees. Confusion and overlap increased during an important part of the postwar period, and, while the trend is no longer increasing, neither are those characteristics declining.

This confusion and overlap are characteristics of systems gathering what we term "entropic information." So the system by 1980 was much better in encompassing a greater supply of information than it was twenty years before. But it did so with less clarity and hence generated less expert information. It is perhaps no accident that the nonpartisan Congressional Budget Office was created in the mid-1970s, during a period of strong growth in entropic information, and the General Accounting Office (now the General Accountability Office) expanded the scope of its expert advice. Committees are probably less trusted in Congress, while the nonpartisan professional agencies have come to play an increasing role in the provision of expert information. In 2011, the Senate's chief deficit hawk, Senator Tom Coburn of Oklahoma, authored a report defending the role of the General Accountability Office against proposed cuts, writing "If the mission of GAO is compromised by excessive cuts, where else can Congress turn to find unbiased data to improve programs and save money" (Coburn 2011)?

The struggle between information as expertise and information as entropy reflects the classic agenda struggle among groups seeking access to the public agenda. Whenever one organization seeks to claim a monopoly of political control, it faces potential challenges from those on the outside who may criticize the incumbents for overlooking important aspects of the question. Unless the government entity—be it a congressional committee or an executive agency—is able fully to understand and master the issue with which it deals, it can at least potentially be attacked for overattention to those aspects it defines as most important to its organizational mission and underattending to those aspects that outside critics might like to see addressed. So while the creation of specialized agencies leads to great gains in expertise and division of labor, it also creates an inherent tension between those who are inside and those who are excluded.

This dynamic is the struggle between information and control. Analysts and journalists pay attention to shifts in organizational mandates and control for many reasons, one of which is the political power-game that they reflect. This can make interesting news. But more important than the personalities involved, different organizations typically "organize in" certain aspects of the underlying social problem and "organize out" others. When a committee with an environmental focus examines regulations on how farmers apply pesticides, and an agriculture committee attempts to keep them out of "its turf," this can make for interesting stories. Worsham and Stores (2012) document the ability of the Congressional Agriculture Committees to stymie efforts to interject issues of civil rights, particularly the blatant discrimination by the Department of Agriculture in its treatment of black farmers in the South, for seventy years. The issue reflects the dynamic we are discussing here: clear jurisdictions imply narrower definitions of what is at stake, what information is relevant, and how this information should be interpreted. Messy and overlapping jurisdictions imply contests about what is at stake, what information is relevant, and what goals we are trying to maximize.

"Seek and Ye Shall Find"

In the first three chapters of this book we distinguished between two forms of information: information that is relevant to the processes of problem discovery, definition, and prioritization, and information as solution expertise. Discovering what problems are relevant in the policy-making environment requires open systems characterized by overlap and confusion. Solution expertise, and the implementation of those solutions, requires closed and accountable systems—that is, control. But more and more expertise about solutions cannot solve the issue of trade-offs among priorities. That requires not expertise but entropic information. As a consequence, the tension inherent in the assignments of congressional jurisdictions reflects the struggle between control and information.

Just as important, the existence of a large supply of entropic information ensures the discovery of problems. A limited supply implies control and containment. The agriculture policy subsystem's ability to shut out attempts to raise the issue of discrimination against black farmers meant that expenditures were controlled and expertise focused on commodities, subsidies, and other technical agricultural business. It also meant that justice would not be done. By censoring the civil rights implications of agricultural policies, decision making was simpler but problems were ignored. The House Agriculture Committee invited almost no witnesses focusing on civil rights between 1945 and the late 1990s, when the issue broke through and was taken seriously (Worsham and Stores 2012, figure 9).

Clearly the opposite is also true. Lots of entropic information leads to lots of problem discovery. The tight connection between seeking and finding inherent in the paradox of search implies that the increased search by congressional committees during the third quarter of the twentieth century led to more problem discovery, and hence more legislation, budgetary commitments, and government expansion. We have seen in this and the previous chapter that important changes in the nature of American government—in both the executive and legislative branches—have been how the institutional structure has been revised in order to incorporate more diversity into the system.

One of the most important transformations of American government in the past fifty years has been the increased relevance of issues of jurisdictional dynamics such as those we are discussing. Greater numbers of institutions mean that more perspectives on issues are systematically organized into the political discussion. This greater richness creates problems of overlap, redundancy, and contradictions within government, as different agencies approach the same issue with different goals in mind. There are constant efforts to clean things up, to clarify hierarchical rules and jurisdictional boundaries. But tensions inevitably rise again because the issues themselves raise myriad problems across a great number of dimensions of evaluation. Organizational clarity promotes control and accountability but restricts information. In the next chapter we shift our focus away from organizational design to the fundamental driving force that created these changes: the increased number of policy initiatives housed in government.

6

The Search for Information
and the Great New-Issue Expansion

Government today is bigger than it was two generations ago, and it is messier. Just as various congressional committees have increasingly found themselves sharing rather than controlling authority within their policy domains, so too do government agencies in the federal executive and in the states and localities find themselves in positions that overlap with the authorities of other units of government. Government has grown both bigger and more diverse—it is involved in many more issues today than in the 1950s. One can imagine government limited in the span of issues it addresses, but involved intensively in those issues. But this is not the pattern, and the decline of clarity in legislative jurisdictions is a primary indictor of this. Clarity has declined as more issues have become institutionalized on various government agendas.

How did this happen? How did government become both more intense in the areas it traditionally operated in and more expansive across issues? It did so in a burst of frenetic policy-making activity that carved a great historical arc of problem-seeking activity and legislative results that peaked and declined, but left in its wake a changed politics, government, and administrative organization. In this chapter we offer evidence of what we term "the Great New-Issue Expansion"—a period of some two decades from the late 1950s to the late 1970s in which the reach of government into arenas previously left to private action expanded on an annual basis. Then the process of issue expansion ceased, and a period of consolidation began. That period, however, did not return the system to the status quo ante. The Great New-Issue Expansion had destroyed that. The residues of the period are easily observable in the shift of congressional activities from legislation to oversight, indexed by a decline of legislative activities and the continuance of oversight at the same level as in the peak of the expansionary period.

Problem Definition and Government Growth

The U.S. government, as measured by inflation-adjusted funds spent per capita, has grown by a factor of four hundred (from $20 to almost $8,000) over the period of 1791 to 2008 (see Jones et al., in press). Other measures might not show exactly the same ratio, but all would point in the same direction: government is huge compared to what it once was. (If we just look at expenditures—adjusted for inflation but not for population growth—government grew by a factor of over thirty thousand.) And the process is ongoing. Government today is more complex even than it was in the 1940s and 1950s. As the country emerged victorious from the Second World War, it experienced large increases in the scope of what we expect from government.

Bigger, more intrusive government is a two-edged sword. Government programs have contributed greatly to the welfare of the general population through the provision of public health, pension systems, and health research; to the conduct of commerce through transportation infrastructure; to the store of human knowledge through research and education; and to many other social goods. It is easy to point to social problems, such as excess poverty among the elderly, that have been substantially reduced or virtually eliminated by such programs as Social Security and Medicare. But we can also point to policies that are not so attractive, such as the farm subsidies that go primarily to a limited number of growers of a few commodities. And even where a social good such as protecting endangered species, wetlands, or open spaces is provided, these may involve objectionable limitations on individual freedoms. Further, of course, even successful programs may not be perfect, and critics may focus on their failures, inefficiencies, or unintended consequences.

Problems can present opportunities to enact policies alleviating the problems, but they can also facilitate the attachment of special benefits that do not address the underlying issues. Moreover, the solutions can become increasingly complex as each new government provision generates attempts to correct or extend the existing policy. Aaron Wildavsky (1979, chapter 3) called this phenomenon "policy as its own cause." Whyman and Jones (2012) give a graphic example:

> The Banking Act of 1933, also known as Glass-Steagall, established the Federal Deposit Insurance Corporation (FDIC), imposed banking reforms to regulate commercial bank securities activities, and limited affiliations between commercial banks and securities firms. The Act effectively curbed systemic risk in financial markets by regulating these and other activities

and managed to do so in just 53 short pages. Fast-forward 77 years, after the repeal of Glass-Steagall, and into the midst of the worst financial crisis to hit the [United States] since the Great Depression and the passage of the Dodd-Frank Wall Street Reform and Consumer Protection Act of 2010. Like its predecessor, this act sought to limit systemic risk and create stability in U.S. financial markets, although it did so in 848 pages.

Laws become more complex for several reasons, but the most important are that both problems and solutions are more complex than in the past. In any case, with the growth of a wide range of policy initiatives has come the need to understand the dynamics of information and size of government.

One of the most striking differences between the government during the period of Truman and Eisenhower and more recent times is the number of issues on the policy agenda. By any measure the range of activities in which the federal government simultaneously engages is overwhelming. Government can deal with thousands of issues simultaneously by hiring more staff and creating more agencies, and this is what has happened. The creation of new agencies, new programs, and new levels of bureaucratic oversight by Congress ensures that a wider and wider range of social processes is systematically monitored. Good data does not necessarily imply better policy, but surely the converse is true: bad or absent data invariably leads to poor policies. In some areas, such as weather prediction, the connection between information and policy is close and obvious. In others, perhaps the economy, the connection is less clear—in part because of the "friction" of ideologies and interests.

New agencies institutionalize systematic attention to particular social problems or aspects of their potential solutions. As more agencies, programs, and incentives in the tax code have been created to address poverty, education, agriculture, health care, energy, scientific research, international competitiveness, and other factors, more and more of the complexities of the social world are systematically monitored. At the same time, the institutional consequence of this greater diversity in government is that it becomes more difficult to coordinate or control these disparate programs. Information and control are in inherent conflict. The more information, the greater the problem of setting priorities or maintaining control.

The expanded range of action has made it more important that we understand the trade-offs between information and control. Because leadership and control are much harder where information is overwhelming, leaders have a tendency to limit information by suppressing or censoring attributes. That is, either policy makers ignore, fail to appreciate, or actively deny aspects of a complex problem that can cause difficulties. This may work for long periods of time, and it may even work forever, but for some issues at some times the suppression strategy will fail, and when if fails, it may fail spectacularly. This is a consequence of what we termed "error accumulation" in *The Politics of Attention*, which at base was about the politics of suppressing attributes. As a consequence of the dynamics of attribute suppression and error accumulation, political systems experience an alternation between relatively stable periods of allegiance to established ways of doing things and other periods during which massive adjustments in the very goals and stated missions of various government agencies occur.

This attribute-suppression process is not the sole province of left or right. In the expansionary period liberals tended to underestimate the long-run consequences of what they proposed; in the conservative contraction that followed, conservatives often denied that some problems even existed, lest they evoke calls for government solutions.

Thickening and Broadening of Government

It is common to view government as growing "bigger" and "more intrusive" as if these were two sides of the same coin. They are not. Since the end of the Second World War, government has both *thickened*, in that it is involved more intensely in the areas it traditionally was involved in, and *broadened*, in the sense that it has become involved in a much wider range of activities than it was previously. Thickening is doing more of the same; broadening is taking on new tasks. These two aspects of government growth are not necessarily tightly coupled. When President Johnson enacted Medicare and Medicaid, most political analysts recognized the Rubicon that had been crossed; government had intruded in a major way into the health care market, and that market could never be the same as before. The establishing of a Consumer Protection Agency independent of bank regulation in the Dodd-Frank Wall Street Reform and Consumer Protection Act of 2010 was a similar broadening, if less dramatic. We present evidence that the thickening process was ongoing in the 1950s (indeed, it is probably characteristic of most policy changes in most eras), but the broadening process happened later, and when it did, it was more intense.

Measures of the size of government can underestimate its scope. A single federal law, regulation, or court decision may impose burdens on all entities within a class of economic actors, and the impact is greater where the action moves into a previously unregulated area. As a consequence, the agenda-setting process, in which political actors begin to see a social or economic condition as a problem ripe for government action, has consequences of greater import than even larger actions later in time. The reason is the path-dependent nature of politics—once government has intruded in a novel economic or social arena, it is unlikely to retreat from that arena. In the next few pages we assess thickening and broadening by looking at the range of activities of government; by range we mean the number of distinct policy issues (e.g., policy agendas subtopics) addressed. We will show that government grew steadily broader during the period when it got thicker as well. In the following chapter we turn to budgetary and other estimates to show similar trends.

The Rise of New Issues

Here we examine the consequences of changes in the supply of information represented in the congressional committee structure that was the focus of our previous chapter. We first develop a simple indicator of agenda expansion that reflects the entropy measures of information presented in Chapter 5, and which can be calculated on most of the measures of policy change coded by the Policy Agendas Project. Then we examine multiple measures of agenda expansion and trace them across time.

We can measure with considerable precision the role of government within various policy arenas and compare this role over time. We do so by calculating the expenditures of government within an area divided by the total size (GDP share) of that area. That requires good measures of the GDP share of health care as well as government expenditures within the area. It is important that we begin to measure the broadening of the policy agenda with an equivalent degree of precision. Indeed, that was the essential motivation for developing the Policy Agendas Project datasets in the first place. We are interested in both the informational components of agenda change—when political leaders begin to conceive of a social condition as a policy problem—and in the policy components of agenda change—when policy changes to incorporate a new policy arena.

The Policy Agendas Project enumerates 226 different topics of governmental activity. Each of nineteen major topics, such as Macroeconomics, Agriculture, and Health Care, is subdivided into a number of more precise subtopics, such as those for Macroeconomics: inflation, unemployment, monetary supply and the Federal Reserve, national debt, and so on. The number of hearings conducted during a year assesses the intensity of congressional activity, but it does not necessarily assess the span of issues that Congress addresses. A large number of hearings could be concentrated on a small

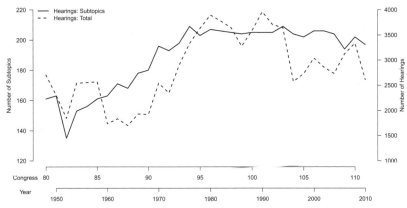

FIGURE 6.1. Number of Policy Agendas Subtopics with at Least One Congressional Hearing
Source: Policy Agendas Project

number of policy topics, which would lead to low entropy and less diversity in information. We use the number of subtopics in which Congress held at least one hearing as a measure of the breadth or span of the legislative policy-making agenda. This measure may be viewed as a rough equivalent of the measure we termed "topic entropy" in Chapter 5. The correlation between the average topic entropy and the subtopic measure is 0.86.[1]

In 1947 Congress held 1,508 hearings, and these were spread across 143 distinct subtopics. During the Korean War hearings activity declined momentarily and only 102 subtopics were discussed in the 828 hearings held in 1952. After this the numbers increased regularly, and by 1975 there were 1,809 hearings and attention had spread to 196 of the 226 possible subtopics. So we see a dramatic transformation, not only in the level of activity but in the spread of congressional action. This spreading out is shown for the full period in Figure 6.1.[2]

The figure makes clear that Congress has not only become more active but also that this attention has spread across a wider range of topics. This spread of attention traces the incorporation of new issues into the polity, and as a consequence U.S. government has moved from generally clear and

---

1. Topic entropy displays higher variability at the upper end of the scale than does the subtopic measure, but the two measures are strongly correlated. See the appendix to this chapter for more information on the reliability of the entropy and subtopic measures.

2. The series above counts the number of subtopics on which at least one hearing was held in a given year. Counting the number of subtopics with at least two, five, or ten hearings produces series very similar to the one shown. Correlations with this series are as follows: 0.972, 0.922, 0.817.

distinct policies within reasonably coherent domains to increased complexity and spillover among policy areas. The trend ended by the late 1970s, and since then the number of subtopics attracting hearing activity has leveled off and slightly declined. We term the period from the mid-1950s to the late 1970s the "Great New-Issue Expansion," as the number of issues and their complexity incorporated into the political sphere increased markedly during that period, but that new-issue expansion has neither continued nor been repeated—at least by the measures we use (policy agendas subtopics subject to hearings and the decline of clarity in congressional committee jurisdictions).

The Great New-Issue Expansion

We are not the first to note that government activity rose in the 1950s or early 1960s and peaked in the late 1970s. Arthur Schlesinger (1986) and Samuel Huntington (1981) both point to the rise and decline of a more progressive and aggressive government between the late 1950s and mid-1970s. Huntington points to a "horseshoe" of political (especially protest) activity. Hacker and Pierson (2010, 99) write, "1977 and 1978 marked the rapid demise of the liberal era and the emergence of something radically different." They offer a list of failures by the huge Democratic majorities in Congress and a Democratic president to enact major reforms in that year as crucial pieces of the evidence. Similarly, Grossman (2011, 2014), based on his analyses of secondary accounts of policy development, refers to the period of the 1960s and 1970s as the "Long Great Society."

These studies fail to distinguish between the expansion of the issue agenda and the level of activity, which are not identical, as Figure 6.1 shows. Our analysis shows the effect of active problem search and agenda expansion on the breadth of government activities, and it leads to a crucial distinction between thickening and broadening of government activities. Because the Policy Agenda Project codes policies similarly across institutions and venues, we can also compare the broadening of government across institutions and begin to understand leads and lags in the agenda-expansion process.

Since the end of the Second World War, the intrusion of scores of "new" issues has transformed the agenda of American politics. What we term "new issues" are those not previously seriously addressed by government. These issues did not enter the system incrementally, however; rather, in a period of two decades these new issues transformed the political space. John Kingdon

(1995) noted that a social condition such as cancer, pollution, or the breakup of the traditional family does not become a political issue until political actors demand that the government do something about it. But the result, as James Q. Wilson (1979, 41) noted in the midst of the Great New-Issue Expansion, is that "[o]nce politics was about only a few things, now it is about nearly everything." Perhaps a major reason for the leveling off of the incorporation of new issues into the political sphere is that politics had invaded so many aspects of life that there were no "new issues" left. That does not mean, however, that agenda politics is dead. In a meaningful sense, agenda setting has moved from a process by which conditions become political issues to one in which a new aspect of the issue becomes salient.

The national political agenda became more crowded as things that were once accepted as social conditions or facts of life became questioned and government resources were mobilized to do something about them. Technological advance has also had a lot to do with it, both directly and indirectly. One consequence of technological advance is that it is possible now to solve some problems, or at least ameliorate them, that were once impossible to address. So technological advances can lead to "new" political problems because they allow the possibility of addressing old problems. Many "new" problems are not really new issues; they are only new to government. Often they have been around, as social conditions, for many decades.

Even within the historical period covered by this book, cancer was once discussed only in hushed tones and usually in private, among family; during the 1950s and 1960s, it was barely a topic of polite discussion, much less political mobilization. Today, medical advances have made it possible for people to mobilize and demand that government declare and win a "war on cancer." Many other issues have arisen as technological advancement has created potentially addressable political issues out of what were once considered to be only unfortunate social conditions. Groups such as the mentally ill or the physically disabled that were once virtually invisible politically are now the objects of significant political attention and massive government programs. The translation of "conditions" into "problems" can stem from social mobilization or from technological advance that makes it possible to do something about conditions that were once accepted as unavoidable.

Technological advances also create new problems, as well as opportunities for new solutions. Increased concern with privacy in the wake of the creation of large databases, telecommunications policy, space, nuclear warfare, cloning, fetal tissue research, and global warming are all examples of new political issues having developed as the consequence of technological advancement. (So some "new" issues really are new.) Technological advancement creates solutions to some conditions, making them ripe for political attention, and it also creates problems of its own.

New issues, and old ones redefined, enter the political system through argumentation and information. Government officials take new information, new claims, new evidence, and new ways of thinking about old problems, and they react. They argue about it, ignore it, deny it, assert it, discount it, discredit it, claim it is not important, or assert it is fundamental to the public debate. In the political system, individuals and groups argue about the relevance of new bits of information. Information is everywhere, and it determines the public response to potential political issues. Technological advance is a major source of new issues in government, though not the only one; social mobilization also matters.

When new issues arise on the government agenda, new institutions are often created to deal with them, or old institutions revise their mandates and missions in order to better take them into account. Similarly, the social transformations that often accompany the rise of new issues (or cause them in the first place) such as mobilization for war, the growth of new areas of the economy, the geographic and economic mobility of the population, and changes in the scope and size of social movements and interest groups serve also to keep them alive in the political realm. As a consequence, it is impossible to understand the evolution, growth, and development of the institutions of American government over the long haul without simultaneously paying attention to the agenda of government: the portfolio of issues with which it deals. Changes in the size and composition of this portfolio have transformed the institutions of government and affected the mobilization of interest groups and social movements outside of government. And as the institutions have changed, so also has their receptiveness to the new political issues.

The Legislative Impact of the New-Issue Expansion

Using the data available in the Policy Agendas Project, we can trace the impact of the new-issue expansion on legislation and on other aspects of government. We begin with the immediate legislative impact of the explosion of issues onto the public agenda.

Figure 6.2 divides hearings into two categories: those in which a bill was considered (termed "legislative hearings") and those in which no bill was considered ("nonlegislative hearings"). This latter category consisted of hearings concerning oversight of existing programs and the implementation of them by the federal bureaucracy (classic oversight hearings) and those di-

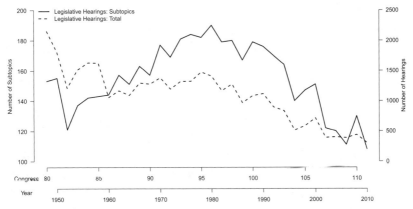

FIGURE 6.2. The Number and Spread of Legislative and Nonlegislative Hearings
Source: Policy Agendas Project

rected more generally at problem definition and illumination of problems that could require legislation.

The figure graphs both the total number of hearings and the number of policy agendas subtopics that see at least one hearing.[3] The pattern is striking. Hearings considering legislation declined from the early 1950s to the end of the period of our data (2008). Each year Congress conducted fewer hearings on potential new legislation. But our measure of the broadening of the policy-making agenda, the number of agendas subtopics with at least one legislative hearing, clearly traces the new-issue expansion of the 1960s and 1970s. During the period of the Great Society and following, Congress not only considered a broader array of issues but it also drafted bills on them and scheduled formal consideration of them. The broadening process peaked in the late 1970s and began to decline steeply in the late 1980s. Congressional lawmaking activity became increasingly focused on a smaller number of topics throughout the 1990s and 2000s.

Hearings on nonlegislative matters display a similar pattern for the period of new-issue ascension to the policy-making agenda, and both the number of hearings and their breadth of content follow the same pattern. As in the case of legislative hearings, hearings on problems and bureaucratic oversight reach a peak, both raw numbers and in breadth of policy topics,

3. House and Senate hearings are combined here. And we present the data by two-year Congress rather than by year because of the seesaw pattern in which there are more hearings but fewer laws in the first session, then more laws and fewer hearings in the second session of a Congress. We repeat this practice in later figures in this chapter for the same reason.

in the late 1970s. After the peak, there is no decline in either measure. It would seem that once legislation is enacted and programs created, Congress expends considerable energy in examining the results of its legislative activity.

Our analyses of other Policy Agendas Project datasets indicate a similar pattern. If we examine the statutes passed since the Second World War, we find that the number of statutes increased during the 1950s, but then declined throughout the rest of the period of study. On the other hand, the number of subtopics with at least one statute—our measure of the broadening of legislation across the issue space—generally follows the new-issue expansion pattern noted in legislative hearing activity.[4] The data show first an expansion as the diversity of the lawmaking agenda increased, then a steady state issue agenda at around 150 subtopics addressed by legislation during the 1970s and 1980s. A rapid consolidation of the lawmaking agenda begins with the 102nd Congress (1993–95), and accelerates in the 103rd Congress with the Republican ascension to congressional control. By the late 1990s, the lawmaking agenda had constricted to about the same size as it was in the mid-1950s.[5]

LAWMAKING

Congress does not exist in some sort of vacuum—rather, the institution is intimately linked with the other governing institutions. As Congress passes laws, it affects other parts of government—clearly the executive branch, but also the courts. Perhaps most importantly, the statutes Congress enacts cumulate to form the corpus of U.S. federal law (which is assembled in organized fashion as the U.S. Code of Laws), and these laws form the framework for rule making in the executive branch, court interpretations of the law, and further lawmaking by Congress. If we examine the pages of statutes passed, which can also be (roughly) interpreted as the addition to the corpus of laws, we can see how much larger the body of law becomes as a result of

---

4. Our findings of a period of increasing agenda diversity, which we termed "the Great New-Issue Expansion" seems to correspond closely to Grossman's (2011) "Long Great Society" era of active major legislation, based on his study of secondary analyses of major legislation. The connection between ascension of issues to the agenda and the passing of major legislation is well worth considering.

5. There are some qualifications to this interpretation. Sometimes Congress repeals parts of the Code, or replaces parts (such as would occur with a reauthorization) or the courts declare parts invalid. But our examination of the Code suggests that the main statutes passed translate directly into the Code.

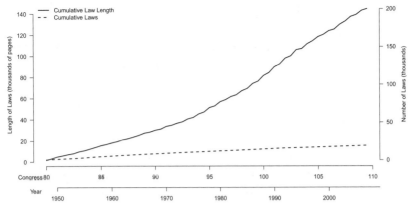

FIGURE 6.3. The Cumulative Number of Laws Passed and the Cumulative Number of Pages of Laws
Source: Policy Agendas Project (number of laws); Michelle Wolfe (pages of laws)

congressional legislative action—and how much more complex law becomes as well.

Figure 6.3 graphs the cumulative number of laws passed and the cumulative number of pages of laws passed annually between 1947 and 2008. The cumulative number of laws passed increases over time, but at a decreasing rate, as Congress passes fewer laws than it did in the past. The cumulative number of pages of law has a different pattern: a distinct upward curvature, as the number of pages per law is considerably higher today than in the past. And it is this cumulative number of pages that best indicates the increase in the corpus of law.

A great increase in the size and complexity of federal law was put in motion by the intense lawmaking activity of the 1960s and 1970s. The number of pages begins to grow at an increased rate during the mid- to late 1950s, and receives another boost in the late 1970s, peaking in the early 1990s. After a decline in the mid-1990s, contributions to the corpus of law decline and stabilize, but remain at a much higher level than before the 1950s and 1960s.

Whyman and Jones (2012) examined fits to the graph separately for the periods 1948–65, 1966–94, and 1995–2007. The cumulative pages of law enacted by Congress experienced a modest linear rate of growth (Congress created an average of 1,371 pages of law per year) between 1948 and 1965, an exponential growth rate between 1966 and 1994, and a linear but more robust rate of growth after 1995 (with Congress creating an average of 3,136 pages of law each year). During the expansionary period, law was cumulating at a much faster rate than during the earlier or later periods, but exponential growth ceased around 1994. The greater growth rate in the later period represents the shift in the velocity of law accumulation as a consequence of the expansionary period.

What is going on? We suggest that early in the expansionary period laws were fairly simple, with few titles and a simple structure. But as government became involved in more and more issues, and as executive branch agencies issued rules to implement the laws, and as interest groups became increasingly involved in claiming particularistic benefits and gaining exceptions to the simple and general statutes, laws became increasingly large and complex. Whereas a statute in the 1950s might affect one or a few of the fifty titles in the Code, today it could affect many. The necessity for reauthorization of programs gives Congress the opportunity to revisit what is working well and not so well, and it gives policy entrepreneurs the opportunity to add provisions to the original law, hence adding complexity (Adler and Wilkerson 2012).

THE SUPREME COURT

It would not be surprising to find the court system affected by the new-issue expansion, and the increase in the complexity of laws generated in it. In a 2011 lecture, Justice Antonin Scalia claimed that declines in the number of cases decided by the Supreme Court were in large part caused by declines in legislative activity by Congress. Because Congress has passed fewer major statutes in recent years, the Supreme Court had a lower caseload (Cohn 2011).

Our analysis of the Policy Agendas Project's Supreme Court dataset offers some support to Scalia's perspective. After an early increase and rapid decrease in cases decided just after the Second World War, both the number of cases and diversity of the Court's agenda increased from the mid-1950s through around 1990, and then both fell off rapidly. The number of subtopics addressed increased from around thirty-five in the late 1950s to a peak in the forty to fifty range from the mid-1970s to the late 1980s. After a rapid decline in 1990, the diversity of the agenda fell back to the midthirties throughout the 1990s and 2000s. The Supreme Court's caseload, and the diversity of topics addressed, generally followed the pattern of new-issue expansion that characterized legislative activity.

THE PRESS

The new-issue expansion also affected press coverage. Not surprisingly, the diversity of coverage of issues in the Congressional Quarterly, which specializes in the coverage of the activity of the federal government, parallels closely the new-issue expansion (and contraction) period detected in our analyses of congressional activity—rapid increases in the diversity of coverage beginning in the late 1950s, a leveling off at around 120 to 140 subtopics from the mid-1970s to the early 1990s, and a rapid decline after 1995.

The Arc of New-Issue Expansion and Contraction

In Chapter 4, Figure 4.2, we showed that the number of reports that the General Accountability Office (GAO) had increased and then declined in a wide arc, peaking in the 1980s. We fit a quadratic curve to that data, which quantitatively describes the arc. Now we ask whether the measures of increases in the policy topics that government has become involved with fits a similar pattern.

Figure 6.4 fits our measure of agenda expansion, the number of subtopics addressed annually, for four different policy agendas datasets: hearings involving legislative proposals, laws enacted, Congressional Quarterly coverage, and Supreme Court cases. The pattern is a broad arc of issue expansion and contraction through time: increase, peak, brief stability at a higher level, and general decline.[6] The steepest increases and declines occur in legislative hearing activity and Congressional Quarterly coverage; the Supreme Court experiences shallowest increase and decline, with lawmaking intermediate. The arcs all peak about the same time—in the 95th or 96th Congresses. Remarkably, the number of GAO reports issued peaks about the same time—in the 97th Congress (1981–83).

Other series from the Policy Agendas Project, however, do not fit the broad arc of issue expansion and contraction. A second pattern characterizes hearings not involving lawmaking (basically oversight hearings), all hearings aggregated, and roll calls in House and Senate. This second pattern is one in which the increase segment of the arc occurs, but the decline fails to materialize or is quite muted compared to the series in Figure 6.4. Figure 6.5 shows the patterns for all hearings and roll calls together on a graph like Figure 6.4. The leveling off after the 95th Congress is clear, as is a downturn late in the period (which may or may not be permanent).

The first pattern, the arc of expansion and contraction, represents the contemporaneous activities of government. The second pattern reflects the residue of the Great New-Issue Expansion. It includes nonlegislative (and total) hearings, and roll-call votes. With increased issue diversity in the

---

6. Each arc is fitted by a quadratic function of the form $Y = a + b\,X - c\,X^2$. Details of the fits are in the appendix to this chapter.

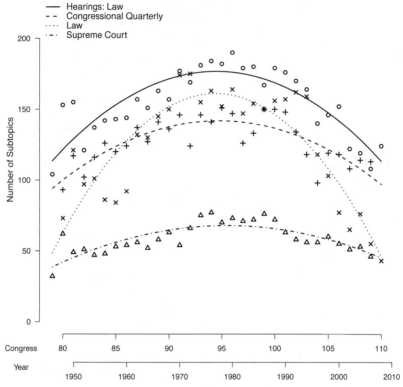

FIGURE 6.4. Issue Expansion and Contraction across Governing Institutions
Source: Policy Agendas Project

agenda (assessed by the number of policy agendas subtopics addressed in hearings), increased intervention in the economy and society occurred (assessed by the number of subtopics addressed in statutes), and other institutions were affected by the increasing span of government involvement (assessed by subtopics addressed in Supreme Court cases and Congressional Quarterly coverage). Most of these measures declined beginning in the late 1980s, but the programs and agencies assembled to implement the legislative expansion remained, as did the need for Congress to oversee the new bureaucracies. As a consequence, nonlegislative hearings continued at a robust pace.

Why did roll-call votes not decline with the decline in lawmaking? (There is evidence of decreasing diversity of roll calls in the Senate, but that is minor compared to the collapses in lawmaking and legislative hearings). The answer is that Congress is taking more votes per measure—because those measures are becoming increasingly complex. The residue of the in-

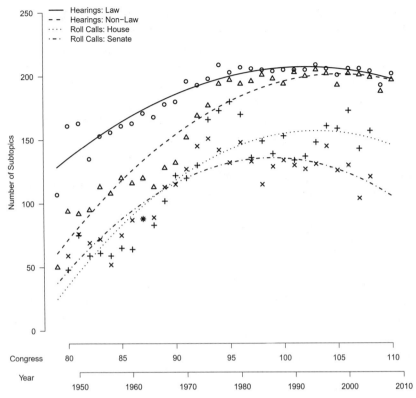

FIGURE 6.5. The Continuity of Issue Expansion
Source: Policy Agendas Project

creasing complexity of statutes is the increasing diversity of roll-call votes on procedures and amendments on bills.

The trends we describe reflect dramatic changes in the nature of political debate. One of the most striking differences across this same period is the rise of partisan polarization in Congress. The most important studies in policy making come from Keith Poole and Howard Rosenthal's methodological innovations in linking dimensional (left–right) positions across Congresses. To estimate polarization, median party positions are calculated for a year or Congress, and then one party median is subtracted from another.[7] There is no doubt that polarization has increased since the 1970s, and

7. This requires some assumptions that probably ought to be questioned more than they have been, because the method uses a linear interpolation to link the scores (and because subtracting ordinal data is not strictly speaking justified), but it is nevertheless an important methodological accomplishment and a very useful tool to track polarization across time.

considerable evidence shows that the polarization has been asymmetrical—that is, Republicans have moved more to the right than Democrats have moved to the left. (For more information on polarization and Poole and Rosenthal's estimates, as well as the underlying data, see voteview.com.)

Most explanations of polarization center on exogenous events that have caused the political parties to become more ideological, or changes in the organization of Congress that have fostered intraparty solidarity (Theriault 2008). These include the realignment of the South, redistricting to maximize partisan gains, a more partisan media, increased mobilization in primary elections, and stronger congressional party leadership, among others. We do not doubt the importance of these factors. But it is also worth considering the role in the Great New-Issue Expansion in provoking a counterreaction from conservatives. Figure 6.6 provides some suggestive evidence that this explanation has some validity. Roll-call polarization drifted upward between the 80th (1947) and 95th Congresses (1977) and then began to rise at a far more rapid rate. The critical burst in polarization did not begin to increase until the Great New-Issue Expansion had peaked. How one might interpret this could vary. On the one hand, it is evidence that the expansionary period was not characterized by particularly large partisan differences. That makes sense, because to some extent both parties were caught up in the wave of policy activity that characterized the period. The polarization is a feature of the postexpansionary period, and hence in one sense the new-issue expansion could not have contemporaneously caused the polarization. On the other hand, countermobilizations do not occur instantaneously. It seems inconceivable that the conservative countermobilization and the consequent asymmetric polarization could have occurred without the new-issue expansion. Moreover, the expansion of the governmental agenda left a much-enlarged administrative state, and these residues are potential contemporaneous causes of polarization—in the sense that they did not go away after the expansion ceased.

Support for the notion that issue development influenced the emergence of partisan polarization comes from a study by Jochim and Jones (2013) of issue-based polarization in congressional roll-call voting. Using Poole and Rosenthal's scaling algorithm, they scaled votes within each of the policy agendas major topic categories for the period 1965–2004, for each Congress. They looked for differences in the power of Poole and Rosenthal's first dimension, which is the strong ideological dimension that has characterized American legislative voting since the dawn of the Republic. That dimension captures debates regarding the degree of involvement of the federal gov-

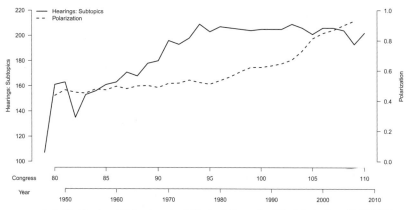

FIGURE 6.6. The Number of Policy Agendas Subtopics Addressed and the Polarization of Roll Call Votes
Source: Policy Agendas Project (subtopics); Voteview (polarization)

ernment in economic and social affairs. They divided the period of study into two parts: 1965–80, and 1981–2004. For almost all of the issues, dimensionality and polarization (assessed by standard intraparty unity measures) increased during the period. However, issue susceptibility to polarization varied greatly. They detected three distinct patterns in the development of polarization. The first set of issues were those that were polarized and of low dimensionality for the full period of study, including economics, housing, and labor and employment. The second set was less polarized during the first period and remained so in the second: agriculture, foreign affairs, transportation, trade, and public lands. The final set were those moving from less polarized to more polarized: health care, education, civil rights, law and crime, and defense. This last set of issues (with the exception of defense) form the core of the new issues that broadened government, not just thickened it.

THE ROLE OF INTEREST GROUPS

It is well established in the interest-group literature that policy change comes first and groups come to Washington afterward. Many more groups descend on the capital after a major policy change has been enacted because of the incentives offered by the new legislation. This does not mean that groups are unimportant during the forging of legislation; it means that legislation stimulates many more groups and their lobbyists after the legislation. While it is common to think that broad social movements mobilize first and then

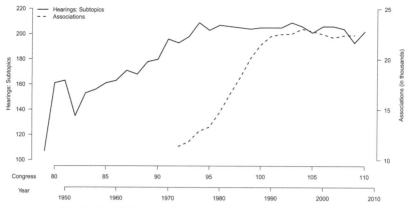

FIGURE 6.7. The Number of Policy Agendas Subtopics Addressed in Congressional Hearings and the Number of Associations Tabulated by the Encyclopedia of Associations
Source: Policy Agendas Project

demand redress from government, it is also clear that groups respond to the creation of new government programs. For every environmental group created before the establishment of the Environmental Protection Agency, there is one created afterward (see Baumgartner and Jones 2009, chapter 9). So, even if the women's movement pressed successfully for change in government and more groups may not have been created in response to government action, this is not generally the case. More groups are created in response to government action for many reasons: they want to protect gains; they are groups of professionals who administer new programs; they want to contest the intrusion of government into another issue area (see Walker 1983, 1991; Baumgartner and Leech 1998, 2001; Leech et al. 2005; Baumgartner et al. 2011). To test these ideas, and to dispel the notion that group organization causes policy change, it is worth looking at Figure 6.7. There we have plotted the number of subtopics addressed in all hearings and the number of associations tabulated by the *Encyclopedia of Associations*. Between the 95th and the 100th Congresses, the number of associations went from about eleven thousand to twenty-three thousand, before leveling off. It is interesting that the number of groups tabulated by the *Encyclopedia* followed the same pattern as the policy-making processes we have monitored through the Policy Agendas Project. But that growth and leveling off occurred many years after the expansion of the policy-making agenda. The graph strongly suggests that interest groups grew after the expansion of the policy-making agenda, not before it.

The Role of Legislative Rules[8]

One possible way to account for at least some of the trends we observe is that there was some sort of congressional rules changes at about the same time we observe the Great New-Issue Expansion. We deem this highly unlikely. First, the changes we observe do not occur all at once, and the patterns of increase and decline follow an understandable historical narrative. Rules changes should lead to more abrupt changes. There were rule changes, however, and some of these may have influenced some of the variables we study. In particular, changes in the rights and responsibilities of subcommittees could have led to more hearings. Most important are the changes wrought by the Legislative Reorganization Act (LRA) of 1970, which decentralized committee power to subcommittees. However some of the reforms of the act were put in place during the 1965–70 period, in both House and Senate. The LRA was a response to the efforts of the Joint Committee on the Organization of Congress that met in 1965 (and continued until 1966 in the Senate). Most of the joint committee's recommendations were signed into law with the LRA of 1970. Fenno (1973, 136) indicates that the House put reforms in place in 1965 and Smith and Deering (1990, 46) write that the Senate did the same thing. Given the sequencing of events, it is more likely that the rules changes were a result of the issue expansion rather than a cause of it.

A second issue is whether the shift from legislative to nonlegislative hearings can be explained by rules changes or other aspects of member behavior. Smith and Deering (1990, 140) show no real change in the percentage of legislation reported out of committee that had been referred to a subcommittee during the period 1969 to 1988. In the 90th Congress, cosponsorship of bills was allowed, and it is possible that this change led to the overall decrease in the number of bills introduced documented by the Congressional Bills Project. A member could simply cosponsor legislation rather than introduce a bill for the purposes of position-taking. It is possible that there were fewer legislative hearings because over time there were fewer bills introduced; however, the correspondence of the behavior of the lawmaking series, with fewer but larger laws being passed, suggests that these trends were both effects rather than causes. We cannot rule out that this rules change had some impact, but given the patterns of the trends we document in this chapter, we think a rules-based explanation to be highly improbable.

8. This section relies substantially on Lewallen (2012).

Chicken or Egg?

There is no doubt that the policy-making agenda expanded during the 1960s and 1970s, and this expansion was not caused by a single factor. It was a period of increasing pressure on government by diverse groups, but it was also a period in which government built its analytical capacity and in which congressional capacity for entropic search increased as the older system of strong control by entrenched committee chairmen gave way to more active subcommittees and party organizations. The increasing diversity of problems that government began to detect, both through mechanisms such as congressional hearings and investigations by executive agencies, and the demands of citizens, led to an expansion and diversification of the policy-making agenda. As the agenda diversified, the arenas in which government intervened to address those problems increased. While it is not invariably true that government expands when the agenda diversifies, certainly that is the general tendency.

We have shown that partisan polarization for the most part followed the period of agenda expansion, and that the number of associations grew mostly after it as well. In a later chapter we explore in more detail the factors that are generally cited as causing changes in policy, such as elections. This obviously does not mean that groups and parties were not part of the issue expansion, but it does mean that the impact of increases in the scope of government had more of an impact on the structure of parties and groups than the other way around.

Maybe the growth of government was a consequence of the preferences of the mostly liberal partisan majorities in the 1960s and 1970s, which caused Congress to become involved in overseeing more programs through hearings. That is, the surge of lawmaking preceded the search process. In a limited sense, this is not the right story, as hearings on a legislative proposal almost always precede laws. If we compare the average entropy from hearings, as presented in Chapter 5, with the number of laws passed per Congress, we find stronger evidence of the link between entropic search and lawmaking.[9] We examine the pattern of correlations across time between the entropy index presented in Chapter 5 and the number of laws enacted. We want to see if the correlation is higher when entropy is measured before laws than when laws are treated as occurring first. This is a rough way to assess

---

9. We use Congresses rather than years because of the year-to-year variability in both hearings and laws, which would bias our analysis toward accepting our hypothesis that search leads laws.

whether search occurs before laws or whether laws stimulate more search. The contemporaneous correlation between entropy and laws is 0.364. If we lag entropy such that Congress's entropy matches up with this Congress's lawmaking, which roughly assesses the situation where entropic search during the last Congress leads to more laws passed this Congress, the correlation increases to 0.492. But if we lag the variables such that earlier laws are associated with later entropy, as would be the case if lawmaking stimulated entropic search, the correlation drops to 0.153.

Two papers relying on more sophisticated analyses add support to the idea that the search process in fact did precede lawmaking. We studied the interaction between committee hearing entropies, our measure of information, and the size of government. Causal flow is primarily from information to programs, and the feedback from government programs to information flow is weak (Jones, Baumgartner, and de la Mare 2005). In a second study, Workman (2012a) examined the influences of both the informational component and the partisan changes in government on the size of the bureaucracy. He found that information caused program increases, but that partisan divisions were not related to either information acquisition or program adoption. He concludes that "changes in the administrative state have much to do with the changing problems facing government."

The likely reason for these findings is that during the period of new-issue expansion Congress aggressively sought out problems that needed addressing—and this held whatever the partisan composition of the legislature or the presidency. Republicans, however, never held both branches of Congress during this time, although they regularly held the presidency and held the Senate for much of the 1980s.

Conclusions

Government, politics, and American society were all transformed in a brief twenty-year period in an explosion of legislative activity. President Lyndon Johnson and the Democratic majorities in 1965 built the legislative platform for the modern American administrative state. What is less appreciated is the vigorous expansion of the policy-making agenda across virtually all areas of American life. Many conservatives react viscerally to this reach, and most liberals think that the work is incomplete and even flawed. Indeed, Ted Kennedy's "the dream shall never die" speech to the Democratic National Convention in 1980 can be seen in hindsight as a reaction to the consolidation process begun in the Carter years—a consolidation bitterly resented by the liberal wing of the Democratic Party.

The Great New-Issue Expansion left not just a panoply of new programs and administrative agencies but a heightened ability of government to detect and define problems in the policy-making environment. The complex, confusing, and overlapping network of federal, state, and local agencies, linked through fiscal federalism and the classic mechanisms of congressional committees and subcommittees, left government better at information processing—in the sense of attending to multiple attributes of complex problems. As we show in the next chapter, it also left government prone to enact more and more intrusive legislation and regulation, because finding and defining a problem is not the same as designing an efficient solution to it. Hence, the modern tension between liberals and conservatives, Republicans and Democrats, was born in the Great New-Issue Expansion. But the burgeoning administrative state transformed the old partisan divisions. Conservatives urged quick and decisive policy-making activities in military and foreign affairs, something alien to the party prior to the 1950s, as well as in such areas as crime and justice, immigration, and even marriage—the Defense of Marriage Act defined marriage rights, traditionally left to the states, for example. Indeed, Workman (2012b) shows that government adopts as many regulations during Congresses controlled by Republicans as those controlled by Democrats, but the agencies issuing the rules shift. Growth, then stabilization of government, has been a bipartisan process.

The Great New-Issue Expansion fundamentally altered the pattern of conflict between the parties, and it forms the basis for the polarized and vitriolic politics of today. We do not deny the contemporary sources of this conflict—redistricting, the emergence of a more partisan media, and the flood of money entering the political realm, for example. But we think our understanding of today's partisan polarization is incomplete without an appreciation of the radical transformation of the agenda during the 1960s and 1970s. It was driven by a self-reinforcing process of seeking and finding, then of suppressing the search for new information in order to stifle the growth of government. None of these trends can last indefinitely, and the strategy of ignoring trends by not monitoring them does not make them go away.

In Chapter 4 we focused on the analytic capacity of the federal government in both the executive and legislative branches, showing the tight links between informational capacity and the growth and spread of government. In Chapter 5 we focused on the organizational structure of Congress as it has responded to, and influenced, this growth. Here, we have focused on the spread of new issues through the legislative system. These three chapters

together have documented many of the linkages among information, organizational structure, and the content of U.S. public policy over the postwar
period. In the next chapter, we link these trends to the growth and spread of
spending, returning, therefore, to a focus on executive branch actions after
this prolonged focus on Congress. The trends we document, of course, move
in parallel.

7

The Thickening and Broadening of Government

Diversity of information is closely connected with the diversity of the public agenda (e.g., the number of different issues being discussed), the diversity of debate (e.g., the number of different aspects of a given issue being discussed), and the diversity of authority (e.g., the degree to which jurisdictions over given issues are shared by many rather than allocated cleanly to a single institution). Cut off the jurisdictional messiness and you cut down on information. Cut down on the range of issues being discussed, and you cut down on information. But the process also works the other way: cut off the flow of information, and you can cut off the rise in new issues and in the size of government itself. The search for information is therefore tightly connected to the growth of government.

One way to halt or slow the growth of government is to cut down on information. This is often a temporary solution, however, as problems continue to develop and eventually make themselves known even to those who are not looking for this unwelcome information. While there is a clear social construction dynamic to shifting people's framing of a situation to a problem with a government solution, there is oftentimes a strong empirical reality behind the problem. Unemployment is unemployment, and in the modern world leaving that "up to the market" is no longer an acceptable response. But at times cutting down on information does limit the needless growth of government; surely government can overreact to a problem that has no obvious government solution or that might better be left to civil society to address. The problem lies in distinguishing these two cases, and cutting down on information may not be the best way forward.

We distinguished in Chapter 6 between the thickening of government, in which traditional functions of government such as national security and transportation grow, and the broadening of government, in which new functions are added. In this chapter, we show the tight link between the breadth of government and its growth. And we show that the process of information search, especially as this is institutionalized in government, is integral to the struggle about the size of government. So those seeking to contain government are correct to focus on new issues as potentially adding greatly to the growth of government. James Q. Wilson (1979, 41) recognized that this could well be the case. He wrote, "Once the 'legitimacy barrier' has fallen, politics takes a very different form. . . . New programs need not await the advent of a crisis or an extraordinary majority, because no program is any longer 'new'—it is seen, rather, as an extension, a modification, or an enlargement of something the government is already doing."

Government gets thicker when it increases its activities within a previously occupied arena. It gets broader when it intrudes in an arena previously unoccupied. The process of occupation opens the way for a subsequent thickening of government within the now-occupied arena. The Civil Rights Act of 1957 was not particularly important as a lawmaking enterprise, but it was a critical agenda breakthrough engineered by Senate Majority Leader Lyndon Johnson—and was recognized as such by Southern lawmakers (Caro 2012). Broadening often leads to subsequent thickening (see also Sparrow 1996).

The process of broadening generates a whole new political landscape. The rise of new issues in politics generally leads to institutional and political changes. Once new institutions are created or revised, and once social movements and interest groups are mobilized around a given issue, the conditions are in place to keep the issue alive for future years. Interest groups come to Washington on the heels of issue expansion—the initial group presence that is important in the politics of initiating programs attracts even more group activity as the program grows. Issues rarely recede from political view as easily or as quickly as they appear in the first place.

Contrary to myth, issues and institutions sometimes do disappear; there is no guarantee of permanence even in government, even if the growth of interest in a new area is typically faster than the decline of interest in an established one. While there are more creations than eliminations, public agencies within the executive branch do sometimes disappear (Lewis 2003; see Figure 7.8 below). Once created or given a new mandate, institutions of government themselves play an important role in maintaining interest in a given policy.

The politics of agenda setting is so important because it determines the broadening of government. The question "Why doesn't the government do something?" is almost always a plea to broaden the scope of government.

Social actors of all kinds attempt to influence the production and discussion of information. Oftentimes the first line of action in broadening are government institutions themselves. They are in a privileged position because government institutions have much greater legitimacy than many other actors. "Official" studies carry more weight than those done by "interested parties" (and government agencies often conduct among the largest and the best empirical studies of various types, such as in collecting economic information). But government agencies are particularly important as information sources because their democratic legitimacy ensures that others will take them seriously. When the administrator of the Environmental Protection Agency focuses on a given environmental problem, others will follow suit. Many of those also involved in the debate may be government officials from rival agencies, states, and localities armed with equal levels of democratic legitimacy, but a different set of concerns. Many may mobilize to resist the implications of the problem focus. More institutions addressing different elements of the same problem increase the likelihood that multiple dimensions of that problem will be addressed explicitly in public discussion and debate. More government institutions and larger government in general assure that a greater range of issues will be discussed. So the broadening and thickening of government are tightly intertwined with the rise of new issues and the supply of information regarding diverse aspects of those issues.

As society has become more complex, government has both broadened and thickened. As Chapter 6 showed, government has broadened by increasing the span of issues it is involved in; government today does many more things than government in the 1950s. It has also thickened through the process of increasing the density of connections among executive agencies, legislative committees, courts, and private actors. The increased overlap, conflict, and competition among government agencies of all kinds are consequences of this, leading to a confusing multiplication of levels of government, unclear jurisdictional mandates, and competition. This makes it harder to control, so there are periodic calls for "clarity" and "rationalizing" government. But messiness is generally healthier in terms of the generation of information. Whether we have too much or too little jurisdictional clarity across our government agencies, there is little doubt about the linkage between jurisdictional "messiness" and information.

Government leaders do not necessarily like the abundance of information that is increasingly part of the policy process. Much of the information may be embarrassing, counterproductive, or supportive of the wrong policy solution. Private actors often do not like the increased informational density either. As a consequence, the politics of information suppression is an important part of the policy process. The rise of new issues in politics has generated much more information in the system, and while the legislative "will" to enact more legislation has declined, the structures generating more information about those issues remain as residues of the "Great New-Issue Expansion."

The Politics of Information in Administrative Agencies

It is common to think of administrative agencies as the implementing arm of legislation, which is the realm of Congress. This is far too simple; indeed, taken too literally its application would lead to a vast undersupply of necessary information. In addition to their duties in the implementation process, administrative agencies act as information processors, focusing on parts of a complex policy-making environment, and feeding that information both into Congress and to their own rule-making operations (Workman 2012b).

Consider the missions of these public agencies: the Civil Rights Office of the U.S. Department of Justice, NASA, the Department of Education, and the Department of Homeland Security (or one of its components such as the Transportation Security Administration or the Coast Guard). Each has a mandate to focus attention on its particular area of federal government policy. Each generates reports, fields or oversees thousands of workers, and undertakes activities designed to further its particular mission. Each also interacts with other government agencies at the national and other levels of government that address the same or related issues, but perhaps from a different perspective or with a slightly different mandate. In fact, the number of different agencies of government addressing different aspects of the same question is a fundamental driver in the political process. Workman (2012a, 35) writes, "[B]ureaucracies monitor the agenda for changes in existing issues, redefinitions of older issues, and the emergence of new issues. They further help to define problems for government action." New government agencies define into the political system institutionalized attention to greater and greater numbers of dimensions of evaluation. Over time institutions and issues interact recursively, with each affecting the other, and each also being affected by related issues, by related institutions, by exogenous events outside of the control of any institutional leader, and by other factors. The growth of agencies, oversight activities in Congress, spending, and bureaucracies at the federal, state, and local level provide the fuel for and are in part explained by the rise of new issues in politics.

When we refer to information, we do not refer only to scientific studies or reports. We also mean the number of different dimensions of discussion that are organized into the political debate for a given issue. The same information, or information along the same dimension, simply repeated many times from multiple sources adds little to the debate. But a greater diversity of perspectives generates a wide diversity of information. This is difficult to interpret and to evaluate as compared to other relevant pieces of information along different dimensions, to be sure—decision making is much easier when less information is available! In any case, one of the most important elements of the "thickening" of government is that government agencies overlapping with others dealing with the same or similar issues will generate a greater diversity of information relating to that issue.

The clear connection between information and an expanding governmental agenda has stimulated an indirect attack on government information by conservatives seeking to limit government growth. At one time, Republicans used to complain that if you search for a problem, you tend to find an answer in a new government program, and surely Chapter 6 offers support for that thesis. If politicians can constrain the range of situations investigated by government, they can limit the subsequent governmental activity in the arena. This process, however, has the unintended consequences of denying the existence of problems that actually need to be addressed. Decision making with less information may be easier but it is not necessarily better. In fact, it may be more likely to lead to mistakes, errors, and inefficiencies. These must be corrected later, often at great cost.

An information-rich system makes leadership more difficult, but may be more adaptive and therefore more efficient. On the other hand, there is little doubt from our analysis that more problem search leads to more government solutions. This puts politicians on the right in an admittedly difficult situation, and we return to this dilemma in the concluding chapter.

THICKENING AND BROADENING IN THE BUDGET OF THE FEDERAL GOVERNMENT

Increases in the size of government through thickening versus broadening leave different traces in the federal budget. Older issues grow mostly through the process of thickening, and hence tend to experience increases in expenditures as policy subsystems buttressed by interest groups and interested congressmen solidify. But they can experience losses in the percentage of the budget they claim as new issues break onto the agenda and new policies are consequently enacted.

We illustrate by comparing two "old" issues—that is, issues that have experienced government involvement for an extended period of time—with two "new" issues—issues that government "invaded" during the Great New-Issue Expansion, using the Policy Agendas Project's tabulations of consistent Congressional Budget Authority data.[1] Figure 7.1 shows that, in absolute figures, the old issues grew during the period of study (from Fiscal Year 1950, after the budgets stabilized from the disruptions of the Second World War, to Fiscal Year 2007, before the disruptions associated with the Great Recession). Transportation spending increased from less than $10 billion (in 2009 dollars) to over $80 billion. It did so in several "steps," the last of which took place in the late 1990s and early 2000s. Agriculture similarly cost the government more in 2007 than in the early 1950s, but it traced a more erratic path due to the manner in which subsidies are calculated. Indeed, the year with the highest absolute level of spending for agriculture was 1974. These changes represent the thickening of government—growth within established policy areas.

The new issues, in comparison, literally leaped onto the budget in the late 1960s and early 1970s. Health grew from around $10 billion in the early 1960s to over $300 billion in 2004—much of this through the Medicare and Medicaid programs. Justice Administration also grew spectacularly—from under $3 billion in the early 1960s to over $50 billion in 2004.

As the Great New-Issue Expansion proceeded, more issues elbowed themselves into a place at the table; as a consequence, older issues grew more slowly. The older issues lost budgetary shares in comparison to the new issues. Figure 7.2 compares the percentage of the total federal budget consumed by the policies. The two older issues, Transportation and Agriculture, are depicted in Panel A; the two newer issues, Health (not including Medicare) and Justice Administration, are depicted in Panel B. The older issues lost budgetary shares during the period, with especially severe declines during the late 1970s. On the other hand, the new issues gained budgetary shares, especially in the early 1970s and after 1988. (Panel B is plotted on dual axes to emphasize the share gains of the areas; the health budget is a great deal larger than the justice budget.)

Like Transportation and Agriculture, Defense and International Affairs both experienced growth during the period—the Defense budget grew by more than a third between 1951, the peak of the Korean War, and the mid-2000s, in real dollars. But the budgetary shares of these programs steadily

1. Congressional Budget Authority is the money that federal agencies are legally authorized to spend. Outlays are the actual expenditures. The Office of Management and Budget presents consistent Budget Authority data beginning in FY 1976; the Policy Agendas Project has extended these consistent figures back to 1946.

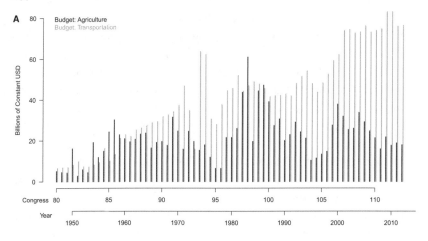

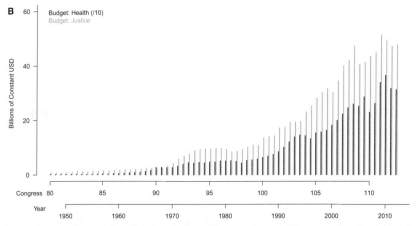

FIGURE 7.1. Inflation-Adjusted Budget Authority for Agriculture and Transportation (Panel A) and Health and Justice (Panel B), 1947–2012

Source: Policy Agendas Project

Note: Health spending is divided by 10, so the series reaches a peak of $364 billion in 2010; justice reaches a peak of $51 billion in 2009. All figures are presented in inflation-adjusted 2009 dollars.

declined—for Defense, from 60 percent in 1951 (and even 40 percent in the peacetime year of 1958) to 20 percent in 2008.

The new issues of Education and Training, Natural Resources, and Income Security (including Supplemental Security Income) follow a roughly similar pattern to Health and Justice. All experienced great growth in the late 1960s (Education) or early 1970s (Natural Resources and Income Security), but unlike Justice Administration and Health, began to lose budgetary shares quickly after becoming established. We might say that they "aged" quickly in comparison to Health and Justice.

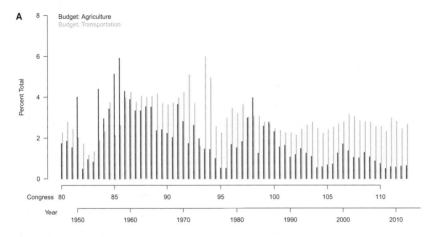

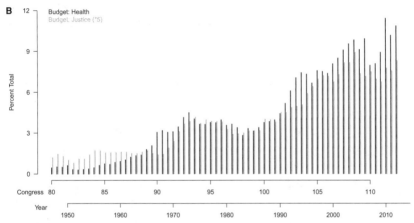

FIGURE 7.2. Changes in the Percentage of Total Budgetary Authority for Agriculture and Transportation (Panel A) and Health and Justice (Panel B)

Source: Policy Agendas Project

Note: In Panel B, justice spending is multiplied by 5 in order to display it on the same scale as health spending. While health spending reaches a peak of 11.42 percent of total spending in 2010, the peak for justice is 1.78 percent, in 2004.

It seems fair to conclude that during the post–Second World War period, the broadening of government was a much more powerful dynamic than the thickening process. While one might think that the activities of subsystem participants—bureaucrats, legislative leaders in substantive areas, and interest groups—would cause government to grow, that is a misleading picture. The old issues have grown in absolute terms, but they have lost ground substantially in relative budgetary shares. The new issues have captured budgetary shares from the older issues. This causes few crowding problems during times of robust economic growth, but can cause a politics of trade-offs in periods of economic stagnation.

We have thus far analyzed the broadening process as separate and distinct from the thickening process, and in many ways this makes sense. But new initiatives within complex policy areas can result in the agenda disruption process that we have documented in Chapter 4 and in the above discussion of budgets regarding new issues. For example, Medicare experienced such a "new issue" disruption with the addition of drug coverage (Part D) to Medicare, and the entire health care system is experiencing such a disruption with the Patient Protection and Affordable Care Act of 2010. Much of the Patient Protection and Affordable Care Act involves the thickening process as the federal government puts in place incentives to institute cost control and increase health care quality. However, the major features of the act, especially the insurance mandate and shift from a Medicaid program based on categories to one based on percentage of poverty, do involve agenda disruptions and, hence, broadening.

Thickening and Broadening in Government Employment

We can look at the growth and spread of government from a number of angles. No matter how we look at it, we can recognize a silent revolution in the structure of government during the roughly thirty years from the 1950s through the 1970s. While various social movements also occurred during this time, perhaps more significant changes were taking place in the structure of government itself. While these trends were related, the trends toward increased government involvement in various aspects of social life began well before the social events of the 1960s. These trends toward broader and thicker government continued through the late 1970s; after that the trends moderated, and the growth in government slowed, but a second burst occurred after 2000, as we shall see. But the transformations that took place during the twenty-five-year period from roughly the mid-1950s to the late 1970s were enough to change the nature of government.

One of the standard conservative mantras is that the federal government is growing out of control. Yet when one looks at measures of overall growth, the pattern is more complex. One measure is the federal workforce. Figure 7.3, a stacked area graph of Defense and Non-Defense workers, shows the postwar federal government's employment.

The impact of the Second World War on *civilian* employment in government, not just defense employment, shows clearly in the figure. Civilian

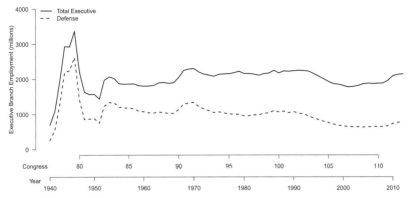

FIGURE 7.3. Defense and Nondefense Civilian Employment in the Executive Branch of Government
Source: U.S. Office of Personnel Management, Federal Workforce Statistics, Historical Tables (http://www.opm.gov/feddata/HistoricalTables/ExecutiveBranchSince1940.asp)

employment in the federal government rose from approximately 443,000 in 1940 to 777,000 in 1947. Military employment, of course, rose much more, but after the war it declined closer to its prewar base. Civilian employment ratcheted up by 75 percent during the 1940–47 period, then remained relatively close to its peak level for years after that. From about 1955 until the late 1970s, civilian employment rose steadily, from 673,000 in 1955 to approximately 1.2 million in 1979. This steady growth corresponded to a period in history when unprecedented numbers of new issues were rising on the government agenda. Finally, these trends were reversed. Federal employment did not grow inexorably but rather was stopped after a generation of steady increases, after approximately 1979. Rapid declines in military employment more than offset increases in civilian employment, and civilian bureaucracies stopped growing after the 1970s as well. Overall federal employment reached 3.4 million in 1945, declined to 1.4 million in 1950, rose to 2.3 million in 1969, then declined to reach a low of 1.8 million in 2000 and increased to 2.1 million in 2009. The trend most of interest in Figure 7.3 is the dramatic increase in civilian employment from the mid-1950s through the 1970s.

Just as dramatic is the reversal of the trend beginning in the late 1970s. Perhaps surprisingly, the overall employment figures for the executive branch is lower today than in the 1980s, or even the 1960s, even though the country is much more populous and richer than then (and these factors are associated with more government). A good part of this is due to the "hollowing out" of government—the replacement of government workers with private contractors. These figures are difficult to trace, so we cannot say much about

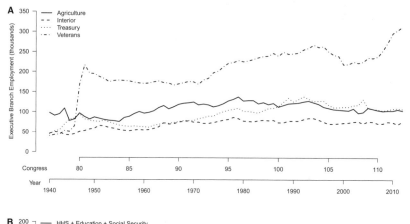

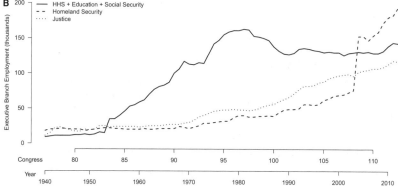

FIGURE 7.4. Civilian Employment, Old Issues (Panel A) and New Issues (Panel B)
Source: Calculated from U.S. Office of Personnel Management, Federal Workforce Statistics, Historical Tables (http://www.opm.gov/feddata/HistoricalTables/ExecutiveBranchSince1940.asp)

this. We can say, however, that the main reason that government employment has not grown since the mid-1960s is the steady decline (until 2006) of civilian Department of Defense workers. This has been matched by a steady growth of non-Defense workers.

If we return to the distinction between thickening and broadening of government, we find that the old issues mostly subject to thickening have added few new government workers, but the new issues that come about through the agenda politics associated with broadening have added workers in a major way. Figure 7.4 charts the growth of federal civilian employment in four older issues (Panel A) and three newer issues (Panel B). In the older issues, Veterans Affairs, Agriculture, Interior, and Treasury, government involvement was established prior to the Second World War. The newer issues, Health and Human Services and Education (tabulated together by OPM), Justice, and Homeland Security, became prominent political issues after the Second World War by taking on major new (and often controversial) responsibilities.

None of the established policy areas increased employees by more than a third. Another older policy area, Transportation, which is not depicted in Figure 7.4 because it was not tabulated separately until 1968, did not grow at all. Among these agencies, the thickening process was modest indeed. The operative policy subsystems perhaps protected turf, but they were not able to add substantial numbers of employees to carry out their assigned responsibilities.

On the other hand, the newer policy areas added employees in great numbers. Justice grew from around 20,000 employees in 1967 to 120,000 by 2007. HHS and Education experienced rapid growth in the 1950s, 1960s, and 1970s before leveling off and even declining. Homeland Security (that is, the agencies that were combined in 2003 into the Department of Homeland Security) began to grow incrementally beginning in the 1970s, but exploded after 2001. Not reflected in the figures is the vast expansion of clandestine intelligence operations, which exploded after 9/11 (Bamford 2008; Priest and Arkin 2011). Indeed, as the overall government figures indicate, the period after 2001 was a period of substantial broadening of government, particularly in the areas of homeland security and clandestine intelligence.

THE GROWTH AND ORGANIZATION
OF CLANDESTINE INTELLIGENCE

There is one area of government growth that is not fully traceable through standard sources: clandestine intelligence. In their book, *Top Secret America*, Dana Priest and William Arkin document the ever-expanding network of government agencies and private contractors that operate under the veil of the highest level of secrecy granted under Executive Order 12356. In addition to the numerous government agencies operating under some form of secrecy, Priest and Arkin documented over five hundred companies who had contracts with these government agencies doing top-secret work. Because of the secrecy surrounding the budgets of clandestine intelligence, both budgets and employment are hard to gauge, and the very large number of contractors in that area make the determination even more difficult. But at a conference sponsored by the Defense Intelligence Agency in 2007, government officials revealed that 70 percent of the classified intelligence budget was spent on contracts (Shorrock 2007). In 2012, almost 5 million people held secret or top-secret security classifications; of those over a million were employed by private contractors and almost 500,000 held top secret clearances (Office of the Director of National Intelligence 2013). Priest and Arkin (2011, 12) write that "Top Secret America, its exponential growth and ever-widening circle of secrecy, had been set in motion by one overwhelming force: the explosion in the number of covert and clandestine operations against al-Qaeda leaders and people suspected of supporting them."

Whatever one thinks about this intrusiveness—necessity to protect Americans from harm, or violation of basic Constitutional rights—the clandestine intelligence services represent probably the broadest and most intrusive incursion into the lives of ordinary Americans in recent years. Second, it was generated by a serious and visible problem. Third, it enjoyed considerable support from members of both political parties. Fourth, the initial growth spurt, and much of the following growth in the area, was generated by agenda politics—a major expansion of the more limited (in hindsight) clandestine activities that were established during the Cold War. This is not to say that subsystem politics—the network of intelligence agencies, congressional supporters, and contractors—did not contribute to the pattern, nor that the parties did not differ on critical components of the issue. At base, however, the discovery and definition of fresh problems are a critical component of government growth, and this example makes clear that the parties have collaborated in many of these expansions. For example, this particular expansion was promoted most extensively by the administration of a conservative Republican president, George W. Bush, and particularly his vice president, Richard Cheney.

The emergence and fading of problems on the agenda as they are defined and addressed by government causes an ebb and flow of attention to these issues at the expense of other issues. In the previous chapter, we documented that process for a cluster of new domestic issues. Figure 7.5 offers a different perspective: the emergence, fading, and reemergence of espionage, terrorism, and civil defense as topics of major interest to Congress. The figure graphs four Policy Agendas Subtopics of relevance. Three of these center on military intelligence, civil defense, and terrorism, and one on civil liberties.[2] Two major peaks of intense interest occur: the 1950s, generated by the Cold War competition with the Soviet Union, and the 2000s, caused by the 9/11 terrorist attacks on the United States. Anti-Government Activities (under the major topic Civil Rights, Minority Issues, and Civil Liberties), peak at a much higher level in 1954, and faded from view by the early 1970s, but all tend to travel together through time.

2. Military Intelligence, CIA, and Espionage (Defense); Civil Defense (Defense); Anti-Government Activities (Civil Rights, Minority Issues, and Civil Liberties); and Terrorism and Hijacking (International Affairs).

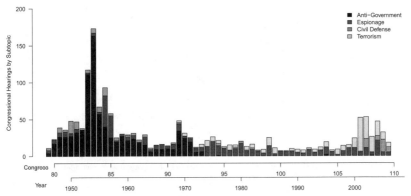

FIGURE 7.5. Congressional Hearings on Espionage, Terrorism, and Civil Defense
Source: Policy Agendas Project

Figure 7.6 details hearings and laws on civil defense issues; not surprisingly, laws passed track congressional interest as indicated by hearings activity.[3] The two strong peaks of hearings are matched by two more intense periods of writing and passing laws. It perhaps should not surprise us that laws follow hearings, but there remain some political scientists and others who maintain that hearings are simply symbolic activities and do not result in more substantive action. Budgetary commitments to the aggregate intelligence activities of the U.S. government cannot be traced reliably, because no figures were released prior to Fiscal Year 1997. At that time, the aggregate intelligence budget was $26.6 billion (CIA FAQs); by 2010, the aggregate budget was estimated to be $80 billion (Global Security.Org).

During each of the two peaks of intense focus, government took on major new responsibilities associated with detecting foreign and domestic threats. In each case, advances in technology were generated by the problem and pushed government's requirements for more intervention. In each case, government grew rapidly as a consequence not of the successes of the intelligence subsystem (that should have resulted in more sustained incremental budgetary growth rather than the apparent bursts of appropriations) but because of the emergence of serious problems that required addressing. Naturally, the proponents of more government within the subsystem utilized the new problem to their budgetary advantage, but the process began with 9/11.

The Intelligence Community (IC) consists of sixteen agencies within six cabinet departments (Defense, State, Treasury, Justice, Energy, and Homeland

3. Laws are presented as percentages of totals because of the tendency for laws to become larger and for fewer to be passed through time.

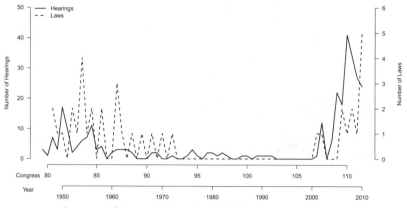

FIGURE 7.6. Congressional Hearings and Laws on Civil Defense
Source: Policy Agendas Project

Security); the Central Intelligence Agency (CIA) is an independent agency. The numerous overlapping intelligence jurisdictions would seem to provide optimal structure for the production of information, and indeed we believe that it does. There are continual calls for hierarchy, structure, and "rational organization" to the sprawling mass, but even in the supposedly more hierarchical arrangement established and reestablished by amendments to the enabling statute, the National Security Act of 1947, and executive orders over the years (most recently by the Intelligence Reform and Terrorism Prevention Act of 2004), considerable bureaucratic autonomy remains.

Nevertheless, there are issues particular to the intelligence domain that make competition among agencies less effective in generating information. In the normal flow of information in systems of overlapping jurisdiction, there is an implicit competition that encourages a potential supplier of information (whether that supplier is a public agency, interest group, or other entity) to produce information. Otherwise the entity loses out to a competitor in the issue definition process. This dynamic is muted in the case of intelligence agencies because of the secrecy surrounding the process. Only a limited number of congressmen have appropriate clearance to receive the information, and they jealously guard this prerogative. As a consequence, jurisdictions are considerably more fixed than in domestic affairs. Moreover, a secret court system, the Federal Intelligence Surveillance Court (FISC), whose proceedings are secret, and legislative committees in which briefings are secret oversee the system.

Leaks of information are punished, which facilitates censoring of attributes. This secrecy leads to accusations of failure to share information and "petty bureaucratic politics." We do not doubt that these very human tendencies are part of the process, but we strongly suspect that the inability of analysts to weigh the value of the information in an environment where the information cannot be made generally available, hence limiting feedback to a few select decision makers, is even more important. While the overlapping jurisdictions may aid the production of information, the secrecy of the system detracts from gaining knowledge from the information.

In 2013, an intelligence contractor with top-secret clearance, Edward Snowden, released documents that indicated the scope of the collection efforts directed at American citizens to a reporter from the *Manchester Guardian*. The incident highlighted the tension between privacy and national security and ignited an international incident as the Obama administration frantically tried to censor the flow of information. While issues of privacy have been debated in Congress and in the media in the past, the Snowden affair suggested just how extensive the censoring of attributes in clandestine intelligence has gone.

Social Problems and Government Growth

Two general conclusions emerge from our analysis of government growth thus far:

Much of the growth of government is due to the broadening of government rather than thickening. Older, more established issues grew more slowly than the newer issues in which government took on new responsibilities. This is true both for domestic issues and defense issues, although they trace different patterns through time. It is also the case that any broadening of government has tended to lead to subsequent thickening.

Much of the growth of government comes about because problems are recognized and addressed, not because one philosophy or platform prevails over another. While many accounts of increases in the depth and scope of government center on differences between political parties, the preferences of elected governmental officials, and philosophies and ideologies of the role of the public sector, we stress a competing account. Much of government growth has only tangentially to do with the prevailing accounts. The one "old issue" that added the largest number of employees is Veterans Affairs, yet that issue has not divided the parties. Among the new issues, the growth in Justice employees was mostly due to the increased federal involvement in crime control, again an issue that crossed the partisan divide. The biggest increases in the scope of government in more recent times have centered on Homeland Security and Intelligence; again, these are increases in government scope that were responsive to problems that most political actors saw as pressing and worthy of vigorous policy action. And in these cases, Republicans have generally been more supportive than Democrats.

This does not mean that these new functions are uncontroversial; often they are. We are not questioning the notion that ideologies and policy preferences are important in politics. But many times preferences are activated within a framework of problem identification, and in the identification of problems information is critical. Nor do we mean to imply that the policy activities directed at the problems are proportional to the intensity of the problem in light of other competing problems that simultaneously require attention. Indeed, the whole notion of "disproportionate information-processing" (Jones 2001; Jones and Baumgartner 2005b) implies that this is almost certainly not the case; rather, the system tends to lurch from under-reacting to a problem (when it is off the policy-making agenda) to overreacting to it. For many analysts the vast buildup of the clandestine intelligence infrastructure and the extreme secrecy that surrounds it is exactly this kind of overreaction (Priest and Arkin 2011).

The Creation of Administrative Agencies

The broadening of government generally results in the development of a much more robust administrative state. Congress creates agencies not only to implement the programs enacted by Congress but also to continue to monitor and alert Congress to any needed changes in programs (Workman 2012b). Figure 7.7 charts the percentage of congressional hearings that included consideration of creating new government agencies. The now-expected pattern emerges: Congress considered agency creation disproportionately during the Great New-Issue Expansion. The process peaked in the mid-1970s and subsequently fell. With ups and downs, the process stabilized at a lower level and continued until the early 1990s, when it ceased for all practical purposes, interrupted only occasionally (such as the debate over the creation of the Department of Homeland Security in 2002).

David C. Lewis (2003) provides the most complete description of the growth of the administrative state in the postwar period. His analysis of the creation, destruction, and design of various administrative agencies puts the emphasis on how agencies are created with the express purpose of insulating them from presidential control. From the National Transportation Safety Board to the Federal Election Commission, congressional and presidential decision makers have wanted to create professional agencies that adhere to relatively neutral standards and are immune from presidential control. Of

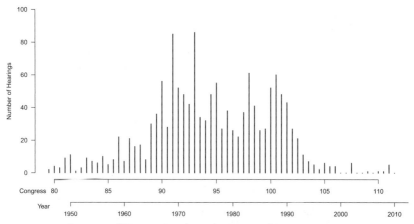

FIGURE 7.7. Congressional Hearings Considering the Creation of Government Agencies
Source: Policy Agendas Project

course, within executive agencies as well, there can be conflict between professional staff and presidential appointees. But one striking element of the postwar period has been the multiplication of independent sources of bureaucratic power. Figure 7.8 shows Lewis's data on the creation (and elimination) of executive branch agencies.

Fifteen executive agencies were created in 1946 and one was eliminated in that year. For the next twenty years, agencies were created and dismantled at such a pace that 146 more such organizations existed in 1974 than immediately after the war. In fact, as the figure makes clear, the idea that organizations are not eliminated once they are created is a myth. From 1946 to 1974, 143 executive agencies were disbanded, according to Lewis's figures. The net growth of 146 new organizations is based on 290 agency creations. Clearly, the two decades that followed the end of the Second World War were a period of great expansion of the federal regulatory state. Agencies of many types were created, from the Air Force and the Central Intelligence Agency to the Maternal Child Health Bureau and the Office of Bilingual Education and Minority Languages Affairs. Just as important, scores of agencies were eliminated. Massive shifts took place in the structure of government, but the net result was a much thicker administrative structure as organizations were created to oversee and implement policies that did not exist before the Second World War or which took on much larger importance as the economy grew, the population grew more diverse, and the state took on scores of new functions.

The distinction between thickening and broadening can be traced in Lewis's data—indeed, agency creation is one direct estimate of administrative

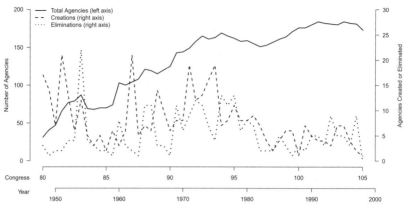

FIGURE 7.8. The Growth of Executive Agencies
Source: David Lewis

broadening. In the late 1970s, the broadening of the administrative state leveled off and declined, and when it resumed a decade later, the process was
far more muted. Legislation comes about as a consequence of government
directing attention to problems; agencies are created both to implement the
programs created by the legislation and to continue to monitor problems in
the area. The net creation of federal agencies parallels the great broadening
of government between the late 1950s and the late 1970s (indeed, Lewis's data
suggests that agency creation may have begun earlier).

A MANAGEMENT EXPLOSION

Modern government is not just bigger but it has more executive-level managers, and the rate of growth in managerial employees has been greater than
growth in general employment. Paul Light (1999, 70–72) shows a 400 percent increase in the numbers of senior administrative positions in the federal executive from 1960 to 1992, with most of the growth coming in the
early part of that period. From 1960 to 1992, the number of employees with
the title "deputy undersecretary" grew from 78 to 518. Similarly, there were
four individuals with the title "associate assistant secretary" in 1960, but 208
in 1992. There were 52 deputy administrators in 1960, and 190 in 1992. In all,
Light counts 452 senior administrators in the federal bureaucracy in 1960
and 2,408 in 1992.

As federal bureaucracies have grown, successive presidential administrations have added new layers of presidential appointees. As the president has
exerted more control through these mechanisms, Congress has reacted by

increasing its oversight of the bureaucracy (Aberbach 1990), further increasing government but also increasing the supply of information about public problems and programs. Congress also responded to the growth in executive employment by creating more independent commissions and agencies that are harder for the president to control. And all the while state and local governments have exploded. The net result of these changes, which were particularly stark during the period from 1960 to 1980, is that the government has both broadened and thickened. It has become denser and more complex as its functions have multiplied.

MORE CONGRESSIONAL OVERSIGHT

As the executive branch grew and as the number of federal agencies blossomed, Congress had to respond or else lose the capacity to be an equal player with the executive branch. As we noted in Chapter 4, lawmaking hearings declined after 1978, but nonlegislative hearings, including oversight hearings, continued unabated. In 1949 Congress held 1,287 hearings, of which 1,043, or 81 percent, were associated with bill referrals (hearings concerned with lawmaking). Just 244 hearings were focused on overseeing federal agencies, assessing the severity of social problems, or on other topics that did not involve active consideration of a legislative bill. These percentages were generally in the area of 60/40 in favor of referral hearings until the late 1960s. In 1971, for the first time there were more oversight than referral hearings, and this trend then accelerated until in 2005 fully 89 percent of the hearings were unrelated to the consideration of a particular piece of legislation. The ratio percentage of oversight hearings has not changed significantly since then.

Why would Congress now devote the bulk of its hearing time to monitoring problems, discussing the severity of various social indicators, and overseeing the activities of federal agencies rather than to considering legislation? Most obviously, there is much more to oversee. With the multiplication of new programs, new agencies, and scores of issues that were once not part of the political agenda, there is simply much more to do.

STATE AND LOCAL GOVERNMENT EMPLOYMENT

With public and congressional pressure to limit the size of the federal bureaucracy, we have seen great use of government contracts, grants, and privatization of services. Paul Light (1999, 38) notes that if we consider not only employees directly employed by the federal government but also adjust for those working on federal contracts, through federal grants, working in states and

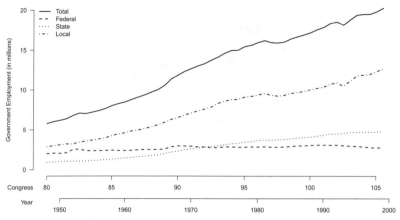

FIGURE 7.9. Local, State, and Federal Government Employment
Source: Historical Tables of the Budget of the United States

local governments on projects mandated (but not necessarily funded) by
the federal government, and adding the Postal Service and the military, we
see approximately eight times greater employment. From 1.9 million direct
civilian employees at the time of his estimate, he suggests a more accurate
total of 16.9 million federal or federal-related employees.

Moreover, most of the growth in public employment has not been at the
federal level but at the state and local levels. Figure 7.9 shows total employment from 1940 to the late 1990s.

Local governments expanded as well in the period following the Second World War. Whereas in 1947 their total combined employment was
only slightly greater than that of the federal government (2.8 million local
government employees, 2.4 million at the federal level), by 1960 the number
of local employees had grown to 4.8 million, whereas federal employment
remained at the same level. By 1980, there were 9.6 million local government employees, 2.9 million at the federal level, and 16.2 million employees
including state governments as well. As Light's analysis reminds us, there
could be others as well working on federal grants or through federal mandates
that are not counted in these estimates. However, the timing and the vast
scope of the expansion is clear no matter what particular numbers we use.

One of the facets of American federalism is that when the federal government initiates new programs, it often relies on the states to implement them.
The primary mechanism is the grant-in-aid, with the federal government
providing monetary incentives to the state to implement programs initiated
at the center and laden with rules and guidelines for the administration of

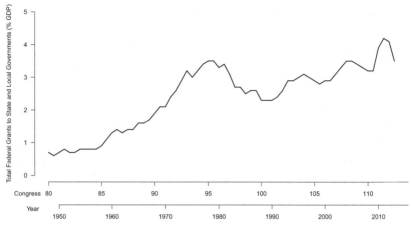

FIGURE 7.10. Total Federal Grants to State and Local Governments as a Percentage of GDP
Source: Office of Management and Budget, Historical Tables, Table 12.1

the program (every federal dollar comes with strings). A major consequence of this is the increasing complexity of programs, with states having substantial discretion in many programs but having to meet federal guidelines.

The "grant-in-aid state" was a product of the 1930s and the New Deal, but the United States vastly expanded its use after the Second World War. Indeed, increases in the total federal grants to state and local governments paralleled the vast broadening of the federal government, as Figure 7.10 shows. In 1957, federal grants as a percentage of GDP was under 1 percent; that percentage rose from 1958 until it peaked at 3.5 percent in 1975. After a steady fall until 1988, the percentage grew with ups and downs until in 2010 it reached 4.1 percent—both as a consequence of declines in the GDP in 2008 and 2009 and because of the impact of the 2009 stimulus bill. The result is a far more complex and overlapping system of government.

NOT JUST MORE GOVERNMENT, MORE GOVERNMENTS

"The government" is made up not just of the three branches of the federal government and the fifty states but also thousands of local authorities and an increasing number of specialized governments, also at the local level. There has been no growth (but also no significant decline) in the number of counties, municipalities, or towns/townships over the past decades. The number of independent school districts actually declined substantially in the decades following the Second World War as thousands of smaller districts merged into "unified" or "consolidated" school districts. Still, when the U.S. Census Bureau surveys and enumerates local governments in the United States, it reports over 87,000 units.

States, counties, and municipalities or towns/townships are relatively stable parts of the structure of federalism in the United States. These multi-function government units employ the police officers, firefighters, building inspectors, judges, bus drivers, and other civil servants that make things work. Nowhere is the American love of localism in government more apparent than the simple fact that we have over thirteen thousand independent school districts (and more than one thousand "dependent" ones, integrated into their city governments). As noted above, these numbers actually declined from over sixty-seven thousand in 1952 to less than sixteen thousand by 1972; this was a period of dramatic consolidation in school districts. As shown in table 5 of the U.S. Census 2002, it is clear that the most common type of government in the United States is one most Americans have never considered: the special purpose district. The country has over thirty-five thousand of these.

A general-purpose government (such as a county) is involved in all types of services. Special purpose governments and school districts, by contrast, have a limited mandate to be involved only in one area of public service. It might be an agency created by several counties together to manage an airport. It could manage a region's public hospitals, libraries, or public parks. It could provide electricity or clean drinking water to a set of municipalities, each of which is too small to provide these services in a cost-effective manner only to its own citizens. Its leaders may be appointed by state officials or elected. With the huge number of local governments of all types, and with the increase in the number of special purpose districts, it is clear that there are not only more government employees but that there are more government entities. Special purpose governments grew from less than 12,500 in 1952 to over 35,000 in 2002.

Too Much or Too Little Government?

At any point in time, it is difficult to judge whether there is too little or too much government intrusion into the economy and society. The adaptive systems perspective, however, suggests that there is some sort of ideal level of intervention—although that level varies greatly by issue and time, is plagued by difficult and often unrecognized trade-offs, and is infused with high levels of uncertainty. Moreover, the practical problems of interested parties bringing biased information to the table and the requirements of supermajorities to achieve action increase the probability that the optimum level of government will not be achieved.

The theory of disproportionate information-processing points to a pattern of under- and overreaction to information, and this leads both to too little and too much government. This variability is inconsistent across issues—in the same administration, one area may be overregulated and characterized by unnecessary spending, and another may be neglected and hence underregulated and suffer inadequate levels of appropriation. Because responses to information tend to be disjointed, inconsistencies develop. Yet, as we have shown, government in some eras searches more aggressively, finds more problems, and produces more public policies than others.

Everyone has his or her favorite story of inadequate government ("Why doesn't the government do something?") and almost as many have anecdotes of overbearing government. These stories may exaggerate, but they are often pretty near the mark. It is difficult, however, to know when government is under- or oversupplied, just as it is difficult to recognize asset bubbles, which occur when prices for assets, such as commodities or stocks, get out of line relative to values. As the housing bubble of the 2000s developed, the Federal Reserve argued whether it was a bubble or reflected underlying economic realities, and Federal Reserve Chairman Alan Greenspan (2004) downplayed indicators that a bubble was developing. Similarly, political actors dispute that an intervention by government is needed on all sorts of issues, some of which clearly were "policy bubbles" in hindsight (Jones, Thomas, and Wolfe 2013). The debate surely reflects interests and ideologies, but it also reflects the certainty that government both underreacts and overreacts and the great uncertainty concerning which it is doing at any one point in time on a particular issue.

One of the key responsibilities of congressional oversight at its best is detecting this pattern of under- and overreaction. The Department of Homeland Security was born out of a sense of urgency following 9/11. It suffered from attempts to focus diverse agencies on a single issue—counterterrorism—when the component agencies performed many diverse functions, leading to declines in performance (May, Workman, and Jones 2008). It centralized management to accomplish this, leading to high variability in output. And, as a recent report from a subcommittee of the Senate Homeland Security and Governmental Affairs (set up by state and local governments to coordinate activities concerning the detection of potential terrorist activities) suggested in a devastating critique at counterterrorism "fusion centers," the program has been enormously wasteful, with the Department of Homeland

Security unable to account for the money it spent, and the local fusion centers producing little useful information and considerable faulty information on innocent citizens. "National security programs tend to grow, never shrink, even when their money and manpower far surpass the actual subject of terrorism" (Sullivan 2012). Yet in an example of the diversity of information that can exist within a multiplicity of jurisdictions, the chairman of the full committee, Joe Lieberman, issued a press release critical of the report's conclusions (Majority Media 2012).[4]

No matter what disagreements there might be on the validity of the critique about our nation's "fusion centers," one could hardly find a better example of overgovernment. There are enough indicators to suggest that the counterterrorism activities of not just Homeland Security but the whole counterterrorism initiative by the federal government is far too large, expensive, and intrusive relative to the task. Overreactions are so consequential that the politics of information suppression are an understandable response, however frustrating to academics and others who would like real problems to be openly addressed and discussed, with proportionate policy responses forthcoming. But, in a way eerily similar to what we noted in an earlier work about the rapid and enthusiastic expansion of civilian nuclear power (Baumgartner and Jones 1991), the policy image of "protecting America" combined with restrictive institutional venues that keep "unqualified" critics away may be enough to ensure that one cherished value—protecting Americans—is overstated while another—maintaining our domestic liberties—gets short bureaucratic shrift. Ideas, institutions, and political agendas intertwine.

Diversity, Attention, and Control

Government today is larger, more diverse, and richer in information than it was two generations ago. It is also more complex, more internally contradictory, more confusing, and possibly more frustrating to those who would like to lead it. Growth in government did not stem simply from existing programs getting bigger; rather, it came from a multiplication of programs and activities in areas where government was once absent. From health care to the space program and from energy to transportation, programs have proliferated in areas where previous decades saw minimal activity or, more com-

---

4. The Permanent Subcommittee on Investigations conducted the investigation at the request of Senator Tom Coburn, the ranking minority member of the subcommittee; the chair of the subcommittee, Senator Carl Levin, issued a statement supporting the report (Media, Permanent Subcommittee on Investigations 2012).

monly, no activity whatsoever. With so many more issues simultaneously a part of the public agenda, and with more dimensions of each issue mobilized into the public discussion, the scarcity of public attention becomes more obvious. As government has grown, agencies have multiplied, and their activities have become spread over so many diverse areas of public policy, the dynamics of attention shifting and agenda setting have become even more critically important now than in the past.

8

Rounding Up the Usual Political Suspects

Broadly speaking, political scientists divide themselves into two camps regarding the role of popular government. Some emphasize primarily democratic control and accountability through partisan mandate, and some, including us, focus more on the role of government in addressing problems. For decades, many of the former group have touted responsible political parties as a major key to the democratic process. Parties lay out clear platforms distinguishing their policy preferences from opponents, voters choose on the basis of these competing "offers," and, once elected, the winning party enacts its policies and implements them through a hierarchical bureaucracy. Some see this model as the only true meaning of democracy itself, for if elections do not lead to new policies, or if voters do not pick parties on the basis of issue preferences, then there is no linkage between citizens and policy response. In any case, most models of electoral democracy imply some kind of successful policy leadership based on electoral legitimation and control of the bureaucracy.

In our view, this concept must be empirically tested against the possibility that leaders respond, as best they can, to shifting social problems. At least we must consider that the linkages between party competition based on ideology and the public policy outputs of government may be indirect or more complicated than a simple electoral mandate model would imply. After all, party platforms cannot lay out each and every policy decision a governing leader will be called upon to make. In a separation of powers system, compromise between leaders exercising shared control may lead to different outcomes than in either of their party platforms. And, most importantly, the world changes as a four-year presidential term goes on, and no platform could encompass all the contingencies with which governments routinely deal. In sum, there are many reasons to expect a slippage from electoral platforms to governing agendas, even if those elected are attempting to implement their proposals.

Whether partisan control matters more than the shifting severity of different social problems, or whether they interact in complex ways, is a new and exciting empirical question. By ignoring the question of long-term developments of public policies and by focusing on election effects, political scientists may well have overplayed the leadership hypothesis and underplayed the problem-solving nature of what leaders do. Much of the time they respond to challenges and opportunities that are thrust upon them, which may or may not correspond to their own partisan preferences in regards to which issues to attend.

Of course, they approach the new problem differently from how a partisan rival might, but leaders in power must respond, like it or not, to those issues that require urgent attention. And this is a swirling mix, constantly changing, not an easily predictable or stable set of policy concerns. Consider President Obama's situation on his arrival in office. While he certainly campaigned on the health care reform issue, and did indeed deliver on that promise, he also inherited two wars that he then had to manage, and had to respond to the financial crisis and the bankruptcy of some of the largest U.S. corporations and banks, and so on. Elections mattered, but so did the facts on the ground.

While the preferences of participants are more influential in choices among policy solutions than the selection of policy problems, solutions are influenced by the flow of information as well. Government grows in response to some combination of the preferences of political leaders (which themselves might be some complex mix of party positions, citizen desires, and interest influence) *and* information. Preferences alone do not determine policy outcomes (which affect the size and vigor of government). Information is critical. In the autumn of 2008, President G. W. Bush's secretary of the Treasury, Henry Paulson, went to Congress at the height of the 2008 financial crisis to request authority to buy troubled assets of financial institutions. Paulson's TARP bill, colloquially referred to as the "Wall Street bailout bill," brought to Congress by a conservative Republican administration, was one of the largest and most important legislative interventions in the economy in modern American history. Yet legislators uniformly claimed that it was not their desire to take this action. John Boehner, House Republican leader, said after the defeat of the first bill, which he supported, "I've got to tell you, my colleagues are angry about the situation they find themselves in. Nobody wants to have to support this bill." Just prior to the

Senate vote, Senator Claire McCaskill of Missouri said she would "hold my nose" and vote for the Senate's version of the Wall Street bailout bill. "The whole thing stinks." That is, legislators claimed they were *not* voting their preferences; they were voting based on the information generated by the Treasury Department and other sources (Jones and Surface-Shafran 2009).

The essence of governance is fashioning policy responses to problems, which are ever changing and dynamic. Holding fast to an alleged electoral mandate can lead to governing disaster. Nevertheless, we expect that the partisan positions and general philosophies of the major political parties influence the conduct of government, but they generally do so in complex interaction with the dynamic and diverse flow of information from the policy-making environment. The political system is adaptive (but not necessarily efficiently so), but its fundamentally adaptive nature pushes politicians toward addressing problems rather than solely imposing preferences.

In this chapter, we round up the standard political suspects often accused as responsible for changes in public policy. We will see that most of them are innocent of the accusation, but that they are clearly coconspirators. And once in a while, when elections move strongly enough in one direction, they are indeed guilty as charged.

The Composition of Government and the Expansion of the Policy Agenda

The Democratic Party in common lore is the party of government expansion; in its typical platform and in the rhetoric of many, if not most, of its political leaders one can find many references to employing government to intervene in social and economic affairs. On the other hand, Republican platforms and rhetoric is replete with references to the problem of big government and calls for limiting its scope. Following from this, we can easily hypothesize that governments unified under Democratic control— that is, the presidency, the House of Representatives, and the Senate—will move more aggressively to expand the scope of government than will either divided governments or unified Republican governments. We will examine two facets of policy-making agenda expansion: the search process, as assessed by changes in the substantive scope of hearings, and the lawmaking process, as assessed by changes in the substantive scope of laws.

We start by examining the scope of lawmaking, hypothesizing that the passing of statutes will be much more aggressive in unified Democratic governments. We are not so interested in the number of statutes passed, because these can represent both the thickening process, in which laws are passed in areas that are traditionally within the purview of government, and the broadening process, which reflects agenda expansion. Rather, we focus on expansions in the substantive focus of lawmaking to capture changes in the breadth of government. Our measure is the number of policy agendas subtopics that experienced one or more hearings (for expansions in the search process) or laws (for expansions in lawmaking). In Chapter 7 we used this measure with considerable success to examine increases in government scope, but we did so within a historical context. For simplicity's sake, we use three categories of government control: unified Democrat, unified Republican, and divided. We count as divided any Congress in which the presidency, House, or Senate are held by different parties. Figure 8.1 depicts the number of subtopics in which government passes at least one law for a two-year Congress. It shows the number of subtopics within which laws were passed for each congress, divided by Democratic unified government (at 2), divided government (1) and Republican unified government (0).

The average number of subtopics in which laws were passed was 125 for Democratic unified government, 113.5 for the two years of unified Republican government, and 127.5 for divided government. While the two coterminous Congresses of Republican rule (108th and 1009th, serving between 2003 and 2007) enacted statutes in fewer subtopics than Democratic or divided governments did, there is a clear tendency for divided governments to expand the lawmaking agenda into more policy categories than do unified Democratic governments. The variability in the aggressiveness of parties in government to expand the scope suggests that there is more to the story than party differences—and indeed there is. History mattered, and quite a bit. Lawmaking reached its largest scope in the first Congress to serve after President Jimmy Carter was elected. That Congress passed laws in 151 subtopics, but the Reagan years also experienced great lawmaking activity—150 subtopics were the subject of lawmaking in the 100th Congress, Reagan's last, as well as in G. H. W. Bush's first Congress.

These are the years that the arc of lawmaking described in Chapter 6 reached its apogee and began to decline. The nature of the arc means that the years at apogee (roughly the 90th through the 101st Congresses) are more similar to each other in expanding the scope of government regardless of the partisan nature of the government in control of the process. Similarly, Congresses before and during the expansion are similar in the aggressiveness with which they expanded the scope of government. (See Figure 6.4.)

Perhaps only some elections send powerful enough signals to shift the policy-making path away from its trajectory. Peterson, Grossback, Stimson,

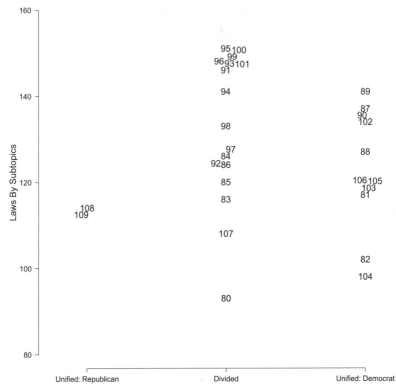

FIGURE 8.1. The Number of Subtopics in Which Laws Were Passed, 80th–110th Congresses
Source: Policy Agendas Project
Note: Numbers indicate the Congress. Vertical placement of the Congress number represents the number of distinct subtopics, on the left scale. These are shown separately for unified Republican, divided, and unified Democratic periods. Slight movements left or right beyond these three categories are only to avoid superimpositions.

and Gangl (2003) make the argument and present supporting analyses that a certain kind of election, which they call *mandate elections*, make a stronger difference in the policy-making activities of government than the typical election. To these authors, mandate elections are in the perceptions—do congressmen perceive the election to have provided a "message about the changed policy preferences of the electorate" since the Second World War (411), and consist of 1964, 1980, and 1994.

The evidence offered by these authors to support their thesis involves roll-call votes. But surely mandate elections should involve expansions and contractions of the policy-making agenda. One of the elections, under the standard electoral hypothesis, should drive the agenda toward broadening government, the other two toward limiting the reach of government. Two

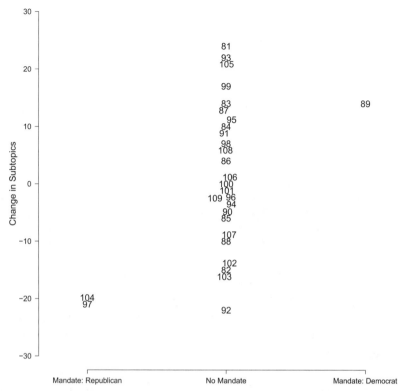

F I G U R E 8.2. Mandate Elections and the Change in the Number of Policy Subtopics in Which Laws Were Passed

Source: Policy Agendas Project

Note: Numbers indicate the Congress. Vertical placement of the Congress number represents change in the number of distinct subtopics, on the left scale. These are shown separately for Congresses following the two Republican mandate elections, nonmandate elections, and Democratic mandate elections. Slight movements left or right beyond these three categories are only to avoid superimpositions.

of these elections took place in presidential years and provided unified government (1964 and 1980), and one (1994) moved the control of government from unified control to divided control. Because the number of laws has decreased over time, we look only at changes in agenda breadth.

Figure 8.2 displays the Congress to Congress change in the number of policy agendas subtopics in which at least one law was passed during the Congress. If that number is positive, then Congress added subtopics to the lawmaking agenda; if it is negative, Congress enacted laws in fewer areas. Toward the left of the graph are the two conservative mandate Congresses (strong votes for Republicans) and to the far right the liberal mandate Congress (strong votes for Democrats). In the center are all other Congresses. In this case, the electoral hypothesis is supported. While there were both

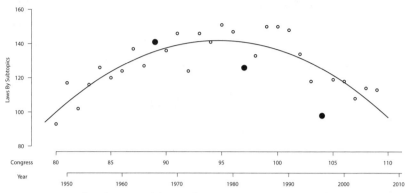

FIGURE 8.3. Mandate Elections and the Arc of Issue Expansion: The Number of Subtopics in Which One or More Laws Were Passed in a Given Congress

Source: Policy Agendas Project

Note: Mandate elections indicated by large black circles.

more aggressive Congresses than the 89th (1965–67 Johnson) Congress, and there were more conservative Congresses than either 97th (1981–83) or the 104th (1995–97) Congresses, in all cases the mandate elections are associated with lawmaking changes in directions consistent with the hypothesis. The Republican-mandate Congresses are more aggressive in cutting back the lawmaking agenda than all, save two: the 92nd (1971–73) and the 109th (2005–07). Somewhat more troubling is the finding for the 89th Congress (1965–67), which was exceeded by four Congresses in agenda expansion.

It is likely that where the mandate Congresses fell along what we called the arc of new-issue expansion in Chapter 6 has a lot to do with the findings above. As a consequence, in Figure 8.3 we present the quadratic estimate for the rise and decline of the breadth of the lawmaking agenda, which we presented in Figure 6.4. The circles indicate the mandate elections. It is clear that the 89th Congress falls a little above the average temporal path, but the 97th and 104th Congresses fall well below the arc. It seems likely that the 89th Congress followed a period of expansion of the lawmaking agenda and hence contributed toward further expansion only minimally. Its success was in passing major legislation, not in overall broadening of the policy-making agenda. On the other hand, the 97th and 104th Congresses did act to contract the lawmaking agenda, and very severely, even when compared to the arc.

A more rigorous analysis confirmed the graphical presentation in Figures 8.2 and 8.3. Table 8.1 presents the results of a regression analysis in which the number of subtopics within which laws were passed is the dependent variable. Predictors include a quadratic trend for new-issue expansion, fit by the

TABLE 8.1. Regression Analysis of Law Subtopics and Mandate Elections

Variable	Coefficient	Std. Error	t
Constant	−1565	202.01	−7.75
Congress	35.96	4.30	8.37
Congress Squared	−0.189	0.023	−8.33
Unified Democratic	−5.31	3.16	−1.68
Mandate	17.49	4.92	3.56
$R^2 = 0.779$	$F = 22.08$	$N = 30$	

Congress and Congress squared variables, unified Democratic rule (assessed by a dummy variable), and mandate elections (with −1 indicating a conservative mandate, and 1 indicating a liberal one). The trend is significant, both in its linear and quadratic components, as is mandate Congresses. But unified Democratic government is not significant.[1]

Even when we adjust for this context, the pattern we observe supports the hypothesis that agenda expansion is directly affected by the partisan control of government, but only in special situations—mandate elections. Once a pattern is in place, it takes a great deal of political energy to shift away from it, but it can be done. Moreover, the deviations themselves help to set the future path.

Is Search Partisan?

We have made the case in this book that aggressive search on the part of government is key in solving problems, but it can also lead to government growth. One may object to the increasing size of government on philosophical grounds, but one may also object on the grounds of practical public policy. Government may overreact to real problems, providing more government than an efficient solution to the problem requires. One way to minimize such mistakes is to slow down the search process; if government does not search for problems, it cannot propose government solutions to them. The cost is obvious: minimizing search will allow real problems to fester and perhaps grow to crises. In an ideal world, search and solutions would be addressed in independent and objective processes, but policy dynamics in real political

---

1. A second analysis with unified versus divided government entered instead of unified Democratic government (measured as 0 for unified Republican, 1 as divided, and 2 as unified Democratic) yielded no differences in results.

systems are more likely to lead to a pattern of policy overreaction interspaced with longer periods of underreaction (Jones and Baumgartner 2005a, 2005b). In any case, a politics of search limitation is absolutely possible, and in the past Republicans talked openly about the problem of aggressive Democrats finding a government solution for every problem they found.

The number of policy agendas subtopics that are pursued in a given year or Congress is a good indicator of the expansion of the policy agenda during that year or Congress. If we study the number of subtopics addressed compared to the party holding the reins of government, we can find out if there is any patterning to the search process. We hypothesize that unified Democratic governments will be more aggressive in searching for problems and hence expanding the policy agenda than either divided governments or unified Republican governments.

Figure 8.4 displays the results. There we plot the three values of government control versus the number of subtopics addressed in the corresponding Congress similar to the approach used in Figure 8.1. While we would expect unified Republican government to pursue fewer policy topics, that is not the case, nor is it clear that Democratic governments pursue more. Nor is it the case that unified governments of either stripe are more aggressive in the search process than divided governments.

We already know that the process of agenda expansion has a strong historical component to it (Chapter 4). Maybe the process is time dependent in the sense that when control shifts from a Democratic-dominated government to a divided or Republican one, slowing down the process of search takes time (and similarly for a change from Republican or divided to Democratic control). Figure 8.5 adjusts for this possibility by calculating changes toward or away from more Democratic (and hence hypothetically more aggressive) government in adjacent Congresses. Left is to the more conservative side (Republican), right toward the more Democratic side, and the middle point is no change.

Note first that the center of the graph (no change) clusters approximately around zero, as we expect. Otherwise, however, Figure 8.5 contains no element of support for the notion that moving to a hypothetically more aggressive government yields a larger expansion of the policy-making agenda. Indeed, governments becoming more Republican (either moving from unified Democratic control to divided government or from divided government to unified Republican government) are actually more likely to expand the agenda than those becoming more Democratic.

Do mandate elections affect the aggressiveness of search in the hearings process? The short answer is no. Figure 8.6 presents the number of subtopics with at least one hearing within it across time, with the three Congresses

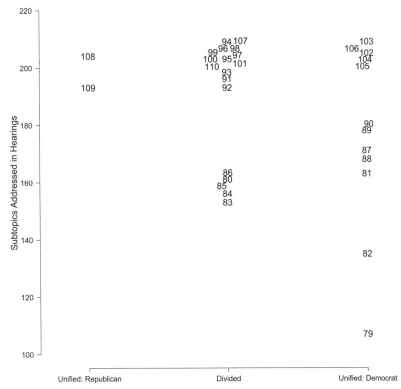

FIGURE 8.4. Subtopics Addressed in Hearings and Party Control of Government

Source: Policy Agendas Project

Note: Numbers indicate the Congress. Vertical placement of the Congress number represents the number of distinct subtopics, on the left scale. These are shown separately for unified Republican, divided, and unified Democratic periods. Slight movements left or right beyond these three categories are only to avoid superimpositions.

following mandate elections denoted by darkened circles. The deviations around the curve depicting the arc of new issue expansion are much tighter than was the case for lawmaking, and within this tighter band the mandate Congresses do not distinguish themselves. Mandate elections do not seem to affect the congressional search process.

Search in a Divided Congress

The most common form of divided government since the Second World War is for the presidency to be held by one party and both houses of Congress to be held by the other. But in some cases, the House and the Senate were themselves divided in regard to party control. This allows us to take

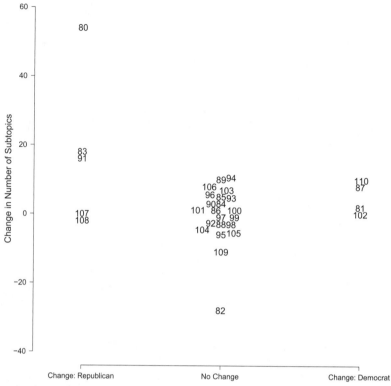

FIGURE 8.5. Change in Subtopics Addressed in Hearings and Change in Party Control of Government
Source: Policy Agendas Project
Note: Numbers indicate the Congress. Vertical placement of the Congress number represents change in
the number of distinct subtopics, on the left scale. These are shown separately for Congresses following a
shift in control to the Republicans (left), ones with no change in party control, and Congresses following
elections putting Democrats in control after a period when Republicans had been in control (right). Slight
movements left or right beyond these three categories are only to avoid superimpositions.

advantage of this natural experiment to examine whether the two houses of
Congress display different search behaviors when held by different parties
at the same time. The period 1981–87 (97th through 99th Congresses), when
Republicans controlled the Senate and Democrats controlled the House,
was the most extended period when the party holding each house of Congress was different. We expect that the Senate will hold hearings on fewer
subtopics during this period than the House.

Figure 8.7 presents the evidence. We graph our reliable variable assessing
issue expansion, the number of policy agendas subtopics on which at least
one hearing was conducted, separately for House and Senate. It is true that
the Senate held hearings on fewer subtopics during the period of divided

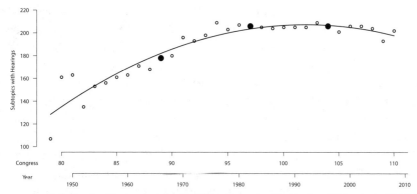

FIGURE 8.6. Mandate Elections and the Arc of Issue Expansion: The Number of Subtopics in Which
One or More Hearings Occurred in a Given Congress
Source: Policy Agendas Project
Note: Mandate elections indicated by large black circles.

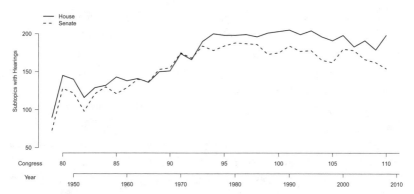

FIGURE 8.7. Subtopics Addressed in Hearings, House and Senate Separately
Source: Policy Agendas Project

congressional control. But it is unlikely that the divided Congress was the
cause of this deviation. The Senate and House began to diverge regarding
the expansiveness of the search process in the 93rd Congress, and this deviation remained in place for the rest of the period of our study. Congress
implemented rules changes for the operation of congressional committees
in the 1970s, and the reform impetus was stronger in the House than in the
Senate (see Chapter 4 for a discussion). Perhaps the most important in regard to the deviation beginning in the 93rd Congress is the Subcommittee
Bill of Rights, which expanded the power of subcommittee chairs to hold
hearings. It likely that these differences in rules for committees accounts for

the House-Senate differences in Figure 8.7. This is supported by the fact that the House began to hold more hearings than the Senate beginning in the 94th Congress, and continued to hold more hearings throughout the period of study. This difference had become quite large by the 96th Congress, with the House holding six hundred more hearings than the Senate.

In general, we find no evidence that the partisan control of government has any effect on agenda expansion or in the number of laws passed. This does not mean that arguments about either growth of government or agenda expansion are not continually made by political parties; it means that partisan control alone does not seem to influence the outcomes we study.

We examine in the next section changes in expenditure patterns that may be associated with presidential elections. This time we look at any directional change in spending.

Are Spending Changes a Consequence of Electoral Changes?

New presidents invariably bring fresh ideas and proposals for changing the way things are currently being done. The size of government and its intrusiveness is a standard topic in presidential campaigns. As a consequence, it would seem logical that when a new president takes the reins of the U.S. budget, especially one replacing a president of the other party, a major priority would be to reallocate money from the old priorities of the rival party to the new ones. Overall, budgets are substantially path dependent, but this path dependency masks considerable programmatic churning (Jones, Zalyani, and Erdi, in press). If presidents bring new priorities to the table, this would imply that extreme budget changes at the program or subfunction level should be higher in the first year of a presidential administration as compared to years when the president is revising his own previous budget. With a continuing president rather than a new one, adjustments might be expected to be more marginal, as the president might continue to reallocate, perhaps more slowly over several years, to those concerns he identifies as his priorities. This does not mean that all new presidents can shift budget priorities. Rather, we test a weaker form of the electoral hypothesis: *if* major budget changes are made, they occur as a consequence of electoral shifts at the presidential level.

Before we move to the test, let us consider a second possibility: the information hypothesis. If the political system acts as an adaptive system, then the main problem for any government leader is the ever-changing nature of the surrounding environment and the complexity of the choices confronting him or her. There is no reason to expect that problems cluster at the beginning of a president's term; rather, they are more likely to occur randomly throughout a presidential term. To the extent that budgets reflect attempts to address dynamic and changing problems, we should expect no systematic differences in large budget changes over the course of a presidential term. Certainly the newly arriving president would *like* to reallocate to his priorities and to demonstrate the differences in his approach from that of his predecessor, especially if it was a partisan rival. On the other hand, he must manage the entire federal budget, not just one or two pet priorities. And if there is a farm crisis caused by drought, a foreign policy challenge, foreboding economic news, or a new idea sweeping through a policy community that leads to a new consensus, these events may well be out of his control. Welfare reform is a policy associated with Democratic president Bill Clinton, but it is more correct to view the policy as driven by the policy entrepreneurship of conservative intellectuals supported by Republicans and steered away from more extreme forms by Clinton. Therefore, while we do not suggest that elections play no role in the political system, we do hypothesize that they will play very little role in the budgetary process when we consider the entire distribution, not just a few carefully selected categories. Presidents, after all, can always point to a few cases where they did indeed choose to make distinctions.[2] Whether they can do this systematically, across the board for the entire federal budget, is another matter.

The test for whether presidents systematically impose greater reallocations across the budget categories is simple enough: we look at the kurtosis for the first year when a new president can affect the budget and compare that with all other years. If the election hypothesis is correct there should be a greater number of extreme changes, and therefore greater kurtosis, in that first year.[3] Table 8.2 presents this comparison.

Whether we look at all newly elected presidents or only at those taking over from a predecessor of the other party, the distribution of annual changes in the budget is barely different in the first year of the new president's authority compared to other years. In fact, the first year appears to

2. Not only do individual presidents want to have something to point to as their major proactive accomplishments but biographers will write books about these dramatic impacts, and political scientists will teach courses and write analyses of these examples to demonstrate that "elections matter"—and they do. However, the desire to find human agency in all matters should not blind us to the need to test agency versus contextual effects in a fair matter. We try to do this by looking comprehensively at all budget matters, not just a few.

3. For these analyses we link the first year of a presidential administration with the first budget over which he has control. By lagging the budgets in this way to correspond to presidential control, we can simply test whether there are more large changes in the first year of a president's control.

TABLE 8.2. Do Newly Elected Presidents Reallocate Spending More than
Continuing Presidents?

A. All new presidents:

Budgetary Year from Election	Number of Observations	L-Kurtosis
First Year	488	0.581
All Other Years	3,149	0.607
Total	3,637	0.605

B. Presidents taking over from a president of the other party:

Budgetary Year from Election	Number of Observations	L-Kurtosis
First Year	423	0.595
All Other Years	3,214	0.607
Total	3,637	0.605

Note: Part A includes Eisenhower, Kennedy, Nixon, Carter, Reagan, Bush I,
Clinton, and Bush II. Part B includes only Eisenhower, Kennedy, Nixon, Carter,
Reagan, Clinton, and Bush II.

show slightly lower kurtosis, though we hesitate to interpret this difference, as it is not likely very meaningful. Figure 8.8 shows that there are no differences across *any* presidential years.

Figure 8.8 shows the number of "extreme changes" in each presidential year and compares the observed values to two reasonable rival hypotheses: a "first-year" hypothesis and a "learning" hypothesis. The first of these, represented by the dashed line in the graph, suggests that a new president would immediately mobilize to make significant reallocations, which gradually decline as a percentage as successive years of the same presidential administration go on. The second, shown in the dotted line in the graph, incorporates the idea that it may take a year or two for the new administration to have its people in place and to affect the budget in the manner it hopes, so the peak reallocations would come in the second or third presidential year, not the first. In either case, reallocations would be expected to decline over the years of a presidential administration, as he is no longer correcting the errors of his partisan predecessor, but rather simply adjusting a budget for which he has increasing responsibility each year.

The data show, of course, that nothing of the sort occurs. Our definition of "extreme" changes for this illustration is the number of changes in the top and bottom 10 percent of the distribution across the entire presidential administration. The data clearly show that the number stays near 20 percent in each year, with only slight random fluctuations around this number whether it is the first or the eighth year of a president's ability to affect the budget.

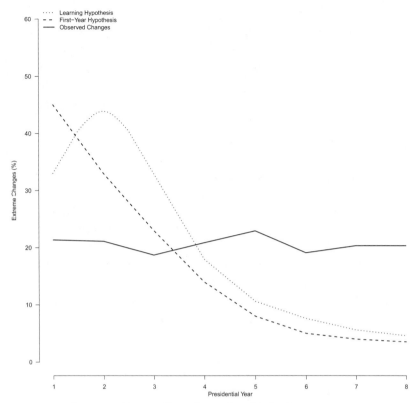

FIGURE 8.8. Percentage of Extreme Changes by Presidential Budget Year
Source: Policy Agendas Project

In sum, the data roundly reject the straightforward expectation that new presidents would reallocate more commonly than continuing presidents (accounting for possible learning effects so that the period of maximum reallocation might be the second or third presidential year, not necessarily the first one). Presidents respond to the shifting environment surrounding them, exerting their preferences, of course, but also responding to changes in the flow of information that outweigh the ability of even the vast bureaucracy of the OMB and the federal budgetary process to predict, manage, and plan change.

Search and Policy: Getting Causation Right

A final but essential issue in rounding up the usual political suspects is whether search does in fact occur prior to policy making, or whether policy making occurs first and search is mostly about correcting errors made in the policy once it is made. This is critical to our argument that search and processing information relative to the detection and definition of problems are critical drivers of agenda expansion and the broadening of government. We have argued that search and processing of information are fundamental to the idea that governments operate on problems rather than impose elite preferences that are selected within the framework of competitive elections. Naturally problem definitions are very much affected by partisan preferences. Nevertheless, it is hard to impose preferences in a democracy without some prior analysis that a problem exists. Elections are critical in establishing the electorate's understandings and prioritizations of problems. But in our approach it is the problem that is the fodder of politics.

As they interact across time, problem search and policy solutions are as bound as the DNA strands of the double helix. Problems generate efforts at forging solutions, but each solution must be imperfect, and as a consequence solutions generate new problems. Nevertheless, we can provide some basic evidence that in this intertwined system search tends to lead policy. We simply tabulate rough search processes by session of Congress. (A "Congress" is the two-year period beginning the January after an election; each Congress is divided into two annual "sessions.") We use two measures of commitment to search. One is the number of hearings conducted in each session. While this conflates what we have termed "entropic" and "expert search" by including all types of hearings, it is justified because we want here to focus on both types of search; the issue is the extent to which any search occurs prior to policy enactment. The second measure of commitment to search is the number of bills introduced per session. We use the number of laws enacted as a measure of policy solutions. We want to know if search precedes policy. That would require the first session of each Congress to be more concerned with search procedures (hearings and bill introductions) and the second session with policy making (enacting laws).

We have averaged each of our three measures for first and second sessions, separately. The table below presents the results (slight differences in the periods covered reflect data availability). In the first sessions of all Congresses, over ten thousand bills were introduced, but less than half that were introduced in the second sessions. A similar pattern emerges for hearings. For laws, the pattern is reversed: 230 statutes passed in the first sessions, but 290 in the second. Table 8.3 presents the results.

This does not tell the full story, because each of the series trends across time, and for bills and hearings the trend patterns are complex. So we present Figure 8.9 below, which shows each of the series on a session-by-session basis. There exists a clear saw-toothed pattern for each series, although the

TABLE 8.3. Bills, Hearings, and Laws by Session of Congress

Bills Introduced, 1949–2008		Hearings Conducted, 1947–2010		Laws Passed, 1947–2010	
First Session	Second Session	First Session	Second Session	First Session	Second Session
10,530	4,835	1,541	1,305	238	390

Source: Policy Agendas Project.

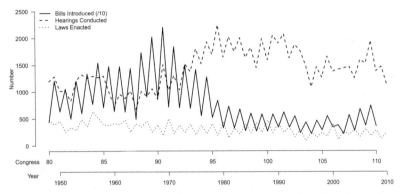

FIGURE 8.9. The Number of Bills Introduced, Hearings Conducted, and Laws Enacted on an Annual Basis

Source: Policy Agendas Project

Note: The number of bills introduced is divided by 10, so its maximum value, in 1969, is over 22,000. The other values are indicated on the scale shown.

hearings series shows this pattern most consistently only after 1960. For bills introduced and hearings, the series have peaks in the first session; for laws, peaks are in the second session. The pattern of search first, policy later is quite clear even while the series are displaying considerably different trends across time. We have also examined hearings involving bills and those that do not consider bills and find that the saw-toothed pattern holds for each series, although it is clearer when bills are not considered. Since these hearings are focused on problem discovery and issues in implementation of earlier laws (oversight hearings), this is not a surprise.

We conclude that problem search is indeed an important component of policy making, and that it most likely leads rather than follows the enactment of solutions. This obviously does not mean that a considerable amount of the business of problem detection and definition does not come later, once statutes are enacted and modifications must be made to them. But it does undermine the contention that policies stem from the preferences of political elites who are chosen through elections to enact these preferences. That would lead to an inference that more policies would be enacted right after an election (the first session of a Congress), which does not happen.

Conclusions

When we round up the usual variables suspected by many of causing changes in the path of public policy, we find little to support an indictment, and where we do, a reduced sentence is probably in order. We find no evidence that unified government affects either the expansion of the lawmaking agenda directly or the propensity to search out new problems that may be occurring in the policy-making environment. We find no evidence that changes in the control of the presidency affect budgetary shifts at the program level. We do find effects for mandate elections—those in which the party taking control of government after the election has received wide support and interprets this support in policy terms—but only for expansion and contraction of the lawmaking agenda.

The likely reason for the lack of direct evidence to support typical political dynamics is the role of context. Politics always occurs relative to what is happening at the time it occurs—the problems that are being addressed and solutions that are currently in vogue. In terms of the framework developed in Chapter 6, it depends on where the political activity occurs on the arc of new-issue expansion. Taking this context into consideration suggests that mandate elections would be important in the lawmaking agenda, but not in the search process, as indeed is the case. It is likely that mandate governments stimulate or winnow policy proposals but are not able to stop problems from accessing the governmental agenda. But the typical election does little to change the trajectory of the lawmaking agenda or any other aspect of the issue expansion process.

PART III

The Implications of Information in Government

We have shown that information is central to government. Control the flow of information and you can control the growth of government. Information is not easily controlled, however, in a democracy, and the framers of the U.S. Constitution seemed to have an implicit understanding that multiple sources of information were a potential route to better decision-making processes. Clarity of hierarchical control is essential for implementing policies that are known to work. A network of professionals loosely coordinating their efforts but each focusing on different aspects of a complex problem is a good way to make scientific advancement in studying a complex problem. The National Institutes of Health supports a vast network of health care researchers through the nation's universities; it does not directly hire all these scientists and give them research tasks through a hierarchical command structure; no one would stand for that in the area of basic science. The U.S. Postal Service directly employs a huge army of employees doing many different things, but it is not a complex structure in the way that health research is: a large but understandable task corresponds to a simpler organizational structure with direct hierarchical control functions. So, understanding the nature of the problems governments face is necessary to understand the structure that government should adopt. The struggle between information and control is key to understanding arguments about the structure and function of government itself.

The tension over the processing of information in government is intimately bound with the classic agenda-setting problem, which centers on how circumstances tolerated by citizens become problems worthy of government action. We have shown how this has played out historically in Chapters 4 through 8. In Chapter 9, we summarize these results and suggest that the process has been critical in the transformation of the American policy-making system. In Chapter 10, we reexamine the paradox of search, particularly asking whether modern complex governments face a Hobson's choice of fostering either organized anarchy or dangerously restrictive search processes.

9

Organizing Information and the Transformation of U.S. Policy Making

Of the proposition that the U.S. policy-making process underwent a sustained change from the mid-1950s to the late 1970s there can be no doubt. Our detailed documentation of the expansion of the policy-making agenda supports other more qualitative and limited quantitative analyses of this process. What has been far less recognized is the role of the processing of information in this transformation. Moreover, the reaction to the broadening of government during what we term "the Great New-Issue Expansion" was intimately bound with the processing of information as well—but in this case the limitation and focusing of information gathering and processing as the policy-making agenda shrank. In this chapter, we review our findings on this transformation and suggest some of the major implications of our focus on the role of information in the process.

Broadly speaking, modern complex governments engage in two types of search behavior. One of the search methods, which we term "entropic search," involves signal detection: what problems (or potential solutions) might be relevant to the organization. The second, termed "expertise," aims at understanding the problem or solution and its potential impacts. This type of search is analogous to the concept of the power of a statistical test: the greater the power of the test, the more likely it is to detect an effect from a variable. The greater the expertise, and the more its resources, the more likely it is to find an effective solution. But only if the problem is understood. For problems that we do not understand, or problems that have numerous interconnected dimensions, greater expertise and more control will not typically lead to better results.

In entropic search, diversity is valuable and the space searched is complex, uncertain, and multidimensional. In expertise-based search, the space searched is simple and unidimensional, but still uncertain (if there were certainty, there would be no need for search). In entropic search, diversity is used to explore potential problems or solutions. In expert search, analytics (in the sense of breaking down a problem and simplifying it) are used to reduce the variance on the dimension being studied.

Each method of search has advantages and disadvantages. Entropic search, by exploring the problem or solution space, can yield too much information, overwhelming the system at the stage of prioritization. Expert search may start with serious attribute suppression, so policy is based on an incomplete understanding of the problem or the nature of how various solutions might work.

We have argued that government organizations are best at entropic search when they incorporate diverse elements and share overlapping jurisdictions with competing organizations. Agencies in competition with other agencies and pushed by legislative committees are more likely to discover problems than those subject to unitary jurisdictions and hierarchical control. But this overlap can lead to prioritization problems in the central decision-making units of government. Moreover, the aggressive discovery of problems can lead to increased pressure to act. Acting can lead to the growth of new government programs and agencies, which can create a backlash after time. On the other hand, a failure to search carries with it equal or greater danger. Problems fester, and error accumulation may occur. This process of accumulating errors leads to a disjointed, punctuated policy-making process (Jones and Baumgartner 2005b). We termed this dynamic the paradox of search.

We developed ways to assess the extent of entropic search, and, using the datasets of the Policy Agendas Project, showed how these methods could be employed to examine the search process in the U.S. government over time. One might think that some sort of simple growth process would lead to increasing complexity in search and that this would create a self-reinforcing process that could continue indefinitely. That is, over time entropic search would increase as a consequence of an increasing number of agencies, programs, and responsibilities assumed by government. As the social system becomes more complex, agencies and programs become more complex. The historical record of search processes in the United States after the Second World War indicates that this account is too simple. Entropic search in Congress increased from the mid-1950s until around 1978, and then, depending on the measure, either dropped precipitously (as it did in the case of the lawmaking process) or leveled off (as it did in nonlegislative hearings and roll-call votes). What happened? Politics intervened to alter the supposedly simple relationship between an increasingly complex society and an increasingly complex information acquisition and analysis process in government. The increase in program density generated a conservative reaction that affected the information-processing capacity of government, a reaction that served as a bromide to the "seek and find" problem. Yet today even conservatives are asking whether the analytic capacity of government has been too limited.

Any organizational structure has limited capacity to expand its subunits that could process information, but the world generating the information is potentially infinitely complex. The potential for information complexity is a function of both the number of attributes one could potentially use to understand the information and the manner in which those attributes might be weighted and interact with each other. But the limits of organization meet the problems of complexity in information long before the organization is overwhelmed. Because of the trade-off between clarity of purpose and supply of information, it becomes clear to political leaders that they quickly lose control if the organization differentiates to cope with incoming complex information flows. Figure 5.5 shows this process at work in Congress. It tabulates entropic search in committees. During the 1970s, Congress coped with increased demands for solving problems by adding subcommittees and muddying committee jurisdictions. By the early 1980s, this process ceased, but at a high level. Then, after 1995, entropic search contracted as the parties, particularly the Republican Party, centralized control in the Office of the Speaker and the party caucus.

Patterns of alteration in the aggressiveness of government policies are oft-noted but ill-explained. We suggest that these patterns are due less to some sort of mysterious societal mood, or in the political party composition, than is often thought. As important as these factors is the unavoidable dynamic of problem solving and its consequent tension between increasing the supply of information on the nature of problems and the control and prioritization of that information. This tension typically does not lead to stable equilibrium but rather an oscillation as political forces supporting control temporally ascend at one time and the forces supporting openness ascend in another. As a consequence, the paradox of search probably creates a cyclical pattern of consolidation and expansion of government as aggressive problem solving leads to more government, which can lead to counterreactions. These cycles may be quite long. In an analysis of the federal budget since 1790, Jones et al. (in press) show that periods of specific growth rates occurred regularly but were also interspersed with periods of consolidation or retrenchment.

As in all complex systems, equilibria are often partial. We have detailed the strong support in our analysis of policy agendas data for one full phase of expansion and contraction in the search and agenda-expansion process during the second half of the twentieth century in the United States in this book. But we also have hints of strong agenda expansion within limited spheres, particularly after 2001 in the vast buildup of the national security state apparatus.

Search and Agenda Expansion and Contraction

Beginning in the mid-1950s, the U.S. federal government entered a period of aggressive and systematic expansion into areas of American life previously left to civic life or to the states. This agenda expansion was closely associated with the expansion of both entropic and expert search, the former assessed by our analysis of committee hearings and jurisdictions in Chapter 5, and the latter by our qualitative examination of policy analysis in the executive and legislative braches in Chapter 4, approximated by the number of GAO reports issued. We assessed agenda expansion using straightforward measures of the number of policy agendas subtopics on which lawmaking (or bill referral) hearings were held and the number of subtopics addressed by the laws enacted. The Great New-Issue Expansion peaked in 1978, and contraction set in, which continued through the period of study (around 2008). The result was a broad arc of expansion and then contraction of the lawmaking agenda—those topics considered explicitly in hearings on bills—and in the enactment of laws themselves.

Both this expansion and its demise had much less to do with preferences and the liberalism of either the mass public or policy-making elites than is generally supposed. Elections and party control mattered little in either the agenda expansion or its contraction, at least in the typically simple fashion that political scientists view the process. The typical view that citizens set the policy agenda by responding to choices offered by political parties in elections, with the winning party then putting into place its programs, is simplistic and misleading at best. If we were to view elections as determinative of the expansiveness of the government agenda, we would be wrong. Elections and parties of course matter, and we show that "mandate elections" have the effect of deflecting the path of expansion and contraction. More importantly, the parties continue a long-term dialogue with each other and the public about the course of policy, and that wider conditioning effect probably has more to do with the general plot than is commonly acknowledged. But even that does not tell nearly enough of the story.

What did change in the second half of the twentieth century was the nature of how government processed information. In the expansionary stage, the process became more diverse and open to new groups and new ideas. One might say that government lost control of the agenda-setting process. This did not mean that government was incompetent; a major characteristic of this expansionary period was the incorporation of systematic policy analytic methods and systems analysis brought to domestic policy from experiences garnered in defense Cold War policy making.

Once agenda control was reestablished in the late 1970s, the nature of search and information processing changed. After 1978, the lawmaking agenda became far more focused than in the preceding period. Laws centered on economics and defense, while human services and education lost ground (Jones and Whyman 2011). Policy analytic capacity declined in the executive branch (Jones and Williams 2008). In Congress the number of hearings fell, but more importantly the process as an open forum declined. With agenda control came atrophied search. Moreover, the shift in control of the legislative branch in 1995 demonstratively and strongly affected the search process by limiting both entropic search (see Chapter 5) and expert search (Chapter 6). Elections have consequences, but the consequences seem to have influenced the agenda-setting process, at least in considerable part, by affecting how information was processed in Congress.

Generally during the postwar period there existed a tight connection between the extent and diversity of search and growth in government. However, during the G. W. Bush presidency, government grew robustly—the expenditure growth in the discretionary budget was comparable to the Great Society. Yet the overall curves for information diversity continued the general trend set in place after 1978: the diversity of legislative search leveled off and declined slightly. What happened, however, is concentrated search: in some areas hearings increased, as did the diversity of their topics. In Chapter 6, we presented information that showed the increased interest in search in the domestic intelligence area during the G. W. Bush years. But government grew domestically as well. Congress passed new major initiatives in health care and education.

Recall that entropy assesses the diversity of the search process. We have generally calculated entropy scores through time, averaging them across policy topics, but we can calculate these scores for a single topic as well. If we examine entropy scores for separate topics for the House of Representatives, we find a divergence in trends. For education and defense, trend scores are higher at the end rather than at the start of the Bush presidency. Health care, however, follows the general trend of lower entropy.

This probably indicates that the search process during the Bush presidency reflected the more focused and controlled process of information acquisition, and this was obviously true in the case of national security. Recognition of policy problems was concentrated in a few areas, and the agenda expanded in those areas. A more generally open approach to search, however, did not occur, and the lawmaking agenda did not experience the more general expansion that occurred during the 1960s and 1970s. One may be tempted to see most of this as a thickening rather than broadening of government, but the expansion of the national security state was so rapid and intrusive that this seems to underestimate the extent to which the expansion of the national security and intelligence apparatus broached Wilson's "legitimacy barrier" (see Chapter 6).

Thickening and Broadening Government

Most discussions of the growth government, either in the academic world or the world of practical politics, ignore a primary distinction. Government grows in two ways: thickening, by augmenting existing programs, and broadening, by taking on new responsibilities. It is adding new responsibilities where entropic search is most important. Where lots of new ideas and perspectives are admitted as legitimate concerns in the political arena, government adds responsibilities. As a consequence, it is imperative that political scientists begin to explore in more detail how government is broadened and refuse to conflate this process with the process of thickening.

It is worth taking stock of our findings regarding broadening. We can summarize them as follows:

- Government grows mostly through adding new responsibilities (broadening) rather than adding new elements to existing programs (thickening).
- The process is generally not in response to economic or international crises, though it can be.
- The process is not a function of some of the "usual suspects." The number of interest groups grew after the Great New-Issue Expansion—caused by it rather than causing it. Elections, even mandate elections, cannot be seen as directly responsible for the expansion.
- The process is not a function of dedicated political parties providing options to the electorate. The period of broadening began during the Eisenhower years and continued through the Nixon years, peaking and declining during the Carter years. The polarization of parties and the increasing approximation to responsible, disciplined parties occurred after the peak of the Great New-Issue Expansion, at least as measured by the activities of the congressional parties.

- The process of broadening was in considerable part generated by an active and aggressive search for new problems rather than the imposition of the predetermined preferences of political leaders. Preferences are indeed important, as they bias the search process and lead to predetermined solutions. But this observation leads to a different understanding of how politics works than the traditional approach of politics as a struggle to impose differing political preferences and philosophies.
- The agenda processes associated with broadening may be government-wide, as they were during the great agenda expansion documented in Chapter 6. But it is also possible for these processes to be channeled toward a more limited set of priorities. To some extent, this happened in the 2000s.
- The broadening of government has resulted in a transformative change in the relative roles of Congress and the administrative agencies. We explore this important implication below.

The Transformation of Congress in the Administrative State

Two aspects or our analysis speak volumes to the transformation of the role of Congress during the second half of the twentieth century. In 1946, three-quarters of congressional hearings involved consideration of bills that could become laws. By 2010, only around 12 percent did so. Congress is no longer primarily a lawmaking body; most of its work is in overseeing the vast executive bureaucracy that it created during the Great Expansion. The second aspect is graphically revealed in Figure 6.5. While lawmaking agenda expanded and then contracted, the oversight agenda did not. Oversight hearings in the 80th Congress (1947–49) addressed less than one hundred policy agendas subtopics; the 100th Congress (1987–89) addressed twice that many. And the number has not declined; once Congress creates programs and agencies, it is stuck with the task of overseeing the growth and development of its creation.

It is too much of a stretch to see Congress as a cog in a vast administrative state because its legislative role is still distinct, especially in the budget and appropriations process. What has disappeared from the legislative process is the ability to make on-the-fly adjustments in legislation, indicated by the disappearance of smaller laws. When Congress acts, and that is less and less often, it tends to do so in big, comprehensive pieces of legislation that leave much to the rule-making process in agencies. Political controversy over the original proposal is carried over into the oversight and appropriations processes. It is not that Congress is a weakened partner in the federal system, but its role has definitely shifted away from the traditional lawmaking function.

We do not claim that changes in the organization of search and information in government are the cause of all policy changes in America. But we do suggest that the process of detecting and organizing information about problems and solutions is a key component of understanding this process. One might say this is part of an era of more aggressive government, and that would be correct. But as we have shown here, the whole process of how government organizes information is a key—perhaps *the* key—component of strong, aggressive government. Moreover, the centralization of authority in the party leadership in Congress had a direct causal effect on the process of circumscribing search in committees and in the congressional analytic agencies. More centralized and ideological parties are antithetical to both types of search, but they are especially antagonistic to entropic search. The tension between information and order plays itself out in the national political arena as well as within committees and executive agencies, and the result is a very different legislative branch.

The vast increase in problem complexity and the resulting political struggle to cope with increases in information flows in modern government obviously has not just affected the legislative branch. These changes rippled throughout the federal system. But our analyses make it easiest to see there.

10

Organizing Complexity

Opening up the process of search adds complexity to government. Overlapping jurisdictions, shared powers of investigation and action, and multiple centers of power all make for a very messy mix. We have traced the implications of open and closed search procedures for the course of public policy in the United States and highlighted the tension between expert search and controlled implementation, on the one hand, and the messy, disorganized problem discovery process, on the other. However, our own analysis and the state of studies in organizational dynamics leave the impression that the choice is between censored, confined, and hence incomplete search versus organized anarchy. In this chapter we reexamine these organizational aspects in light of the empirical findings we have presented.

Some may think that increased complexity and interaction among component parts in a system lead to gridlock and an inability to act. That is not the case. Many quasi-independent venues for policy making and problem discovery and definition lead to dynamism and change, as we argued more than twenty years ago in *Agendas and Instability in American Politics*. Our finding presented in this book that agenda expansion was associated with increased entropic search in the legislative branch of the U.S. national government is an elaboration of this old theme. And, as expected, contraction of entropic search and the associated imposition of central control by the parties in Congress constrained the policy-making agenda. Complexity leads to agenda and subsequent policy expansion; simplification and control lead to agenda contraction. Complexity leads to disorder and confusion; simplification leads to attribute censoring and problem festering.

Issue Dynamics

Issues become more complex in the absence of government policy as private actors act in innovative ways to bring new products and services to consumers. Some of these products are unalloyed benefits, but many have both beneficial and detrimental consequences. One need look no further than the burst of innovative financial products that acerbated the housing bubble of the mid-2000s. Government becomes more complex because the social system becomes more complex. But a second process is at work, one that has implications for both broadening and thickening: a feedback process in which government activity itself adds to social complexity; issues and solutions invariably become more complex as government addresses them.

ISSUE EVOLUTION

Any issue addressed by government incorporates seeds of its own complexity. That is, an issue may become more complex because of government action. Consider transportation. At one time, transportation policy concerned providing infrastructure to where people lived, worked, and shopped. But over time it became clear that providing infrastructure promoted certain living and shopping arrangements, and that these developments could be counterproductive from the perspectives of traffic congestion and energy use and that they "hollowed out" many core cities or the main streets of many small towns. Moreover, the dispersed nature of American cities has become distasteful to many as they seek the benefits of a more urban lifestyle. So transport policy becomes part of energy policy, urban development, and even education (Should the bus go to the school or should the school be located on the bus line?) and may be used as a tool to move the locations of residences and businesses. This is less than comprehensive planning, because it need not be comprehensive, but it is more than the traditional role for transportation policy. It requires not just expertise (in the sense of building better transit systems) but information (in the sense of designing systems that promote goals beyond moving people). Whereas designing a bus line is relatively simple, organizing urban space is complex.

SOLUTION COMPLEXITY

Not all governmental complexity stems invariably from issue dynamics. It may also stem from solutions. When lawmakers demand that employers use E-Verify to ensure that they do not hire illegal immigrants, they are not only adding a regulatory burden to businesses, they are adding a layer of complexity to government. But this time the complexity stems not from the nature of the issue but from the availability of a convenient solution. It implies entropic development in the relationship between problem and organization just as much as the issue-driven process does. The E-Verify solution conflates immigration policy with business regulation. How should responsibility for administering the program be assigned to agencies? How should congressional jurisdiction be assigned? It puts business owners on the front lines of enforcing immigration policy, and it requires that the massive database in the E-Verify system work quickly, robustly, and with few errors, lest an effort to create controls on illegal immigration turn into a misguided policy that stifles private-sector hiring.

In the United States, solution complexity reaches its highest form in the tax code. One might wish for a simple tax code focusing on raising revenue, with positive government action limited to direct subsidies. For politicians, right and left, using the tax code to achieve social or economic goals is apparently irresistible. Rather than direct payments to the working poor, the United States uses the Earned Income Tax Credit. Rather than pay homebuilders a subsidy, the United States grants an income tax deduction for mortgage interest. Rather than provide health care directly, the United States offers businesses that offer health care to employees a tax deduction. No consideration of the U.S. welfare state is complete without a consideration of such tax expenditures (Faricy 2011; Mettler 2011).

This causes potential confusion in agency responsibility and legislative oversight. While Congress generally assigns oversight responsibility to tax committees for such positive policies, this is an arbitrary distinction that nevertheless generates spillovers for welfare, health, and housing committees (witness the struggles to deal with the employer-provided health system in the 2010 Patient Protection and Affordable Care Act).

The Politics of Information

Generally we have approached the role of information in politics in the broadest sense, by looking at how macropolitical forces have played out as information flows change. But there is also a narrower meaning of "politics": the struggle to gain advantage in contests over who runs government and what gets done. Changes in information patterns obviously affect this process. While many attempts to censor attributes stem from attempts to focus priorities and ensure clean implementation of policies, some aim directly to gain immediate advantage in a political fight.

EXPLICIT CENSORING: DENYING THE FACTS

Even when information is available and convincing, political leaders frequently deny its relevance. Both right and left are guilty of this. On the right, climate change and the notion that tax cuts will "pay for themselves" (Jones and Williams 2008) are two of the most important of these. It is easy as well to find left denial—we point to the tendency of the left to deny labor market effects of welfare programs. But it seems to be true that constraining overall search processes seems a strategy that is more prevalent on the right; certainly our data support that contention.

One obvious reason is that powerful economic interests make money from the existing system, and pay well to keep it that way. But it is unlikely that the system is that crass. More likely are psychological and ideological sources. Denial is part of what psychologists call the *confirmation bias*: the human tendency to search for information that supports a preferred point of view. But are conservatives more prone to the confirmation bias than liberals? Perhaps not. A second potential cause for the difference is that we are looking at a time period in which conservatives are disproportionately in denial, but in another era (perhaps the 1970s) liberals could have been more subject to denial. And liberals tend to underestimate foreign threats and regulatory costs to business, for example. So the mix of issues currently most controversial could account for this difference.

Our findings provide another potentially important source for denial. We have shown that well-articulated mechanisms for information processing are disproportionately responsible for generating more government programs and agencies. At one time, Republicans used to complain that if one searches for a problem, one tends to find an answer in a new government program. Certainly the evidence supports this view. If politicians can constrain the range of situations investigated by government, they can limit the subsequent governmental activity in the arena. Explicitly censoring facts can limit the ascension to the agenda of problems whose solutions will lead to more government.

But this is a false solution. Under such a regime real problems can fester and grow, providing fodder for a larger policy reaction in the future. The solution surely is a heightened ability to refuse to act *after* explicit consideration of the issue when action is not warranted. That is difficult in a world where not acting can have consequences worse than acting. Moreover, many analysts continue to rate the "productivity" of Congress and the "success" of the president based on how many laws (or "big" laws) they get passed. Passing laws that address problems too little and too late, or problems that are not properly understood, surely should not be counted as productive or useful. So it may be that conservatives have a harder job, because the demand for government action too easily follows from any configuration of facts that may emerge in a search process.

This trap argues strongly for what we might term the "Coburn solution," in recognition of Republican senator Tom Coburn's spirited defense of funding for GAO and the analytic capacities of the legislative branch. Surely solution search ought to be strongly supported by conservatives. Indeed, while we have emphasized the theoretical trade-off between control and information, suggesting a trade-off between entropic and expert search, that is not how the historical record played out. Our analyses in this book show that expert, policy analytic search and entropic search rose and fell together. These two different mechanisms for processing information ought to be treated as separate and distinct, and both conservatives and liberals ought to be able to find common ground in funding increased analytic capacity in government.

THE POLITICS OF INFORMATION: THREE ILLUSTRATIONS

The political power of information means that collecting information is often at the core of politics itself. While the government collects considerable information with broad bipartisan support (e.g., crime statistics, economic data of all sorts, weather forecasting data), sometimes these efforts become highly charged partisan battles. Then the issues of attribute suppression and denial of the obvious become part of politics. Three examples are gun violence, education-research standards, and racial profiling on the highways.

In the 1990s, the U.S. Centers for Disease Control (CDC) became aware of a growing set of studies looking at gun violence as a public health problem. The number of deaths from handgun violence was large and growing, and the CDC was convinced that a public health perspective on the issue could help it devise strategies to combat needless death. M. Christine Cagle and J. Michael Martinez (2004, 282) describe the CDC's actions and the response of the National Rifle Association (NRA) and its congressional supporters in these terms:

> Beginning in the 1990s, CDC officials began to consider violence as a significant public health issue owing to studies that suggested that firearm-related injuries had reached epidemic proportions. With Americans becoming increasingly concerned about the corrosive effects of escalating violence, an opportunity arose for the CDC to step into the debate and carve out a public health domain far beyond its previous parameters. When the NRA objected

to the methodology and conclusions found in the studies cited by the agency, the stage was set for a battle . . .

There might be no surprise that the result of the battle was that the NRA mobilized supporters of gun rights in Congress and the legislature stripped $2.6 million from the CDC budget and prohibited the CDC from funding any research on gun violence in 1996 (see Cagle and Martinez 2004, 298–300). Authors of the January 2013 report by Mayors Against Illegal Guns entitled "Access Denied: How the Gun Lobby is Depriving Police, Policy Makers, and the Public of the Data We Need to Prevent Gun Violence" write:

> The U.S. Centers for Disease Control and Prevention (CDC) leads the world in research on how violence affects public health, and how to stop it. But it conducts almost no research on the role of firearms in killing nearly 32,000 Americans every year. . . . The U.S. Department of Justice was once a world leader on research into how guns find their way into dangerous hands. As recently as the 1990s, the Department published critical reports that shed new light on firearms trafficking patterns and helped law enforcement at all levels detect and deter crime. In the decades since, the Department has failed to update these seminal studies or conduct new ones, at least publicly. Long after the Internet fundamentally changed the marketplace for firearms, our gun laws are informed by data that are as much as twenty years out of date. The National Institute of Justice, the principal research arm of the Justice Department, has seen its firearms portfolio weather on the vine. Between 1993 and 1999, it funded thirty-two gun-related studies. It has not funded a single public study on firearms during the Obama administration (Mayors Against Illegal Guns 2013, 2–3).

The mayors continue, giving examples of NRA-backed efforts to eliminate various sorts of data collection, information the mayors contend police departments need in order to understand and combat the problem of illegal gun trafficking. Of course, if one has followed the arguments in this book so far, it comes as no surprise that attention to a problem will lead to studies of the severity of the problem, and that these studies, in turn, can be used to support efforts to eliminate the problem. As these can be costly or burdensome to some stakeholders, they fight not only against the policies and the regulations but against information itself.

The field of education research is home to thousands of studies each year, some large-scale, some smaller, some qualitative, some quantitative, some welcome by school administrators, and some, of course, unwelcome.[1] The

---

1. Thanks to University of North Carolina School of Education professor Lora Cohen-Vogel for bringing this example to our attention.

U.S. Department of Education has recently promoted standards designed to ensure certain quality standards in education research. Its National Center for Education Statistics promotes such ideas as that studies should not be relied upon if they have survey response rates of less than 75 percent, if population census data is less than 95 percent complete, and so on (see http:// nces.ed.gov/statprog/2002/std2_2.asp, accessed 18 October 2013). The Department's Institute of Education Sciences maintains a "What Works Clearinghouse" designed to separate the research wheat from the chaff. These efforts promote the idea that the experts will review existing studies, evaluate the methodology, and promote attention only to those studies that reach certain scientific standards, with the goal being to see education reform being made on the basis of "evidence-based decisions" (see http://ies.ed.gov/ncee/wwc/default.aspx, accessed 18 October 2013).

This may be the largest government-oriented project of which we are aware where the goal is to eliminate "extraneous" bits of information so that only "good" information can be incorporated into the debate. Without evaluating the intentions of those involved, it is clear that the "What Works" program serves to eliminate or discredit considerable amounts of research. We are not education policy experts, so we take no position on the merits of any particular studies. As social scientists we are certainly in favor of high survey response rates and the best research methodologies. But as scholars of information we question whether a government clearinghouse to eliminate information from policy debate is a positive step. It is highly unlikely that such decisions can be made in government without some idea that fewer studies will lead to fewer demands for uncomfortable or unwelcome policy changes.

A third example comes from North Carolina's efforts to gather official statistics to investigate the possibility of racial bias in traffic stops. Racial profiling on the highways rose to prominence in national discussion during the 1990s when the concept of "driving while black" or "driving while minority" entered the popular vocabulary. The *New York Times* published just three articles containing the term from 1960 through 1997, but sixteen in 1998 and 156 in 1999, as the issue surged into the nation's consciousness (see Baumgartner and Epp 2012). At the request of Congressman James E. Clyburn (D-SC), chairman of the Congressional Black Caucus, the GAO issued a report on the topic in March 2000 (GAO 2000). The report noted that at least fifteen states considered legislation during 1999 mandating the collection of police-stop information, and North Carolina was the first in the nation to pass such a law. Since January 1, 2000, the North Carolina Department of Justice has collected information on every traffic stop from law enforcement agencies throughout the state.

The North Carolina law, however, did not require the state Department of Justice actually to analyze the law, and no reports were ever issued. In concert with an effort to analyze racial disparities in general, Baumgartner and a graduate student analyzed over 13 million traffic stops from 2000 through 2011 and showed that the difference in likelihood of being searched after having been pulled over for a traffic violation was 77 percent greater for African American drivers and 96 percent greater for Hispanics as compared to white drivers (see Baumgartner and Epp 2012). These and other similar statistics led the attorney general to convene a commission to look further into the matter (and, as of this writing in October 2013, that commission remains active).

They also led to the introduction of NC Senate Bill 923 by Republican North Carolina senator Thom Goolsby filed on 29 May 2012, whose title is self-explanatory: "An Act to Repeal the Requirement that the Division of Criminal Statistics Collect Traffic Law Statistics." While the bill died quickly, it indicates a common response in politics and one that is at the core of our argument. Information on such things as racial disparities can only lead in one direction: to highlight the problem and to suggest that more needs to be done to combat it. Such information is highly political. One solution, the one we would assert is a favorable one, is to look into serious social problems with the best information available. However, such investigations often lead to efforts to reduce the severity of the problem, and these efforts may involve costly programs or intrusive regulations. So another solution is the one described in detail by Walter Williams and explored in Chapter 4 and favored by Senator Goolsby in this example: eliminate the unwelcome information.

Rational Organization Design and Search

Any attempt at control, hierarchy, and accountability invariably requires the suppression of attributes of complex problems. When the issue of excess business regulation is raised, immigration control advocates tend to center on the response that this is "trivial" effort on the part of employers—the attribute of business regulation is suppressed. Of course one might just estimate the total benefit of asking employees to enforce immigration laws thorough E-Verify versus the cost of the added regulation. But these are incommensurate attributes and therefore difficult to balance.

Attribute suppression is not just an artifact of strategically dealing with complex problems. It is rooted in the cognitive architectures of humans. The tendency for people to suppress attributes in a complex problem accounts for the difficulty in implementing a net-benefits criterion for decision making (which rational decisions would require). Suppression comes from the inability of people to address multiple aspects of a complex problem because of severe limits on short-term memory (Jones 2001) and the tendency of people pursuing goals to be overconfident (Kahneman 2011). But in simplifying a complex problem to make decisions easier, the decision maker has added to potential future complications if those attributes become relevant in the future. Even at the individual level, his or her attempt to control an issue leads to declines in the use of available information.

Within the field of public administration, scholars have long understood the problems of ambiguity and complexity that make "rational" design of large bureaucratic institutions subject to periodic failure. But even there, the temptation of a cybernetic or comprehensively rational approach recurs. We, as well as authors from Simon, Lindblom, Wildavsky, Landau, and Sabatier, have complained about these tendencies, but scholars of public administration have often responded to these critiques by asserting that better management or more rational organization can "cure" the complexity of the world around us. Unfortunately these "cures" run into both the inherent trade-off between control and information and the limits of human cognition, even when aided by organizational arrangements and management tools that can alleviate some of the difficulty.

The tension between information and control is reflected in public administration as a debate between descriptive and analytic theories of choice under ambiguity and complexity, on the one hand, and normative and applied theories of rational, comprehensive, cost-benefit analysis (e.g., hierarchical control), on the other. No wonder the applied microeconomic textbook models that are now the staple of public policy programs of how one "should" make administrative decisions rarely describe what really occurs in government. And, no wonder that descriptive models such as the garbage can, which takes ambiguity to its logical (or some would say absurd) maximum, frustrate public managers who need to exert their authority over public budgets and attempt to the best of their ability to solve pressing problems. It is simply not helpful to them to suggest that human agency has its limits: their job is to overcome those limits, period.

In previous chapters we have paid considerable attention to the increased overlap and redundancy in the organizational structure of the U.S. government. Redundancy appears to be inefficient, and if the U.S. government faced well-understood problems and knew exactly what the best technologies were for addressing them, then a hierarchical control system of clear authority would be best. But as long as value judgments differ about the most important problems facing society, technical ambiguities persist, making it difficult to know in fact which problems are most serious (even if we agree, in principle, about the need to address the most severe social problems facing us), and as long as problems remain complex, ensuring that solutions may address only part of the problem and create unintended secondary consequences, then we will be better off with some degree of ambiguity and overlap in our organizational structure as well. This is how the framers designed it, and for good reason.

Compared to the organizational clarity inherent in a system with fixed jurisdictional rules and bright boundaries around the activities and mandates of different institutions, overlapping, ambiguous, conflicting, and redundant systems provide more venues within which policy is debated, and, as a consequence, offer a richer supply of information relevant to policy choices. In any case, one of the most important consequences of the long-term growth of government, whether we look over two hundred years or just back at the more recent period, has been to complicate the structures of government. There are more government institutions today, they overlap in their mandates more than before, and they interfere with each other's activities. Many have decried these developments, as they complicate the process of government. There is no question that they do complicate matters, especially for those who would prefer to have clearer authority to make authoritative decisions.

Detecting, Defining, and Addressing Problems

At the time of the founding of the Republic, the framers already understood issues of complexity and ambiguity in government. They knew that any single view of the national interest, especially one imposed by a small group of leaders, might be opposed by others, and that differences of opinion and interest would cause inevitable divergences in political preferences. They set institution to work against institution, guaranteeing that in the struggle for control over the direction of public policy, argumentation and building coalitions would matter. As the state has grown to thousands of times its original scope, and has become involved in a multitude of issues that were not even imagined at the time, the connection between diversity and institutions has become even more important. Any system with multiple independent sources of power creates competition. This competition creates more information, as each independent actor within and around government seeks to use arguments and evidence to bring public attention to one or another social problem or possible solution. This potential competition among policy venues provided a central part of the story we developed in *Agendas and Instability in American Politics*.

As more and more information swamps a system, making sense of it becomes harder and harder. As we noted when discussing Figures 2.1 and 2.2 and reinforced with empirical evidence throughout the middle chapters of this book, the only administrative solution to the overwhelming amount of information is to ignore some part of it. But those bits of information that are ignored have a way of coming back if they are indeed important, creating crises that eventually have to be addressed. So we see periods when government seems to be on a stable equilibrium, but these can be interrupted at unequal intervals by the sudden discovery of crises. Good government allows the full airing of public issues but is nevertheless able to distinguish between problems that are both solvable and amenable to government action, on the one hand, and those that are best left alone, on the other. This is difficult indeed for humans passionate about politics, and cannot be guaranteed by any particular mechanism. While diversity ensures that issues are aired, the subsequent dynamics can easily lead to the continued growth of government. As a consequence, the supply of information is a critical part of the model of disproportionate information processing, as political systems swing between ignoring signals in some part of the environment and overreacting to them (Jones 2001; Jones and Baumgartner 2005a, 2005b). This overreaction can lead to oversupplying government programs.

The Implications of Complexity

In the second half of the twentieth century some spectacular changes in the overall contours of American government occurred. Two things stand out: the general growth in the size of government and the increase in the diversity of the institutional agenda—the number of different issues to which government attends. During the postwar period, government moved from a relatively narrow agenda, focusing on just a few issues, to a much larger and more complex institutional structure with simultaneous attention to scores of issues that were previously not on the government agenda at all. This is clear-cut and unmistakable.

Compared to 1951, when David Truman wrote his magisterial work *The Governmental Process*, we must pay far more attention to the internal dynamics of government in order to understand its functioning and reactions to changing social conditions. In particular, we need to pay careful attention to what we call agenda dynamics. That is the process by which issues sporadically become the objects of attention in the broad political system. As government has grown, it has become more diverse, with hundreds of distinct issues being debated and thousands of policies variously being implemented, revised, and developed. Most issues, most of the time, are discussed, implemented, and revised within communities of specialists, acting with more or less autonomy from related communities working in different spheres and from the broader political system.

As the number of these specialized policy communities has multiplied, so have their overlaps, and it has become increasingly difficult to define independent policy jurisdictions and clear lines of authority. Many issues fall across the jurisdictions of many local, state, and federal executive agencies, requiring coordination and allowing competition and diverse views to proliferate, even within government. Influential commentators have repeatedly pointed out the increased constraints implied by the various conflicting and interacting demands on government, and we might add, emanating from within government itself. Richard Neustadt (1976, 23–24), in his classic study of the powers of the president, noted several of these factors, including the growth of government following the Great Society, as major new programs such as Social Security in the 1930s, housing in the 1940s, highways in the 1950s, and others steadily accumulated over the decades. As the presidential purview grew broader, necessarily the job became more complex. Neustadt went on to note the end of the long period of economic growth from the 1940s to the mid-1970s; greater resource constraints; more interdependence across areas of policy activity; and the end of international bipolarity, all of which led generally to reduced presidential power.

Neustadt and other commentators have focused on the constraints that they place on the freedom of action of the president and government more generally. However, the multiple and overlapping agencies, policy communities, and congressional committees generate more information, more conflicting information, and more overlapping jurisdictional coverage. These are not all bad things. They may lead to better decisions, as they are based on a greater range of diverse inputs. In any case, they are fundamental characteristics of modern government and increasingly important to understand, but only recently recognized.

Neustadt noted that the greatest power of the U.S. president was the "power to persuade." In a system of interrelationships characterized by no clear powers of authority and some clear constraints based on separation of powers, no president could expect to dictate policy outcomes; the most effective presidents have been those who understood and mastered this "power to persuade." That does not mean that various presidents would not like to have greater powers or that they have not tried to gain them. But we can take Neustadt's conclusions for the president one step further and note that the president may be the single actor with the greatest power to persuade others, but he is not the only one limited to this mode of action. Further, as the size and diversity of government has grown since the Second World War, larger and more diverse constituencies of the public, interest groups, and specialized professionals in diverse policy communities, as well as a wider range of congressional leaders, must be brought along. Each also has a certain power to persuade the others.

This is a much more difficult environment for leadership and decision making, and political leaders have been quick to complain of it. But the larger diversity of opinion that today is incorporated into the policy process brings with it vast resources in terms of information. The informational richness of modern American government compensates for its organizational complexity; in any case, the two are contrasting elements of the same thing. In fact, the difficulties in leadership and top-down control that complexity generates are the mirror image of trends toward incorporating more information into the policy process. Complexity may cause difficulties in leadership, but it is a mistake to argue against incorporating information into the policy process.

The complexity inherent in modern government makes inevitable certain inefficiencies, underreactions, overreactions, and frictions in the translation of signals from the policy-making environment into government responses in the form of programs and agencies. This is not to say that government in the time of President Truman was perfectly efficient—far from it. But the dynamics by which hundreds of issues come to be winnowed down to the few that will be the object of intensive attention have more important consequences now. Leadership decisions intended to purposefully restrict the flow of information in government, or the legitimate participation by those with diverse views, may be tempting in the short run. It is certainly easier to make decisions if one considers fewer rather than more diverse elements of debate.

Governmental complexity affects its information-processing capacity. On the one hand, more complexity generates more information. There are more sources of information because there are more actors, agencies, and oversight committees that have motivation to produce information (from diverse perspectives, not just the same information repeated). On the other hand, complexity leads to more distortion in the translation of information into policy outputs. How government leaders combine information from various sources is a major problem. One temptation they constantly have is simply to reduce the supply of information: to let it be known that they only want to hear information that justifies their current policies, for example. This has been much in the news since September 11, 2001, and various discussions about the G. W. Bush administration's use of intelligence in the period leading up to the Iraq War. But the tension between multiple conflicting sources of diverse and often conflicting information and the need to make sense of it all is always present. In the long run, we see evidence that from 1947 to about the early 1990s trends were consistently toward greater diversity. There were more agencies, more hearings, greater jurisdictional overlap, more interest groups, and more independent sources of information of many sorts. More recently, these trends have reversed. The trade-off between multiple independent sources of information and making sense of these discordant sounds is constant. Leaders often prefer less information, in fact. Government is healthier when there is more of it, even if this makes decisions more difficult to reach.

In spite of the temptation to limit information so that decisions are easier to reach, ignoring uncomfortable information, for example about unintended harmful consequences of proposed policies, does not make these consequences any less likely to occur. And if they do occur then some later government will face increased pressure to deal with them in a process of lurching from one imperfect policy solution to the next that we have described elsewhere. We believe that no government policies are ever likely to be perfect, at least not the large and complex ones we discuss in this book. The ability to consider multiple streams of information is fundamental to the policy process, however. More information means that problems are detected more quickly. More communication means that political leaders can decide if diverse consequences of a policy that may succeed on one dimension but create problems along another are in need of revision, fine-tuning. This process may be more or less efficient, and government, never likely to be perfect, may make small adjustments or it may lurch from one drastic overreaction to the next.

It is possible to ignore the complications and organize the complexity out of politics and government by imposing tight lines of authority on jurisdictions. One can certainly suppress attributes in a multiattribute problem through jurisdictional assignment, as happened in the Department of Homeland Security (May, Workman, and Jones 2008). The results are usually not what the creators expect, as they were not in the Department of Homeland Security. The attributes suppressed in the organizational structure led to deteriorated performance on the other dimensions, and calls to remedy that omission. If problems are complex, simple organizational designs will fail to address them properly.

The general openness of governmental search processes can vary across time. We found considerable indirect quantitative and qualitative evidence that the supply of information generated by the open, overlapping process that was constructed after the mid-1950s was limited sometime after 1978. This probably happened in both the legislative and executive branches. We studied the congressional committee system in detail, and it may be that congressional bureaucracies (the Congressional Budget Office, the General Accountability Office, and the Congressional Research Service) supplemented the decline in committee search. But there is little question that the committee system as an information-gathering and assessment system has atrophied (Coburn 2011).

Information and the Health of Democracy

Government is a complex adaptive system, adjusting to demands from its environment and from internal components as well. Adaptability varies across political systems, and some internal decision-making structures are more adaptable than others. The capacity to detect and interpret potential problems is surely an adaptive trait in governance.

One of the consequences of separated powers is the incentive for both branches involved in lawmaking and policy implementation to construct information-processing systems to ensure against being overly reliant on the other branch. If that is all there was to it, then incentives would all encourage better systems for detecting problems and designing solutions. Unfortunately, in some cases a sense of urgency seizes the political system, and hasty policy making occurs. Some policy actors may want to limit the search process to thwart the information-policy connection.

In some cases, the ideological predispositions, economic self-interest, or other "blinders" to the flow of information can lead to denial even where the strength of the incoming signal about a problem is strong. The notion that tax reductions "pay for themselves" by increasing economic growth and hence need not be offset by spending cuts to make them revenue neutral is an argument that is simply not true, as many academic studies and governmental reports have repeatedly shown (Jones and Williams 2008; Hungerford 2012). There is not much a strong information-processing system can do about these sorts of arguments, especially since they are so convenient for politicians. It should be clear, however, that seeking to shut down the capacity to detect problems is in no way a solution.

Our assessments of the search processes of the U.S. government over time suggest that there has been an attenuation of this capacity during the last thirty or so years. Certainly the social and economic systems have not gotten less complex, yet the capacity of government to assess problems has leveled off and declined, according to our measures and considerable qualitative evidence. The process underlying this seems to be a politics of attribute suppression, a self-conscious attempt to limit serious discussions of aspects of complex problems through a net of formal and informal restrictions. These include limiting of the hearing capacity of Congress and defunding of policy analytic staffs in executive agencies, as we have documented. We would speculate as well that ideological shifts and the influence of money in elections have reinforced these "do less" and "know less" trends as well.

We will end on whether we must choose between organized anarchy and circumscribed, and hence deficient, search. We offer two propositions:

Complexity is in itself no bar to vigorous policy action. It is possible to construct complex systems that cannot act. Many contemporary commentators view modern developments in the U.S. national government this way. But that is not the normal manner in which complex systems operate, so long as balance between independent, deconcentrated power, on the one hand, and "friction" or resistance to hasty action through some degree of independence, on the other, is maintained. Today federalism operates that way in the United States. So we need to distinguish between systems that have become imbalanced in one direction or another and refrain from decrying all complexity as detrimental to democracy.

Expert search need not be limited even if the politics of attribute suppression works against entropic search. While one can see how attribute suppression might be fostered in a political debate to stem unwarranted expansions of government intrusiveness, such suppression should never spill over into the realm of expert search. That could undermine the very objective of limiting policy oversupply by detracting from the ability to seek more efficient policy solutions.

In the end, we come down on the side of vigorous information-processing systems that are capable of detecting problems and prioritizing them for action. That approach may lead to overgovernment, but the answer is not to shut down the process or try to limit the access of others to the process. Doing so can only be effective in the short-term. Governments, for good or ill, are complex adaptive systems evolving in concert with even more complex environments. We must learn to understand them as such.

Appendices: Appendix to Chapter 4

Figure 4.2 presents a quadratic fit to the number of GAO reports over time. It is estimated through least-squared fits for the quadratic equation $Y = a + bX - cX^2$. The table below presents parameter estimates and goodness of fit statistics between the estimates based on the parameters listed for the polynomial equation and the actual data. N = 25 (88th–112th Congresses).

Parameter	a	b	c	R^2
Estimate	−172718	3468	−17.12	0.77

Appendix to Chapter 5

Tables 5.A1 and 5.A2 show the number of hearings by each committee in Congress from 1947 to 2006. The first table shows hearings by committee for the House of Representatives and the second one shows the same for the Senate. Blanks in any row indicate that the committee had not been created at that time, had ceased to exist, or held no hearings.

TABLE 5.A1. Hearings by Congress for the Main Committees of the House of Representatives, 1947–2006

A. 80th–94th Congress

Committee	Congress														
	80th	81st	82nd	83rd	84th	85th	86th	87th	88th	89th	90th	91st	92nd	93rd	94th
Administration	13	6	9	3	15	40	5	3	5	5	0	3	4	5	4
Agriculture	74	69	50	59	93	84	62	54	55	57	61	45	40	78	65
Appropriations	75	96	99	76	92	94	95	91	89	94	93	116	135	155	171
Armed Services	337	257	101	139	136	131	89	81	73	89	71	71	73	88	67
Banking	41	26	16	18	31	16	24	25	37	42	37	43	33	56	86
Budget															29
Commerce	167	36	21	54	44	70	59	61	59	53	50	117	116	113	164
District of Columbia	131	64	32	46	43	47	10	11	21	22	37	27	16	44	29
Education	58	21	16	22	19	35	36	66	48	72	53	89	94	91	123
Fisheries	75	52	33	47	74	59	36	29	27	34	34	62	37	49	48
Government Reform	62	32	56	72	95	124	40	54	50	60	67	96	90	91	103
Homeland Security															
International Relations	12	27	4	17	14	76	37	35	44	57	35	66	88	117	141
Judiciary	82	132	151	185	254	280	31	42	34	31	25	48	52	103	88
Post Office	44	15	39	29	40	54	57	52	55	57	51	41	55	58	95
Resources	378	374	312	337	332	319	31	32	38	44	43	52	57	81	94
Rules	139		1	1	5	5			4	13	5	7		3	2
Science							48	47	21	21	25	32	32	59	124
Small Business	9	10	11	2	20	21	17	8	18	19	14	20	21	29	34
Transportation	51	25	30	45	21	18	25	23	29	38	35	52	42	37	63
Un-American Activities	27	49	40	100	59	34	28	22	15	12	16	29	17	17	
Veterans Affairs	53	22	24	36	36	18	31	13	9	20	19	15	13	14	24
Ways and Means	26	11	19	28	25	20	16	24	23	24	27	54	42	64	102
All Others	3	12	14	10	2	2	1	3	4	0	2	23	16	10	98
Total	1857	1336	1078	1326	1450	1547	778	776	758	864	800	1108	1073	1362	1754

(continued)

TABLE 5.A1. (continued)

B. 95th–109th Congress

Committee	Congress														
	95th	96th	97th	98th	99th	100th	101st	102nd	103rd	104th	105th	106th	107th	108th	109th
Administration	1	3	5	5	4	4	10	16	8	4	2		12	16	24
Agriculture	90	85	103	101	60	115	94	100	99	49	64	68	26	39	40
Appropriations	186	217	214	181	183	169	155	150	170	171	170	167	159	162	162
Armed Services	97	86	83	72	75	126	86	82	56	53	53	67	48	46	153
Banking	107	85	109	120	111	99	192	155	178	51	78	75	87	117	125
Budget	48	37	40	36	23	24	41	67	26	29	10	19	34	26	20
Commerce	196	244	205	195	183	242	220	166	171	119	137	168	143	134	147
District of Columbia	23	19	27	14	23	13	13	12	9						
Education	131	132	156	160	152	115	133	138	120	80	151	134	85	74	61
Fisheries	55	54	47	58	60	95	123	107	126						
Government Reform	116	124	146	166	159	161	155	148	141	210	217	280	248	286	256
Homeland Security														59	107
International Relations	151	178	168	160	193	192	204	176	179	206	210	194	120	161	239
Judiciary	88	104	146	156	109	147	161	130	100	133	132	178	113	117	166
Post Office	81	116	57	63	84	74	87	67	60						
Resources	75	72	71	92	93	106	118	123	136	110	120	79	160	107	63
Rules	2	6	4	3	4	3	4	6	5	7	7	3	6	2	
Science	124	182	180	152	165	154	169	171	174	78	96	111	91	69	64
Small Business	67	70	63	58	49	76	86	93	110	91	67	73	67	83	64
Transportation	52	63	74	74	53	73	83	81	83	80	81	103	105	84	100
Un-American Activities															
Veterans Affairs	43	58	82	61	62	62	58	54	59	28	47	51	56	51	64
Ways and Means	121	135	90	112	104	91	127	135	108	93	95	130	98	73	86
All Others	130	131	91	135	159	162	141	150	15	3	1	1	5	1	0
Total	1984	2201	2161	2174	2108	2303	2460	2327	2133	1595	1738	1901	1663	1707	1941

Note: The table shows numbers of hearings held in each standing committee. Blank cells indicate the committee did not exist in that period or that it held no hearings. Committees with few hearings or intermittent existence are combined in the "All Others" category.

TABLE 5.A2. Hearings by Congress for the Main Committees of the Senate, 1947–2006

A. 80th–94th Congress

Committee	Congress														
	80th	81st	82nd	83rd	84th	85th	86th	87th	88th	89th	90th	91st	92nd	93rd	94th
Aeronautical	31	43	10	41	40	3	16	10	8	9	25	19	15	17	17
Agriculture	56	42	35	40	43	42	25	27	14	27	30	24	38	53	67
Appropriations	70	111	104	136	131	47	47	45	50	51	63	76	91	101	125
Armed Services	95	73	52	83	86	64	55	101	50	45	39	40	50	66	65
Banking	64	62	42	81	62	53	57	70	64	71	80	104	81	92	120
Budget														2	16
Commerce	47	62	91	82	55	67	77	92	71	85	93	134	120	150	129
District of Columbia						79	108	101	75	73	73	59	41	20	17
Energy	97	87	36	133	122	102	64	124	139	130	124	92	168	189	177
Environment	16	19	13	15	23	33	18	21	22	35	56	85	51	79	62
Finance	16	20	23	23	23	27	27	43	23	26	19	40	30	57	65
Foreign Relations	62	85	50	88	96	77	61	41	69	66	81	86	50	63	59
Health	38	52	28	36	42	23	44	36	49	88	86	190	161	157	132
Homeland Security	34	25	20	143	46	16	24	43	48	77	62	65	39	82	72
Judiciary	44	96	62	207	180	124	113	132	78	115	120	177	128	139	142
Post Office	67	53	56	25	44	29	36	53	40	36	27	23	16	27	19
Rules	7	5	24	16	7	12	26	18	58	39	23	3	7	11	12
Small Business	22	8	46	22	20	21	29	19	16	14	39	20	16	16	62
Veterans Affairs													18	17	18
All Others	31	13	12	1	6	108	80	40	31	17	22	125	81	110	73
Total	797	856	704	1172	1026	927	907	1016	905	1004	1062	1362	1201	1448	1449

(continued)

TABLE 5.A2. (continued)

B. 95th–109th Congress

Committee	95th	96th	97th	98th	99th	100th	101st	102nd	103rd	104th	105th	106th	107th	108th	109th
Aeronautical															
Agriculture	74	103	55	70	35	57	61	39	40	28	43	47	42	17	48
Appropriations	106	114	87	94	91	83	90	70	73	72	35	75	81	72	99
Armed Services	68	61	72	75	46	43	39	36	47	36	15	44	46	39	18
Banking	130	127	82	68	56	71	119	85	101	45	46	65	79	63	48
Budget	17	17	17	13	12	20	14	15	4	9	11	6	6	4	8
Commerce	159	150	151	118	95	125	165	127	119	82	109	132	159	37	66
District of Columbia															
Energy	154	170	134	111	97	136	135	113	110	106	105	151	86	92	108
Environment	94	72	78	69	67	94	95	75	66	39	46	63	59	41	30
Finance	106	110	139	156	122	107	111	109	84	78	58	64	73	61	76
Foreign Relations	76	72	100	71	43	37	53	84	44	55	59	95	64	117	80
Health	162	133	123	137	97	98	113	129	104	72	50	87	99	55	61
Homeland Security	112	179	162	103	81	109	127	130	108	70	100	68	112	102	167
Judiciary	126	132	167	156	141	104	109	103	80	108	125	122	119	101	117
Post Office	3														
Rules	8	5	4	3	2	5	2	1	2	3	1	4			
Small Business	63	68	41	43	25	30	31	37	26	30	7	31	17	12	8
Veterans Affairs	23	27	21	15	14	18	26	19	22	10	10	7	18	12	44
All Others	102	87	91	76	59	101	121	107	92	86	98	140	101	128	93
Total	1583	1627	1524	1378	1083	1238	1411	1279	1122	929	918	1201	1161	953	1071

Note: See Table 5.A1.

Appendix to Chapter 6

The arcs in Figures 6.4 and 6.5 are estimated through least-squared fits for the quadratic equation $Y = a + b X - c X^2$. The tables below present parameter estimates and goodness of fit statistics between the estimates and the actual data. In each case the dependent variable is the number of distinct subtopics on which activities occurred. All of the coefficients are significant at $p < 0.001$. This simply means that a rise and then a decline characterizes the arc in every case.

TABLE 6.A1. Number of Distinct Subtopics with Activity, per Congress

Parameter Estimates	All Hearings	Non-Legislative Hearings	Legislative Hearings	Lawmaking	Supreme Court	CQ Coverage	House Roll Call Votes	Senate Roll Call Votes
a	−1343	−2071	−2175	−1589	−917	−4062	−2280	−2278
b	30.40	43.22	49.79	36.55	20.63	89.47	47.33	48.78
c	−0.149	−0.205	−0.263	−0.193	−0.108	−0.474	−0.230	−0.246
R^2	0.89	0.94	0.74	0.65	0.62	0.79	0.82	0.81
N	32	32	32	30	31	31	29	29

Source: Calculated by authors from Policy Agendas Project datasets.

TABLE 6.A2. Average Entropies

Parameter Estimates	House Average Topic Entropy	House Average Committee Entropy	Senate Average Topic Entropy	House Average Committee Entropy
a	−3.474	−2.043	−3.529	−2.727
b	0.0798	0.0475	0.0793	0.0622
c	−0.00039	−0.00021	−0.00038	−0.000298
R	0.87	0.86	0.87	0.90

Note: Entropies were averaged across all major topics or committees for each Congress.
Source: Calculated by authors from Policy Agendas Project datasets.

The Reliability of the Subtopic Measure

In this book we developed the concept of entropic search to capture the notion that diversity is desirable in search processes in which the problem space is ill-defined, and we used Shannon's entropy coefficient to assess this type of search in congressional committees. For many of the areas we studied, we employed a more convenient measure, the number of Policy Agendas Project subtopics. Figure 6.A1 shows how these two measures correlate.

Figure 6.A1 is a scatterplot that compares average topic entropy to the number of subtopics on which one or more hearings were held, per Congress. Average topic entropy calculates entropy across the major topic categories of the Policy Agendas Project, of which there are 19, whereas the number of subtopics can peak at 226. The scatterplot suggests good statistical fit but some ceiling effects, as average entropy varies quite a bit at the upper end of the subtopic scale.

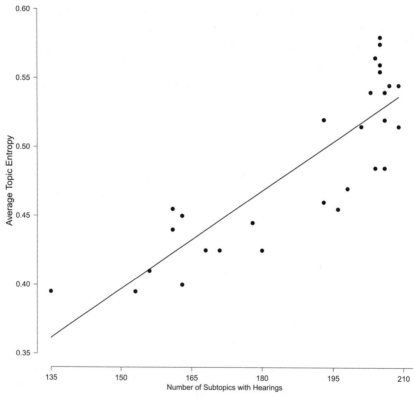

FIGURE 6.A1. Subtopics and Entropy

Note: The figure shows, for each Congress from the 79th to the 109th, the number of subtopics on which a hearing was held, and the average entropy across policy topics in that same Congress. The best-fit line shows that Entropy = 0.04161 + 0.0023693 (Subtopics) + e. R^2 = .741; N = 31.

References

Aberbach, Joel D. 1990. *Keeping a Watchful Eye: The Politics of Congressional Oversight.* Washington, DC: Brookings Institute.

Adler, E. Scott. 2002. *Why Congressional Reforms Fail.* Chicago: University of Chicago Press.

Adler, E. Scott, and John Wilkerson. 2012. *A Governing Theory of Legislative Organization.* Cambridge: Cambridge University Press.

Bamford, James. 2008. *The Shadow Factory.* New York: Doubleday.

Baumgartner, Frank R. 2013. Ideas and Policy Change." *Governance* 26, 2: 239–58.

Baumgartner, Frank R., and Derek A. Epp. 2012. "North Carolina Traffic Stop Statistics Analysis. Final Report to the North Carolina Advocates for Justice Task Force on Racial and Ethnic Bias." University of North Carolina at Chapel Hill. February 1.

Baumgartner, Frank R., and Bryan D. Jones. 1991. "Agenda Dynamics and Policy Subsystems." *Journal of Politics* 53 (November): 1044–74.

———. 1994. "Attention, Boundary Effects, and Large-Scale Policy Change: Air Transportation Policy in the Twentieth Century," in Roger Cobb and David Rochefort, editors, *The Politics of Problem Definition.* Lawrence: University Press of Kansas, 50–66.

———. 2009 (1993). *Agendas and Instability in American Politics.* 2nd ed. Chicago: University of Chicago Press.

Baumgartner, Frank R., Bryan D. Jones, and Michael C. MacLeod. 2000. "The Evolution of Legislative Jurisdictions." *Journal of Politics* 62: 321–49.

Baumgartner, Frank R., Heather A. Larsen, Beth L. Leech, and Paul Rutledge. 2011. "Congressional and Presidential Effects on the Demand for Lobbying." *Political Research Quarterly* 64, 1 (March): 3–16.

Baumgartner, Frank R., and Beth L. Leech. 1998. *Basic Interests: The Importance of Groups in Politics and in Political Science.* Princeton, NJ: Princeton University Press.

———. 2001. "Issue Niches and Policy Bandwagons: Patterns of Interest Group Involvement in National Politics." *Journal of Politics* 63, 4 (November): 1191–213.

Bish, Robert L. 1970. *The Public Economy of Metropolitan Areas.* Chicago: Markham.

Boydstun, Amber E., Shaun Bevan, and H. F. Thomas III. 2012. "Measuring Attention Diversity." Working paper.

Brady, David W., and Craig Volden. 1998. *Revolving Gridlock: Politics and Policy from Carter to Clinton.* Boulder: Westview.

Brudnick, Ida A. 2001. *The Congressional Research Service and the Legislative Process.* Washington, DC: Congressional Research Service.

Cagle, M. Christine, and J. Michael Martinez. 2004. "Have Gun, Will Travel: The Dispute between the CDC and the NRA on Firearm Violence as a Public Health Problem." *Politics and Policy* 32 (2): 278–310.

Caro, Robert A. 2012. *The Passage of Power: The Years of Lyndon Johnson.* New York: Knopf.

CIA FAQs: "How Many People Work for the CIA and What Is Its Budget?" https://www.cia .gov/about-cia/faqs/index.html. Accessed July 12, 2012.

Cobb, Roger W., and Charles D. Elder. 1972. *Participation in American Politics: The Dynamics of Agenda-Building.* Baltimore, MD: Johns Hopkins University Press.

Coburn, Tom. 2011. *Shooting the Messenger: Congress Targets the Taxpayers' Watchdog.* Investigative Reports. http://www.coburn.senate.gov/public/?p=OversightAction. Accessed September 24, 2012.

Cohen, Michael, James G. March, and Johan P. Olsen. 1972. "A Garbage Can Theory of Organizational Choice." *Administrative Science Quarterly* 17: 1–25.

Cohn, Bob. 2011. "Scalia: Our System is Designed for Gridlock." *Atlantic Monthly* (October 6). http://www.theatlantic.com/national/archive/2011/10/scalia-our-political-system-is-de-signed-for-gridlock/246257/. Accessed October 8, 2011.

Cooper, Joseph. 2013. Personal Communication. June 15.

Dahl, Robert. 1967. "The City in the Future of Democracy." *American Political Science Review* 61: 953–70.

Davidson, Roger. 1981. "Subcommittee Government: New Channels for Policymaking," in Thomas Mann and Norman Ornstein, editors, *The New Congress.* Washington, DC: American Enterprise Institute.

Deering, Christopher J., and Steven S. Smith. 1997. *Committees in Congress.* 3rd ed. Washington, DC: Congressional Quarterly.

Derthick, Martha, and Paul J. Quirk. 1985. *The Politics of Deregulation.* Washington, DC: Brookings Institute.

Dodd, Lawrence. 2012. *Thinking about Congress.* New York: Routledge.

Dodd, Lawrence, and Richard Schott. 1979. *Congress and the Administrative State.* New York: John Wiley.

Downs, Anthony. 1957. *An Economic Theory of Democracy.* New York: Harper and Row.

———. 1972. "Up and Down with Ecology: The Issue Attention Cycle." *Public Interest* 28: 38–50.

———. 2008. "How Rational Citizens Reduce Information Costs." http://keithoughts-kwc .blogspot.com/2008/10/how-rational-citizens-reduce.html. October 8. Accessed May 13, 2012.

Faricy, Christopher. 2011. "The Politics of Social Policy in America: The Causes and Effects of Indirect versus Direct Social Spending." *Journal of Politics* 73 (1): 74–83.

Fenno, Richard F., Jr. 1966. *The Power of the Purse: Appropriations Politics in Congress.* Boston: Little, Brown.

———. 1973. *Congressmen in Committees.* Boston: Little, Brown.

Fishkin, James S. 1991. *Democracy and Deliberation: New Directions for Democratic Reform.* New Haven, CT: Yale University Press.

———. 2011. *When the People Speak: Deliberative Democracy and Public Consultation.* New York: Oxford University Press.

GAO. 2000. "Racial Profiling." GAO/GGD-00-41. Washington, DC: General Accounting Office, March.

Gilligan, Thomas W., and Keith Krehbiel. 1987. "Collective Decisionmaking and Standing Committees: An Informational Rationale for Restrictive Amendment Procedures." *Journal of Law Economics and Organization* 3 (2): 287–335.

———. 1989. "Asymmetric Information and Legislative Rules with a Heterogeneous Committee." *American Journal of Political Science* 33 (2): 459–90.

———. 1990. "Organization of Informative Committees by a Rational Legislature." *American Journal of Political Science* 34 (2): 531–64.

GlobalSecurity.Org. N.d. FY 2010 Intelligence Budget. http://www.globalsecurity.org/intell /library/budget/index.html. Accessed August 20, 2013.

Greenspan, Alan. 2004. "Remarks Made At America's Community Bankers Annual Convention, October 19th." Washington, DC: Board of Governors of the Federal Reserve System, Speeches of Federal Reserve Officials. http://www.federalreserve.gov/newsevents /speech/2004speech.htm. Accessed October 3, 2012.

Greenstein, Fred I. 1982. *The Hidden Hand Presidency: Eisenhower as Leader.* New York: Basic Books.

Grossman, Matthew. 2011. "American Domestic Policymaking since 1945: The Aggregate View from Policy History." Paper presented at the Midwest Political Science Association Annual Meeting. Chicago.

———. 2014. *Artists of the Possible: Governing Networks and American Policy Change since 1945.* New York: Oxford University Press.

Hacker, Jacob S., and Paul Pierson. 2010. *Winner-Take-All Politics.* New York: Simon and Schuster.

Hammond, Thomas. 1990. "In Defense of Luther Gulick's 'Notes on the Theory of Organization.'" *Public Administration* 68: 143–73.

Hardin, John W. 1998. "Advocacy versus Certainty: The Dynamics of Committee Jurisdiction Concentration." *Journal of Politics* 60 (2): 374–97.

Hungerford, Thomas L. 2012. *Taxes and the Economy: An Economic Analysis of the Top Tax Rates since 1945.* Washington, DC: Congressional Research Service.

Huntington, Samuel. 1981. *American Politics: The Promise of Disharmony.* Cambridge, MA: Harvard University Press.

Jochim, Ashley E., and Bryan D. Jones. 2013. "Issue Politics in a Polarized Congress." *Political Research Quarterly* 66, 2: 352–69.

Johnson, Simon, and James Kwak. 2011. *13 Bankers.* New York: Vintage.

Jones, Bryan D. 1994. *Reconceiving Decision-Making in Democratic Politics: Attention, Choice, and Public Policy.* Chicago: University of Chicago Press.

———. 2001. *Politics and the Architecture of Choice.* Chicago: University of Chicago Press.

Jones, Bryan D., and Frank R. Baumgartner. 2005a. "A Model of Choice for Public Policy." *Journal of Public Administration Research and Theory* 15: 325–51.

———. 2005b. *The Politics of Attention: How Government Prioritizes Problems.* Chicago: University of Chicago Press.

Jones, Bryan D., Frank R. Baumgartner, and Erin de la Mare. 2005. "The Supply of Information and the Size of Government in the United States." Seattle: Center for American Politics and Public Policy, University of Washington.

Jones, Bryan D., Frank R. Baumgartner, and Jeffery Talbert. 1993. "The Destruction of Issue Monopolies in Congress." *American Political Science Review* 87: 657–71.

Jones, Bryan D., Heather Larsen-Price, and John Wilkerson. 2009. "Representation and American Governing Institutions." *Journal of Politics* 71: 1–14.

Jones, Bryan D., Tracy Sulkin, and Heather Larsen. 2003. "Punctuations in American Political Institutions." *American Political Science Review* 97: 151–69.

Jones, Bryan D., and JoBeth Surface-Shafran. 2009. "Do Legislators Sometimes Vote against Their Preferences? Some Thoughts and a Research Program." Paper presented at the American Politics Workshop, University of Chicago. January 26.

Jones, Bryan D., Herschel Thomas III, and Michelle Wolfe. 2013. "Policy Bubbles." Austin: Policy Agendas Project, Department of Government, University of Texas.

Jones, Bryan D., and Michelle Whyman. 2011. "Lawmaking and Agenda-Setting in the United States, 1948–2007." Austin, TX: Policy Agendas Project.

Jones, Bryan D., and Walter Williams. 2008. *The Politics of Bad Ideas.* New York: Pearson.

Jones, Bryan D., Lazlo Zalyani, and Peter Erdi. In press. "An Integrated Theory of Budgetary Politics and Some Empirical Tests: The US National Budget, 1791–2010." *American Journal of Political Science.*

Kahneman, Daniel. 2011. *Thinking, Fast and Slow.* New York: Farrar, Straus, and Giroux.

King, David C. 1997. *Turf Wars: How Congressional Committees Claim Jurisdiction.* Chicago: University of Chicago Press.

Kingdon, John W. 1995 [1984]. *Agendas, Alternatives, and Public Policies.* 2nd ed. New York: Harper Collins.

Krehbiel, Keith. 1991. *Information and Legislative Organization.* Ann Arbor: University of Michigan Press.

Krusten, Maarja. *The History of GAO: Working for Good Government since 1921.* GAO Web site, last modified September 10, 2001.

Kutler, Stanley I. 1992. *The Wars of Watergate: The Last Crisis of Richard Nixon.* New York: Norton.

Landau, Martin. 1969. "Redundancy, Rationality, and the Problem of Duplication and Overlap." *Public Administration Review* 29, 4 (July–August): 346–58.

———. 1971. "Linkage, Coding, and Intermediacy." *Journal of Comparative Administration* 2: 401–29.

Leech, Beth L., Frank R. Baumgartner, Timothy La Pira, and Nicholas A. Semanko. 2005. "Drawing Lobbyists to Washington: Government Activity and Interest-Group Mobilization." *Political Research Quarterly* 58, 1 (March): 19–30.

Lewallen, Jonathan. 2012. "Memorandum on Legislative Rule Changes." Austin, TX: Policy Agendas Project.

Lewis, David E. 2003. *Presidents and the Politics of Agency Design: Political Insulation in the United States Government Bureaucracy, 1946–1997.* Stanford, CA: Stanford University Press.

Majority Media, Senate Committee on Homeland Security and Governmental Affairs. 2012. "Fusion Centers Add Value to the Federal Government Counterterrorism Efforts." Senate Committee on Homeland Security and Governmental Affairs. October 3. http://www.hsgac.senate.gov/media/fusion-centers-add-value-to-federal-government-counterterrorism-efforts. Accessed October 4, 2012.

March, James G., and Johan P. Olsen. 1983. "Organizing Political Life: What Reorganization Tells Us about Government." *American Political Science Review* 77: 281–96.

Martin, Douglas. 2012. "Roger Boisjoly, 73, Dies; Warned of Shuttle Danger." *New York Times.* February 3.

Matthews, Donald R. 1960. *U.S. Senators and Their World.* New York: Random House.

May, Peter J., Samuel Workman, and Bryan D. Jones. 2008. "Organizing Attention: Responses of the Bureaucracy to Agenda Disruption." *Journal of Public Administration Research and Theory* 18: 517–41.

Mayors against Illegal Guns. 2013. "Access Denied: How the Gun Lobby is Depriving Police, Policy Makers, and the Public of the Data We Need to Prevent Gun Violence." http://www.demandaction.org/detail/2013-01-access-denied-how-the-gun-lobby-is-depriving-police. Accessed October 18, 2013.

McCarthy, Scott. 2009. "Kennedy Pushed Airline Deregulation, Changed U.S. Air Travel." *Wall Street Journal.* August 26. http://blogs.wsj.com/middleseat/2009/08/26/kennedy-pushed-airline-deregulation-changed-us-air-travel/tab/print/. Accessed August 1, 2013.

Meier, Kenneth, and John Bohte. 2000. "Ode to Luther Gulick: The Span of Control and Organizational Performance." *Administration and Society* 23: 115–37.

———. 2003. "Span of Control and Public Organizations." *Public Administration Review* 63: 61–70.

Mettler, Suzanne. 2011. *The Submerged State: How Invisible Government Policies Undermine American Democracy.* Chicago: University of Chicago Press.

Moynihan, Daniel P. 1973. *The Politics of a Guaranteed Income.* New York: Vintage.

Neustadt, Richard E. 1960. *Presidential Power and the Modern Presidents: The Politics of Leadership.* New York: John Wiley.

The 9/11 Commission Report. 2004. New York: W.W. Norton.

Office of the Director of National Intelligence. 2013. *2012 Report on Security Clearance Determinations.*

Ostrom, Elinor. 1976. "Size and Performance in the Federal System." *Publius* 6: 33–73.

———. 1986. "An Agenda for the Study of Institutions." *Public Choice* 48: 3–25.

———. 2005. *Understanding Institutional Diversity.* Princeton, NJ: Princeton University Press.

Ostrom, Vincent, Charles M. Tibout, and Robert Warren. 1961. "The Organization of Governments in Metropolitan Areas." *American Political Science Review* 55: 831–42.

Page, Scott E. 2008. *The Difference.* Princeton, NJ: Princeton University Press.

Patterson, James T. 1996. *Grand Expectations: The United States, 1945-1974.* New York: Oxford University Press.

Peterson, David A., Lawrence A. Grossback, James A. Stimson, and Amy Gangl. 2003. "Congressional Response to Mandate Elections." *American Journal of Political Science* 47: 411–26.

Peterson, R. Eric. 2008. *Legislative Branch Staffing, 1954-2008.* Washington, DC: Congressional Research Service.

Polsby, Nelson. 2004. *How Congress Evolves.* New York: Oxford University Press.

Priest, Dana, and William M. Arkin. 2011. *Top Secret America.* New York: Little, Brown.

Redford, Emmette S. 1969. *Democracy in the Administrative State.* New York: Oxford University Press.

Rhode, David. 1991. *Parties and Leaders in the Postreform House.* Chicago: University of Chicago Press.

Schlesinger, Arthur. 1986. *The Cycles of American History.* Boston: Houghton Mifflin.

Schuman, Daniel. 2010. "Keeping Congress Competent: Staff Pay, Turnover, and What It Means for Democracy." Washington, DC: Sunlight Foundation. December 21. http://sunlightfoundation.com/blog/2010/12/21/keeping-congress-competent-staff-pay-turnover-and-what-it-means-for-democracy/. Accessed March 26, 2014.

Schuman, Daniel, and Alisha Green. 2012. "Keeping Congress Competent: The Senate's Brain Drain." Washington, DC: Sunlight Foundation. November 30. http://sunlightfoundation.com/blog/2012/11/30/keeping-senate-competent/. Accessed March 26, 2014.

Shannon, Claude E. 1948. "A Mathematical Theory of Communication." *Bell System Technical Journal* 27: 379–423, 623–56.

Shannon, Claude, and Warren Weaver. 1971. *The Mathematical Theory of Communication.* Urbana: University of Illinois Press.

Shepsle, Kenneth A. 1978. *The Giant Jigsaw Puzzle.* Chicago: University of Chicago Press.

Shepsle, Kenneth A., and Barry R. Weingast. 1981. "Structure-induced Equilibrium and Legislative Choice." *Public Choice* 37: 503–19.

———., eds. 1995. *Positive Theories of Congressional Institutions.* Ann Arbor: University of Michigan Press.

Shorrock, Tim. 2007. "The Corporate Takeover of U.S. Intelligence." *Salon.* June 1. http://www.salon.com/2007/06/01/intel_contractors/. Accessed September 23, 2013.

Simon, Herbert A. 1946. "Proverbs of Administration." *Public Administration Review* 6: 53–67.

Sinclair, Barbara. 1989. *The Transformation of the U.S. Senate.* Baltimore, MD: Johns Hopkins University Press.

———. 1995. *Legislators, Leaders, and Lawmaking.* Baltimore, MD: Johns Hopkins University Press.

Smith, Steven S., and Christopher J. Deering. 1990. *Committees in Congress.* Washington, DC: Congressional Quarterly Press.

Souter, Justice David H. 2010. Text of Justice David Souter's speech, Harvard Commencement remarks (as delivered). May 27. http://news.harvard.edu/gazette/story/2010/05/text-of-justice-david-souters-speech/.

Sparrow, Bartholomew. 1996. *From the Outside In: World War II and the Development of the American State.* Princeton, NJ: Princeton University Press.

Stiglitz, Joseph E. 2000. "The Contributions of the Economics of Information to Twentieth Century Economics." *Quarterly Journal of Economics* 115: 1141–78.

Stimson, James A. 1999. *Public Opinion in America: Moods, Cycles, and Swings.* 2nd ed. Boulder, CO: Westview.

Sullivan, Eileen. 2012. "Expensive Counter-terror Offices Produced Little Valuable Intel." Associated Press. October 3. http://www.keprtv.com/news/national/Expensive-counter-terror-officesproduced-little-valuable-intel-172469071.html. Accessed October 3, 2012.

Talbert, Jeffery C., Bryan D. Jones, and Frank R. Baumgartner. 1995. "Nonlegislative Hearings and Policy Change in Congress." *American Journal of Political Science* 39: 383–406.

Theriault, Sean. 2008. *Party Polarization in Congress.* New York: Cambridge University Press.

———. 2013. *The Gingrich Senators.* New York: Oxford University Press.

U.S. Census Bureau. 2002. *2002 Census of Governments: Vol 1. No. 1. Government Organization.* Washington, DC: GPO. GC02(1)-1. http://www.census.gov/prod/2003pubs/gc021x1.pdf. Accessed May 14, 2012.

U.S. Senate. 2011. Senate Committees. http://www.senate.gov/artandhistory/history/common/briefing/Committees.htm. Accessed April 20, 2011.

Walker, Jack L., Jr. 1983. "The Origins and Maintenance of Interest Groups in America." *American Political Science Review* 77: 390–406.

———. 1991. *Mobilizing Interest Groups in America: Patrons, Professions, and Social Movements*. Ann Arbor: University of Michigan Press.

Weiss, Carol. 1989. "Congressional Committees as Users of Analysis." *Journal of Policy Analysis and Management* 8: 411–31.

Whyman, Michelle C., and Bryan D. Jones. 2012. "Building Blocks and Bursts in US Lawmaking." Paper presented at the Comparative Policy Agendas Project, Reims, France, June 14–16.

Wildavsky, Aaron. 1964. *The Politics of the Budgetary Process*. Boston: Little, Brown.

———. 1979. *Speaking Truth to Power*. New York: Transaction Publishers.

Williams, Walter. 1990. *Mismanaging America: The Rise of the Anti-Analytic Presidency*. Lawrence: University Press of Kansas.

———. 1998. *Honest Numbers and Democracy*. Washington, DC: Georgetown University Press.

———. 2003. *Reaganism and the Death of Representative Democracy*. Washington, DC: Georgetown University Press.

———. 2008. Personal communication.

Wilson, James Q. 1979. "American Politics, Then and Now." *Commentary* (February): 39–46.

Wilson, Woodrow. 1885. *Congressional Government: A Study in American Politics*. New York: Houghton, Mifflin and Company.

Workman, Samuel. 2014. *The Dynamics of Bureaucracy in the U.S. Government: How Congress and Federal Agencies Process Information and Solve Problems*. New York: Cambridge University Press.

Worsham, Jeff, and Chaun Stores. 2012. "Pet Sounds: Subsystems, Regimes, Policy Punctuations, and the Neglect of African American Farmers, 1935–2006." *Policy Studies Journal* 40: 169–89.

Zelizer, Julian. 2004. *On Capitol Hill*. New York: Cambridge University Press.

Index

Page numbers in italics refer to figures and tables.